Luhmann Explained

IDEAS EXPLAINED™

Hans-Georg Moeller, *Daoism Explained*

Joan Weiner, *Frege Explained*

Hans-Georg Moeller, *Luhmann Explained*

IN PREPARATION

Graham Harman, *Heidegger Explained*

David Detmer, *Sartre Explained*

Rondo Keele, *Ockham Explained*

Paul Voice, *Rawls Explained*

David Detmer, *Phenomenology Explained*

David Ramsay Steele, *Atheism Explained*

Luhmann Explained

From Souls to Systems

HANS-GEORG MOELLER

OPEN COURT
Chicago and La Salle, Illinois

Volume 3 in the Ideas Explained™ Series

To order books from Open Court, call toll-free 1-800-815-2280, or visit www.opencourtbooks.com.

Open Court Publishing Company is a division of Carus Publishing Company.

Library of Congress Cataloging-in-Publication Data

Moeller, Hans-Georg, 1964-
    Luhmann explained : from souls to systems / Hans-Georg Moeller.
        p. cm. — (Ideas explained series ; v. 3)
    Summary: "An introduction to Niklas Luhmann's social systems theory. Discusses key concepts and relevant philosophical issues, and presents a case study. English-language translations of three of Luhmann's essays and bibliographies of works by and on Luhmann are included"—Provided by publisher.
    Includes bibliographical references and index.
    ISBN-13: 978-0-8126-9598-4 (trade pbk. : alk. paper) $ 39.00
    1. Luhmann, Niklas. 2. Social systems. 3. Social systems—Philosophy.
4. Mass media—Social aspects. I. Title. II. Series.
HM701.M634 2006
301.092—dc22
                                                              2006014930

It had always been clear to me that a thoroughly constructed conceptual theory of society would be much more radical and much more discomforting in its effects than narrowly focused criticisms—criticisms of capitalism for instance—could ever imagine.

—NIKLAS LUHMANN, *Protest*

Contents

Preface   ix

Introduction   xi

PART I:
A NEW WAY OF THINKING ABOUT SOCIETY   1

1. What Is Social Systems Theory?   3
   (a) Systems Theory   3
   (b) Social Systems   21
   (c) History   41
   (d) Globalization   52

2. What Is Real?   65
   (a) Making Sense, Making Reality   65
   (b) Second-Order Cybernetics   71

3. What Happens to the Human Being?   79
   (a) Beyond Humanism   79
   (b) Problems of Identity   83

4. What Can Be Done?   99
   (a) Limits of Activism and the Conformism of Protest   99
   (b) Negative Ethics   108
   (c) Subtle Subversions   115

PART II:
MASS MEDIA   119

5. The Mass Media as a System   121
6. Beyond Manipulation   141
7. The Reality of the Mass Media   149
8. Individuality and Freedom   157

PART III:
PHILOSOPHICAL CONTEXTS   163

9. Kant   167

10. Hegel   173

11. Marx   177

12. Husserl   181

13. Habermas   187

14. Postmodernity, Deconstruction, and
    Techno-Theory   193

15. Conclusion: From Metanarrative to Supertheory   199

Notes   203

References   209

Glossary of Key Terms   215

Appendixes: Translations of Key Luhmann Texts   227

   A. From: *The Society of Society*   229

   B. Cognition as Construction   241

   C. Beyond Barbarism   261

Luhmann Bibliography   273

1. Works by Luhmann in English   275

   (a) Books   275

   (b) Articles   276

2. Works on Luhmann in English   281

3. An Annotated List of German Manuals for
    Luhmann Studies   290

   (a) Dictionaries   290

   (b) Introductions   290

   (c) Luhmann's Influence in Other Fields   292

   (d) Bibliographies   292

Index   293

Preface

Niklas Luhmann's theory of social systems is discomforting to many and irritating to some. In a society that puts so much emphasis on the individual and defines itself as "civil," Luhmann's basic claim that, in fact, society does not consist of human beings can be seen as shocking, as going against common sense, or as absurd. The present book is an attempt to counter such reactions and to show that, quite to the contrary, Luhmann's theory is not at all at odds with our social reality—particularly in North America—but rather, in my view, the best theoretical description of it that is presently available. I will explain Luhmann's functionalist model of society in detail in the main body of this book, but I would like to address the issue of Luhmann's "scandalous" antihumanism right away. Yes, social systems theory denies the human being a central role in society, but this is not because of a lack of respect for humans, their bodies, their feelings, their rights, and their values. It is rather because of the insight that the human being is, in reality, such a complex assemblage that it cannot be adequately understood in terms of a single concept. Human reality is too complex to be subsumed under the single heading of "human being." Luhmann's theory should be read, I believe, not as a denial of human experience, but as an attempt to sort out and do justice to the extreme multiplicity, or, to put it more dramatically, the existential division of such experiences. In a certain sense, the project of modernity can be described as the attempt to reunite the Cartesian subject that was split into mind and body with the help of an overarching humanism. Luhmann gives up this attempt and rather tries to grant all the different dimensions of bodily life, of conscious experience, of communicative practice their own right of existence. Luhmann is neither a monist nor a dualist, he is a thinker of multiplicity and difference and in this respect he is more "postmodern" than "modern."

Luhmann is, and this has to be kept in mind, also a thoroughly historical thinker. His antihumanism is not an essentialist replacement of "human nature" with systems. Social systems theory does not describe reality as it "essentially" is, but as what it has actually become—and it could have come out otherwise. In fact, Luhmann points out again and again the contingency and even the unlikelihood of the present state of affairs. Given all the infinite evolutionary possibilities, what is actually the case was by no means necessary. The "strange" nonhuman functionings that we are all part of, for instance, the present forms of the global economy and the mass media, are not more "essential" or "substantial" than a human being, they are mechanisms that managed to evolve and, most likely, they will perish again. Present systems are not the end of human beings and not the end of history; they are temporary and transitory forms of life, consciousness, and communication.

Unlike Luhmann's systems, some people have been truly essential at least in preparing the manuscript of this book. Ryan O'Neill did, once more, take on the task of straightening out my English and put together most of the bibliography. Hannes Bergthaller, Bruce Clarke, and Kerri Mommer at Open Court provided detailed suggestions for revisions and changes. Several students and colleagues took the trouble of reading through the manuscript at various stages and I'd like to thank everybody who in the long period of its development contributed to the completion of this project. I am grateful to Brock University for funding my research work and enabling me to meet in person with some of the most important Luhmann scholars in Germany, and I am, of course also thankful to these, among them Dirk Baecker, Peter Fuchs, Rudolf Stichweh, and the philosopher Peter Sloterdijk, for sharing some of their expertise and time with me.

—Cedar Bay, 27 February 2005

Introduction

In their "revolutionary" bestseller *Empire*, authors Michael Hardt and Antonio Negri (2000, 13 and 15) state that Niklas Luhmann, along with John Rawls, was a main influence on their work. Just as Hardt and Negri's project does, Niklas Luhmann's social theory presents a challenging, avant-garde view of contemporary society. The present book will highlight its unique relevance in regard to current social and political issues. At the same time, it attempts to provide English-speaking readers with a comprehensive introduction to his work, for it is not yet as accessible in English as it is in German, Spanish, and Italian. This is not to deny that major achievements have already been made. Luhmann's earlier magnum opus, *Social Systems*, was translated into English as early as 1995, and in the past few years a good number of other works have become available. In addition, there are also some very fine secondary studies, for example, by William Rasch (2000), and Michael King and Chris Thornhill (2003). There is also the highly recommended introduction to *Social Systems* by Eva M. Knodt, and a concise synopsis of Luhmann's theory by Gotthard Bechmann and Nico Stehr (2002).

No single work, including this one, can pretend to exhaustively present all of Luhmann's ideas—that would be too much to cover in a brief introduction. My special focus will be not only the avant-gardism and relevance of Luhmann's social theory, but also the more philosophical issues touched on by his writings. I will, moreover, concentrate to a great extent on the later Luhmann, particularly on his grand treatise *The Society of Society* (*Die Gesellschaft der Gesellschaft*, 1997), on *Introduction to Systems Theory* (*Einführung in die Systemtheorie*, 2002, a posthumously published transcript of a 1991/92 lecture series), and on *The Reality of the Mass Media* (*Die Realität der Massenmedien*, 1996).

This book proceeds from simplicity to complexity. Part 1 begins with a general description of systems theory as it was understood and adapted by Niklas Luhmann. The first two sections in chapter 1 are written for those who struggle with the difficulty of Luhmann's theory and concepts. I myself have gone through this struggle for many years, and I do not claim that it is over—I hope, however, that my experiences may have led to an exposition that might ease the struggles of others. Chapters 2, 3, and 4 of part 1 are a little more advanced and specific; they deal with how some more or less traditional philosophical topics—reality, humanity, and the distinction between good and evil—are seen from a Luhmannian perspective. Part 2 is a case study of one of Luhmann's case studies that I find particularly interesting—it is a reflection on the mass media as a social system. Part 3 describes the philosophical context of Luhmann's thought.

The appendix contains three articles by Luhmann in English translation. I chose to include these three relatively short essays because they directly relate to the issues discussed in this study and because they are—quite atypically for Luhmann's otherwise notoriously difficult, lengthy, and sometimes even rather associative style—relatively concise and reader-friendly while still theoretically dense and of a general significance. I have also provided a bibliography of works by and on Luhmann in English and a few notes on Luhmann research materials in German.

PART I

A New Way
of Thinking
about Society

1

What Is Social Systems Theory?

(a) Systems Theory

In recent years complaints about an increasingly less humane world seem to be on the rise. When dealing with institutions, even within schools or hospitals, one often feels reduced to a mere number. Economically, all that matters is money—but what about the individuals behind the monetary figures? Politically, many people, even in the "free world," decry the lack of "true" *democracy*, a lack of a true rule *by the people*. Organizations such as multinational corporations—or at least the political parties influenced by their donations—seem to be gaining increasing control of the governments at all levels, from local to global, and to be taking power out of the hands of individual citizens. And then, of course, there is the issue of technology and the mass media; computers and TV sets occupy more and more human space and time. It seems as if highly sophisticated machines are finally pushing human beings toward the fringes of society. All this is topped off by the rising fears of a biological dehumanization of humankind: genetic engineering seems to be able to take reproduction out of the hands (or more precisely: the reproductive organs) of the human body. In the not too far future, birth and death may no longer be individually contingent events of human life, but rather well planned technical operations. Facing all these "problems," people are calling more loudly and intensely for ethics and religion to come to the rescue of human values. This is, for instance, evidenced by the emergence of "applied" or "professional ethics"—a new academic "metaprofession" created to reintroduce humaneness into all professions![1]

Interestingly, and paradoxically, such a negative outlook on the future of humankind is paralleled by more optimistic and sometimes enthusiastic assessments. In the view of many, the impending progress of genetic engineering may finally put an end to human pain, sickness, and even death. Creating the biologically perfect human being may become possible. Likewise, computer technology may immensely increase the intellectual abilities available to humankind. And communication technology has already built the "global village" envisioned by Marshall McLuhan, the Canadian technology apostle of the 1960s. McLuhan viewed new technological developments as extensions of human capacities, and, in the same vein, current technology advertisement, be it for communication or bio-technology, hails great prospects for the full realization of human potential in a new information age. Similarly, there is continued hope that the expansion of the market will eventually bring prosperity to everyone, that more effective education programs and health systems will enable future generations to live better lives, that more professional governments and refined social institutions will increase our freedom and well-being.

Both attitudes, a pessimistic gloom in the face of waning humaneness and an optimistic embracing of human prospects, are often found in the same person. An American president, for instance, may in the same speech appeal to the humanist and religious values of his subjects *and* praise the new achievements of technological and social engineering. One and the same movie or TV character may well be, on the one hand, a thoughtful person who cares about family and human warmth *and*, on the other hand, uses a computer to conduct overseas financial transactions. The humanist pessimist and optimist are only mutually exclusive when it comes to newspaper editorials or academic articles: here one has to take sides. But, in real life, both attitudes seem to go together quite well. There is a fair share of both humanist optimism and pessimism in most of us. This may simply be because they have more in common than what is obvious at first sight— they are both "humanist." Both attitudes somehow realize the immense gap between present-day society and the traditional conception of it as a "human" world. In order to close the gap, the pessimist in us, feeling a certain nostalgia, longs to change the *world*—it should be more human again to fit our good old conception of it. The optimist in us takes another road and wants to change the *attitude*—why can't we be a bit more welcoming to our age and simply "extend" our understanding of what is human so that we may see the wonderful possibilities in store for humanity? Neither of the two, however, seems to be willing to do away with the traditional conception of a *human society* and replace it with a new one. This is left to social systems theory.

Systems theory recognizes that the world—or rather: *society*— can no longer be aptly understood as a human one. Unlike the cultural pessimists, it does not blame society—or any of its individual agents—for this. And, unlike the optimists, it is not willing to celebrate the dehumanization of the humane as the greatest human perfection.

The primary starting point of social systems theory—or its "turning point" in comparison to its humanist predecessors—is that it no longer holds that current society can be successfully analyzed on the basis that it is (or should be) fundamentally humane, and that it is, on principle, an assembly of individual human beings. This sounds, at first, rather counterintuitive. But this oddness may turn out to be due to the fact that traditional ("Old European") descriptions of society still dominate public education and the mass media more than our actual experiences of social life.

Old European philosophy (one may think of, for example, Plato's *Republic*) tended to define society in terms of a group of people: the *polis* was, in the words of Allan Bloom, "a community of men sharing a way of life" (1991, 439–40). This did not substantially change in early modern social theory, when notions of a society based on a "social contract" between its individual members were put forth (Hobbes, Rousseau). Nor did it change in later modernity when thinkers, like the famous British utilitarian Jeremy Bentham, rationalized (or "technicized") the idea of a community of individuals so that it became a mathematical sum of individuals whose interests could be calculated with the help of statistics. Even in the twentieth century, consensus theories of "communicative action" (Habermas) or of "fairness" (Rawls) still conceived of society on the basis of the group model and of communication *between human beings*. There is a strong "anthropocentric" tradition in European and North American social philosophy that is certainly

hard to overcome and informs the "common sense" understanding of what a society is.

However, is it really more convincing to describe what happens
when one buys a chocolate bar at a store or stock on the Internet
as instances of "human interaction" than to describe them as
events in the function system of the economy? On what factual
grounds can one hold that zapping to a TV channel or acting in a
soap opera is a way of taking part in the life of a community rather
than taking part in the systems of mass media? And to what extent
is the mechanical counting of a vote in an election more an act of
recognizing the individual intentions of a citizen than an element
of a social procedure to distribute power? If one opts for the second description in each case, one steps towards social systems theory and one of its most basic assumptions: *human beings do not
and cannot communicate—only communication can.*

As opposed to the traditional Old European attempt to
describe society on the basis of its *members* (that is: a group of people or a community), systems theory tries to describe society on
the basis of its *events:* it looks at what actually happens. When
someone buys a chocolate bar or stock, this is understood as economic communication; when someone watches TV, this is understood as mass media communication; and when a vote is cast and
counted, this is understood as political communication. These
examples already show that communication is not restricted to language; often one can communicate equally well, for instance, with
money or ballots. (While social systems theory is certainly influenced by the "linguistic turn," it is also strongly influenced by
semiotics. Ferdinand de Saussure and George Herbert Mead are at
least as important to it as Richard Rorty and Ludwig Wittgenstein).
But, isn't it—as not only traditional European social theory suggests, but also, and maybe even more importantly, Indo-European
grammar suggests—still "one," that is, an individual being, who
communicates? When "one" casts a vote—isn't it in the final analysis the "one" that counts rather than the vote?

Once I had lunch at a self-service restaurant in downtown San
Antonio. I had just paid for my meal when the next customer
approached the cashier. Coincidentally, both the customer's and
the cashier's cell phones rang, more or less, at the same time, and
both men started a phone conversation. I could not overhear their
conversations, but let us assume that the well-dressed customer

was speaking with a client of his law firm, while the cashier was speaking with his wife. The two phone conversations went on for quite a while, and both men kept talking while the dinner was paid for. So both men were simultaneously taking part in two communications. The customer was communicating economically (paying for his food) and, at the same time, in the legal system (assuming that he was talking to a client). The cashier was communicating economically with the customer and, in the intimacy system, with his wife (if it was her who called). As a matter of fact, it can be said of both men that, at the time I saw them, they each were "*one* who communicates economically" and "*one* who communicates otherwise." They both were *ones* who were, systemically speaking, *two*.

I do not expect that either of these men later suffered an identity crisis and felt the need to consult a psychoanalyst. On the basis of the traditional social models mentioned above, they would, however, have undergone a severe personality split. They both had lost their *in-dividuality* for a short time and turned into "dividuals." The communication-performed-by-individuals model can explain this short scene in only one way: both men quickly switched back and forth between communications. While such switching may have happened in their *minds*, so that their respective mental individuality was preserved, it did not emerge in the *communication* I observed. In fact, all communications, between customer and cashier, and between them and their respective callers, went on smoothly. There was no rapid back and forth, no short break between segments visible in the communications. The economic communication was at no time interrupted by the phone conversations, it did not even seem to be obstructed or prolonged by them—and vice versa.

What I am trying to demonstrate with this example is that individuals and their thoughts are not an integral part of the events of communication. If individuals and their thoughts were an integral part of communication events, then the *three* communications in the cell phone example could not have gone on *simultaneously*. They could only have unfolded in turn. But this was not the case, at least it was not what I *observed*. I witnessed two individuals each performing two separate and uninterrupted communications at the same time. This observation illustrates the previously mentioned assumption of social systems theory. It is, *empirically* speaking (from an observer's perspective), communication that constitutes communication, and not human beings as individuals. Of course, human beings are necessary for communication to take place—but it is not they who are "operating" within communication. They are, rather, the external condition *sine qua non* of communication, but not an internal element of communication and society. What went on in the minds of the two men when they were having their phone conversations was quite irrelevant in regard to the economic transaction that I saw—they were preoccupied with other things, but that did not prevent the economic exchange from functioning well. To explain what was going on economically, it would not help much to investigate the two men's thoughts—instead one would have to describe the structures and dynamics of the exchange that took place.

Niklas Luhmann therefore states:

> Within the communication system we call society, it is conventional to assume that humans can communicate. Even clever analysts have been fooled by this convention. It is relatively easy to see that this statement is false and that it only functions as a convention and only within communication. The convention is necessary because communication necessarily addresses its operations to those who are required to continue communication. Humans cannot communicate; not even their brains can communicate; not even their conscious minds can communicate. Only communication can communicate. (1994a, 371)

When we talk to each other or when we buy something or when we vote in an election, we say that "we" communicate—but it is, empirically speaking, always only the communication that communicates. When two people talk to each other—even the most intimate lovers—their minds and bodies are still outside of the communication, not inside it. In her foreword to the American edition of Luhmann's book *Social Systems*, Eva M. Knodt illustrates this point with the following example from literature:

> In the opening scene of Danton's Death, the nineteenth-century German playwright Georg Büchner dramatizes what is easily recognized as the primal scene of hermeneutic despair. In response to his lover's attempt to reassure herself of the bond of understanding between them, the protagonist makes a silent gesture toward her forehead and then replies: "—there, there, what lies behind this? Go on, we have crude senses. To understand one another? We would have to

break open each other's skulls and pull the thoughts out of the fibers of our brains." (Luhmann 1995a, xxiv)

This is the perennial empirical problem—the "hermeneutic despair"—with the traditional semantics of communication and society being "interpersonal." We can, in communication, only connect to the communication of others, but never to their minds or brains, much less to the "human being" as such in any given case. While communication cannot take place without human beings, human beings are, paradoxically enough, still totally inaccessible within communication. This is true even for the single individual: "I don't know if I mean what I say. And if I knew, I would have to keep it to myself" (Luhmann 1994a, 387).

Systemically speaking a theory that conceives of society as the system of communication has to locate minds and bodies—and, of course, "human beings"—outside the operational realm of society. This is the "scandal" of social systems theory when looked at from the perspective of traditional "Old European" humanisms.

By excluding minds and bodies from society, systems theory establishes three main types of systems: systems of communication (social systems), systems of life (bodies, the brain, and so on), and systems of consciousness (minds).[2] Each system is in the *environment* of others. Communication needs the environment of living and psychic systems, just as a fish needs water. But this is also true vice versa: To be a system, a system must have an environment. In one of his articles, Luhmann uses a diagram to illustrate the three main types of systems that are "mutual environments" (1990a, 2; table modified):

Figure 1.1. Types of Systems

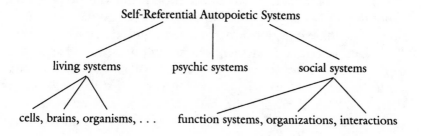

Any system is, for itself, somehow "individual." A mind is always individual, it is a unique and singular psychic system. Similarly, human bodies are unique and, to a certain extent, singular systems. Even communication systems may be called "individual"—the economic system is also "unique"—it is entirely different from all the other systems and "singular." There is only one economic system—systemically speaking, the USA and Canada, do not have separate economies. Thus individuality still exists in systems theory, but as systemic individuality. The traditional "human being" is not such an individual, it is rather divided into at least three segments that each form individualities. A human being is born with an individual body, it builds up an individual mind, and it will partake in many individual communication systems. Social systems theory does not deny that there is a kind of individuality to the mind or the *psyche* (the "soul" in Old European philosophies). But, unlike in Old European philosophies (most notably, the Cartesian tradition), this individuality can neither claim to be the "essential" element nor the only true "individual" aspect of a human being. From a systemic point of view, the bodily and communication systems have the same degree of "individuality" as the psychic system—and these individualities do not converge or exist in a hierarchical relation. Unlike Old European philosophies, there is no mind-body dualism. There is rather a mind-body-communication trinity, and within this trinity no system can "take control." It was common in Old European philosophy (Plato and Descartes are prime examples) to claim that the "intellect" should somehow rule over the body. Given the systemic "individuality" of both systems, they are unable to exert control over each other from the perspective of systems theory.

The human being "as such" has no theoretical place in systems theory. When there is talk about "human beings," systems theory would have to ask: do you mean the social *person* who is addressed in communication? The *body* that can be seen over there? Or the *mind* that thinks and feels within this body? Of course, we usually do not ask these questions when we communicate with each other. But when we talk to someone, we also do not assume that we talk to brainwaves or to thoughts and feelings. We usually assume that we are talking to another person. Once more: this by no means denies that the human being has a body and a mind outside of communication—*it is rather to absolutely confirm this, and to say that human beings exist as much bodily as they exist mentally and socially*—but rather that none of these three realms can claim to include the other two. Neither body nor mind nor society are the definite "home" of the human being—when we love someone, we do not love this person's cells or hormones (which we can't see or feel, no matter how much we may claim to love that person's "body") or mental operations (which we can't hear or know, no matter how much we may claim to be so "likeminded"). It is impossible to reduce a person's social life to his or her bodily data and/or mental activity. And it is also impossible to require a person's mind to control all of their bodily and communicational functions. Likewise, a sociological analysis of a person cannot claim to know all that goes on in the mind and body. While minds, bodies, and communications can be "individual," a human being cannot. The "human being" does not exist as a singular entity.

According to systems theory, the traditional notion of the "human being" is a simplification of the actual complexity of human existence. The single term "human being" does not live up to all that human beings are. The Old European philosophical tradition and Indo-European grammatical habits have contributed to the establishment of the "conventional assumption" that human beings can communicate—but it is an empirical fact that the "essential" elements of what is understood to constitute the human being cannot. Neither brains nor minds can communicate. We cannot say what our brainwaves are "oscillating," and we can't even say what we think. What is said in communication is never equal to what is thought and felt in the mind. It is impossible for me to adequately represent on this page what is going through my mind—intellectually, emotionally, "perceptionally"—while I am writing this sentence. And the same is true for every sentence I say or write—there is no one-to-one correspondence between communication and the mind. I suppose the same is true in regard to your reading of what I write. What you think and feel while reading this sentence will be, in each single case, entirely different from what is communicated in this sentence. Communication systems and mental systems are operationally separate. The "human being" can be reduced to none of them. Thus, social systems theory holds that if "we" want to understand how society functions or operates, we cannot reduce it to such an extremely broad and "metasocial" notion as that of the "human being."

Holding that living systems (bodies), psychic systems (minds), and communication systems (society) are separate does not prevent systems theory from recognizing relations between them. Social systems theory is just one branch of systems theory—there is also biological systems theory, and there may well be, among others, a psychological systems theory. A core concept of social systems theory is derived from biological systems theory: the concept of *autopoiesis*. Chilean biologist Humberto Maturana came up with the concept to explain how biological systems such as cells are a product of their own production. The word is a neologism made up of the two ancient Greek components *autos* ("self") and *poiesis* ("production," see Maturana 1981, 21–32; see also Mingers 1995). Luhmann explains:

> Why autopoiesis? Maturana once told me how this expression came to his mind. Initially, he had worked with circular structures, with the concept of a circular reproduction of the cell. The word "circular" is a common one that does not create further terminological problems, but for Maturana it lacked precision. Then a philosopher, on the occasion of a dinner or some other social event, gave him a little private lecture on Aristotle. The philosopher explained to him the difference between *praxis* and *poiesis*. *Praxis* is an action that includes its purpose in itself as an action. Aristotle here meant the ethos of the life in the polis, its virtue and excellency, called *arête*, whose importance is not due to its contribution towards the creation of a good city, it rather already makes sense on its own. Other examples would be swimming—one does not do it in order to get somewhere—or smoking, chatting, or the reflections in universities, which too are actions satisfying as such without leading to any results. The very concept of *praxis* already includes self-reference. *Poiesis* was explained to Maturana as something that produces something external to itself, namely a product. *Poiesis* also implies action; one acts, however, not because the action itself is fun or virtuous, but because one wants to produce something. Maturana then found the bridge between the two concepts and spoke of *autopoiesis*, of a *poiesis* as its product—and he intentionally emphasized the notion of a product. *Autopraxis*, on the other hand, would be a pointless expression, because it would only repeat what is already meant by *praxis*. No, what is meant here is a system that is its own product. The operation is the condition for the production of operations. (2002a, 110–11)

Francisco Varela, another Chilean biologist who closely cooperated with Humberto Maturana, explains the concept of autopoiesis in connection with the biological cell:

> If you, for instance, try to understand what a cell is as the smallest living system without intending to explain how it is structured, that it reproduces itself, that it develops, etc.—if you simply want to say what it really is—then you will come to the following very simple answer: A living system is an organization that preserves itself as a result of its organization. How does it do this? It produces components that produce components that produce components. This is no mystery: enzymes produce enzymes. The boundary of the cell is its membrane. The membrane again is a process that limits the diffusion and thus preserves the internal network of production that produces the membrane. Everywhere you see systems that exist due to a kind of Münchhausen-effect: they manage to grab themselves by the hair and pull themselves out of the swamp. . . . This is the case in many areas. (Biological) autopoiesis is only one example. Other examples are language, and, possibly, families, firms, etc. (1997, 148–49)

In the last sentence of the above quotation, Varela alludes to social systems theory that has taken up the originally biological concept of autopoiesis. The growth of a social system, be it society in general or singular social systems such as families or firms, can be explained with the same concepts as and in a similar way to the growth of biological organisms. At least, this is what social systems theory tries to do.

The concept of autopoiesis, even though based on a neologism, is not necessarily "revolutionary" in itself—models of self-organization or self-production have been introduced by older philosophies and cosmologies[3]—but it certainly contradicts traditionally influential "creationist" models. If one conceives of the world on the basis of notions of causation and deliberate design, then production is likely to be conceived of as the result of an external "producer," be it a demiurge (as in Plato's *Timaios*), a "first mover" (as with Aristotle), or a Creator God (as in Christianity). Systems theory diverges from such classical models and replaces the notion of external agency or "input" with the notion of self-construction. Reality is no longer a created one (neither a *created* one nor a created *one*) but a constructivist complexity. Every system produces itself and thereby its own reality. The world ceases to be a general "unit" or "oneness." Reality is not an all-embracing whole of many parts, it is rather a variety of self-producing systemic realities, each of which forms the environment of all the others. There is no common "world" in reality, because reality is in each instance an effect of "individual" systemic autopoiesis. Reality is transformed from created oneness to constructed difference.

I left out four important sentences from the passage by Varela quoted above. After describing the "Münchhausen-effect," Varela continues: "This is the core of autonomy. And this is also exactly what is meant by operational closure. My shortest definition is: The results of systemic operations are once more systemic operations" (1997, 149). The autonomy and autopoiesis of biological systems goes along with their *operational closure.* That a system produces itself implies that it produces its own boundary between itself and its environment. It practices a closure by producing—in the case of the biological cell—a membrane. Its autopoietic production consists of producing a boundary or membrane that produces its own operational closure. Once there is a membrane, all operations within the cell happen within the cell, they do not directly connect with operations in the outside environment. There is no literal "input" into the cell. The membrane does not allow for the environment to directly take part in the cell's biological operations. This idea distinguishes the autopoietic model of operational closure from traditional input-output models, which suppose that operations can transgress systemic boundaries. Varela says:

> Let me explain the difference between an input-output model and an autonomy model with the help of an example. Classical immunology studied how the body reacts to inputs of antigens by producing antibodies. This was the classical input-output description. There were attacks and responses to them: viruses and immunity. But the longer research on the immune system continued the less sense the term "antigen" made. It became increasingly difficult to say what an "antigen" is and what it is not, because this was defined differently for every system. Besides, it turned out that most antibodies reacted to most antibodies. The whole immune system is literally a giant network of antibodies and molecules that are in contact with one another and constitute an enormous operational closure.
>
> Where could antigens be fit in? Very simply: as something that is somewhat similar to the internal antibodies. They are not defined as

something alien. The immune system does not function like a military camp with people on all sides watching for the enemy to approach. It is most of all concerned with the constructive and positive aspects to preserve itself in its molecular conditions. Of course, interactions have some effects. But these do not define the system. If one wants to understand its dynamics, how antibody levels are regulated and how pathological situations are coped with, one has to abandon the input-output model. Instead, one has to assume that the immune system is operationally closed. This makes a dramatic difference, because now other questions have to be asked and other experiments have to be conducted, and everything has to be conceptualized with different notions. (1997, 150)

Biological systems theory did away with the input-output concept that assumed a direct interaction between systems and their environment and thus, so to speak, a shared operational reality. From the perspective of biological systems theory, living systems each produce their own systemic reality. Anything that happens in their environment can produce a systemic "response," but only within the boundaries and operational means of the system. There is neither a direct input into the system nor an immediate output.

Social systems theory borrows not only the concept of autopoiesis from biological systems theory, but also the concept of operational closure. The theory views social systems as *operationally closed* because, like biological systems, they are self-producing "organisms" of communication that consist of the connecting of system-internal communication with system-internal communication. Economic communication, for instance, can only connect to economic communication—otherwise it ceases to be economic communication. Once a system has established itself, be it biological or social, it can only continue its autopoiesis by its own operational means. It cannot import other means without losing its systemic integrity and its "membrane" and thus its reality.

The notions of autopoiesis and operational closure make, as Varela pointed out, a "dramatic difference" to traditional concepts of biological life and reality. They also make a dramatic difference when they are applied to the realm of social theory. Luhmann describes the "paradigm shift" that occurs:

I think that the concept of autopoiesis and the theory of autopoietic systems. . . . are underestimated in regard to the radicalism of this approach. This radicalism goes back to the hypothesis of operational closure. This hypothesis implies a radical shift in epistemology, and also in the ontology it supposes. If one accepts it and also relates to it the concept of autopoiesis and treats the latter as a further formulation of the theory of operational closure, then it is clear that it also breaks with the epistemology of the ontological tradition that assumed that something of the environment enters the understanding and that the environment is represented, mirrored, imitated, or simulated within a cognizing system. In this respect, the radicalism of the new approach can hardly be underestimated. (2002a, 114)

The theory of autopoiesis and operational closure—and this is true for both its biological and sociological applications—breaks with the notion of a common reality that is somehow "represented" within all systems or elements that take part in reality. According to systems theory, systems exist by way of operational closure and this means that they each construct themselves and their own realities. How a system is real depends on its own self-production, and how it perceives the reality of its environment also depends on its self-production. By constructing itself as a system, a system also constructs its understanding of the environment. And thus a systemic world cannot suppose any singular, common environment for all systems that can somehow be "represented" within any system. Every system exists by differentiation and thus is different from other systems and has a different environment. Reality becomes a multitude of system-environment constructions that are in each case unique. This is the radical shift away from traditional Old European epistemologies and ontologies that Luhmann speaks of.

The operational closure of autopoietic systems does not prevent them from being "open" to their respective environments. Operational closure rather enables systems to generate an openness towards their environment, but no operational openness. A system cannot come into immediate contact with its environment by way of its own operations. The biological operations within a cell, for instance, are only connected to and in continuation with the other biological operations within it. The same is true for psychic operations within an individual mind and for communicational operations within a communication system. The biological operations of the brain are connected to and continued by other biological operations of the brain. Similarly, a thought or a feeling is connected to and continued by other thoughts or feelings. A mind cannot continue a thought with a brainwave. And a communication can, of course, only be continued with more communication. You cannot communicate with me with your mind or brain, you will have to perform another communicative operation such as writing or speaking.

The operational closure of autopoietic systems allows them to build up mechanisms—biological, mental, or communicational—with which they can observe their environment. Thus the observation of an environment depends on the differentiation of a system from this environment. Luhmann points out: "If you want to formulate it radically, you may say that cognition is only possible because there are no relations, no operative relations to the environment"(2002a, 93).

Luhmann explains the relation between the operational closure of systems and their openness to the environment with a biological example. Brains function on the basis of operational closure, but, with the help of the eyes and the ear, a brain is open to what it sees and hears:

> (A brain) has a small variety of sensibilities that reduce that which can be seen, that limit the spectrum of colors, and also reduce that which can be heard. Only because this is so, the system is not overburdened with external effects on it. And only because this is so can there be learning mechanisms in the brain that allow it to build up more complex structures. We observe a low variety of external contacts going along with an enormous development of the structural capacity of the brain and an enormous capacity for processing the few irritations that are available to the system. And we see that this is again compatible with its autopoietic structure, with its operational closure. Everything depends on the system not establishing contact with the environment, but only being photo-chemically or acoustically stimulated. Then, from these irritations and with its own apparatus, the system produces information that does not exist in the environment but only has correlates out there—that can again only be seen by an external observer. (2002a, 122)

How an eye sees the environment, what a brain makes of the visual irritation it receives, is entirely dependent on its own structure. It reduces the complexity of what can be seen in a specific way—and thus builds up internal systemic complexity. While it reduces the spectrum of visual stimuli—the eye cannot see most of what is "out there"—it is also able to construct itself as a very complex mechanism of seeing. This is why every eye, in accordance with its own internal structure, sees things differently. To each human being the world looks slightly different, and the difference in the "world views" of people as compared to horses, or people as compared to ants is even greater. But who sees the world correctly? Who "represents" it more adequately? These questions become obsolete in systems theory. The specific openness towards the environment is, in the case of autopoietic systems, always an effect of the internal activity of those systems. The external complexity of the environment is reduced by systemic operations, and this reduction is accompanied by an internal increase of systemic complexity.

A brain is not in direct contact with what it sees or hears. It produces the information of what it sees and hears by its own internal means. Likewise, what we think or feel about what we see or hear is produced by the system of consciousness, not by the physiology of the brain (there is more than one thought or feeling possible as a correlate to a specific physiological state). And how we communicate a thought or a feeling is again decided in communication. There is not one specific form of communicating one specific thought or feeling. The brain is operationally closed—and therefore it can have cognition of the external world. Our consciousness system (our "mind") is operationally closed, and therefore it can have cognition of the physiological events in the brain. And when communicating, we can, for instance, observe our thoughts or feelings in communication. Operational closure allows for constant environmental "irritation" of autopoietic systems. The systems, by means of their operational mechanisms, can then produce information about the environment within themselves.

Bodies, minds, and society, being biological, psychic, and communication systems, respectively, are operationally closed and thus open towards each other. They are also "structurally coupled." The concept of *structural coupling* is another one that social systems theory borrowed from Humberto Maturana.[4] Obviously, communication can only go on when there is consciousness and life. Dead bodies and empty minds have nothing to say. Communication systems are dependent on being structurally coupled with consciousness systems (minds), and these in turn are dependent on being structurally coupled with life systems (bodies). Luhmann believes that the emergence and existence of consciousness and communication is due to their structural coupling:

> One cannot imagine that a consciousness could have evolved without communication. Similarly, one cannot imagine that there would be meaningful communication without consciousness. There must have been a kind of coordination, that, because it relates to different forms of autopoiesis, lead, on the one hand, to an increase of complexity within the realm of possible mental contents and, on the other hand, within the realm of social communication. It seems to me that this mechanism of coupling is language. (2002a, 122)

Structural coupling is a state in which two systems shape the environment of the other in such a way that both depend on the other for continuing their autopoiesis and increasing their structural complexity. In the case of the structural coupling of consciousness and communication, these two systemic realms could mutually build up their complexity by sharing the medium of language.[5] We can think in language and we can communicate linguistically. Spoken or written communication can irritate the mind quite impressively—what we read or hear usually makes us think and feel about that which we read or hear. The mental irritation of linguistic communication, for instance, is hard to avoid. We can experience this when we try to study for an examination while someone talks loudly in the next room. It is hard for the mind not to "listen" when there is talk. Conversely, we have difficulty continuing a conversation when our mind is preoccupied with certain thoughts or feelings. When a loved one dies, we find it hard to concentrate on a television program.

Yet the structural coupling between psychic and communication systems does not turn thoughts into communication or communication into thoughts. We cannot continue a conversation by simply thinking about what someone else says. Psychic and communication systems, however, operate simultaneously and cannot improve in complexity without the other. The examples of Kaspar Hauser and other feral children clearly demonstrate that a mind that is not continuously "irritated" by social communication is unable to develop the specific complexity necessary for social communication. You cannot simply teach somebody to speak who has never been exposed to society. In these cases communication is likely to fail because mental correlates have not been developed.

(Of course, minds like that of Kaspar Hauser will likely have built up *other* psychic complexities in correlation to the environment in which they evolved.) The more complex society becomes, the more complex is our reflection upon it. And the more complex our thoughts become, the more complexly they are "expressed" in communication. (Again: of course, the thoughts are *not really* "expressed" in communication; a mind cannot express itself in communication—but more complex minds allow for communication *itself* to become more complex.)

The structural coupling between the brain as a living system, the mind as a psychic system, and society as a communication system seems to be of a specific structure with the mind somehow "in-between" the other two systems. Whatever "happens" within our brains seems to be first somehow "translated" into conscious information (feelings, thoughts) before it can, in turn, irritate communication and be processed by communication as social information. It seems that the mind is some kind of filter between the brain, on the one hand, and communication on the other. Luhmann says: "We can . . . conclude that society only couples itself with its environment through consciousness, and that thus there are no physical, chemical, and also no purely biological effects on social communication. Everything has to pass through that eye of the needle of communication" (2002a, 123). If consciousness functions as the needle's eye of communication this means that nothing can irritate communication that was not somehow processed as information in the mind. The mind, in turn, seems able to be irritated by both communication and the brain/body, so it can produce information out of communication as well as out of bodily events. We can try to cure a mental disorder by communicational irritation (psychotherapy) as well as by physical irritation (psychopharmacology). The mind is open to both kinds of systemic stimuli—but as psychiatric practice shows: each mind "resonates" differently in reaction to these irritations. Being operationally closed, autopoietic systems, organisms, minds, and social systems continuously irritate each other, but they eventually cannot but produce their own operations all by themselves.

The structural coupling between mind and body, and between body and communication as envisioned by systems theory is somewhat comparable to the three-tiered matrix in the popular *Matrix* movies (at least to the first movie in the series). In this film, human bodies function as batteries or fuel for computer programs that in turn function as the masterminds of a virtual society. All three systems seem to function autopoietically and, more or less, as operationally closed. It does not seem to be the case that the biological functioning of the human bodies as such determines the operations of the computer programs. And the computer programs seem to be so advanced that they do not determine exactly what happens in the virtual society. This society seems to be free to perceive itself as free and act in its own fashion. Of course, there is structural coupling; without the human batteries, the programs cannot run, and without the programs, this society cannot communicate. And vice versa, without the society, the computer programs would have no "substance," and without the computer programs, the human bodies would lose their function.

It seems that the human batteries in the film are somewhat similar to Luhmann's view of the biological system, while the computer programs seem similar to his view of the psychic system, and the "virtual" social sphere reminds one of his view of society. In the movie, of course, there is a hierarchy of exploitation and domination among these three spheres, where the computer program has enslaved the "authentic" realm of human bodies, and the story hinges on the notion that a liberation of this realm is possible and necessary. This is precisely the kind of humanist fantasy that Luhmann's theory is meant to debunk. Instead of an ultimately human and singular world, there is a plurality of systemic realities. And this can again only be realized within this systemic reality. We will return to this last aspect in the second chapter.

(b) Social Systems

Social systems theory recognizes psychic and biological systems as the necessary environment of social systems—and it borrows the terminology of biological systems theory to analyze the "life" of society. Of course, the word "life" is here used metaphorically, because society does not literally live—only living systems can live—but communicates. Just as society is no longer literally, but only metaphorically, described as an "organism," it is also no longer literally, but only metaphorically, described in terms of "consciousness." While some social theories, such as Herbert Spencer's Social Darwinism, understood society as a quasi-biological entity, some philosophers, such as Hegel, described it as an aspect of the unfolding of a larger consciousness or "spirit." While such theorists, perhaps especially Hegel, at times came close to a systemic conception of society, they nevertheless denied society its own systemic realm. In Hegel's philosophy, for instance, society is but an expression of spirit and is explained on the basis of concepts that pertain to consciousness. Social systems theory denies both a biological and a "spiritual" grounding of society. Life and consciousness are not parts of society. They operate, so to speak, outside the "membrane" of society (again, a *biological* metaphor) that is constituted by operations of communication. Social systems theory assumes that communication can—analogously, but independently—establish its own systemic autopoiesis through its own operational means.

I have pointed out frequently that social systems theory cannot accept the common assumption that society consists of human individuals—or of their minds or bodies. It consists, operationally speaking, of communication "events" such as communication by language, gestures, or money. Communicational sequences can then establish their own "individuality." They can grow into very specific shapes.

Orderly communication, in which we can *first* expect to be understood by others and *second* to understand them, emerges from *double* contingency.[6] Not anything, but any communication goes on, but it goes on only if and when it is able to establish some kind of order, when the problem of double contingency on both sides of the "understanding" of that communication is solved. Communication that is not mutually understood will not continue. "Buying" is only possible when the buyer can expect that the seller will give him/her goods for a piece of paper called "money," and when the seller can expect that the buyer will understand that he/she has to "pay" for these goods. Economic transactions can only happen when the possibility of *not* communicating economically on both sides of the transaction is overcome.

In this way, communication can be established as a unity of announcement (*Mitteilung*[7]), information (*Information*), and understanding (*Verstehen*). Within a simple economic transaction such as paying for a meal, it is *understood* by the seller that, by putting his tray on the counter, the buyer *announces* that he is ready to pay. Also, that which is on the tray visibly *informs* the seller about the goods the buyer likes to purchase. Even if both people do not talk to one another, their communication (as the unity of announcement, information, and understanding) may well continue, and the buyer will *understand* the seller's *announcement* that he has to pay six dollars when he gets this price *information* by looking at the display on the cash register.

Communication only continues and grows if it establishes certain patterns that allow for it to continue in that certain way along with that certain order. All emerging patterns of communication (of announcement, information, understanding)—or social order—can be explained as a solution to the problem of double contingency. What is communicated and how it is communicated is totally contingent: there is no basic a priori condition for communication. Communication is therefore always contingent in the sense that it could always have been otherwise. Why did society invent money or economic transactions at all? It could have invented something completely different. How do we know that Martians have an economy or money? But even if they do not have these things, they may still have communication.

Once communication goes on, however, how it goes on is contingent upon those patterns that have been established. Once an economy and money have been established, then economic communication is dependent on these patterns. Once a communication system "takes off," one's ability to communicate is contingent upon its order. In a society that has an economy, you can only communicate economically by communicating economically. Nobody can buy anything with noneconomic communication. Even if one gets something for free or steals something, then "getting something free" or "stealing" are economic terms.

Socially established communication patterns are identified by social systems theory as the individual elements that constitute society. Society consists of social systems, of certain communicational "organisms" that emerged and have established their own specific types of operations. These can connect to each other and continue the operations of this communicational organism—similar to a cell that by its bio-chemical operations creates its own autopoietic "being." A social system "is" nothing else but the autopoietic reproduction of itself. A social system, such as the economy, consists of nothing but economic communication that connects to

itself. It is only by economic communication that the economy continues and further constructs itself—and thus builds its own communicational "membrane" by which economic communication can
be distinguished from other types of communication.

According to social systems theory, society has evolved to a state
in which it consists of a variety of large communication systems
that can be identified by the *functions* they perform. Such *function
systems* are, for instance, economy, politics, law, and mass media:
buying a meal is communication functioning economically; the
casting and counting of a vote is communication functioning politically; presenting an argument in court is communication functioning legally. Since all these systems are operationally closed, they
are the intrasocial environment of the others. They are "subsystems" of society. Each function system has its own social perspective and creates its own social reality. They are all, so to speak,
subrealities of a general social reality. Still, they are not, strictly
speaking, "parts" of a "whole": society does not become less
"whole" when a system ceases to function and it does not become
more "whole" when a new one emerges. Before the mass media,
for instance, society was not "less" than it is today. There is also no
fixed "super-system" of which these functions are integral elements. Society, as such, does not function "less" when a system
ceases to function, and it does not function "more" when a new
system emerges. Again: the emergence of mass media did not make
any super-system function better.

Society looks different from the perspective of each subsystem
and its function, and there is no perspective, or super-system, that
can "supervise" the subsystems. The economic reality is different
from the world as seen in education or politics. But there is no
social reality that can claim to present the "whole picture." Even
religion has lost this privilege. In this sense, society consists only of
subsystems.

According to social systems theory, the subsystems of society
cannot be supervised or regulated by any social super-system. If
this was the case, these systems would not be autopoietic function
systems; they would not have their "individual" operational identity. Without a single social super-system, each system can look at
the others through its own means. The economy can look at all

others systems from an economic perspective and can "interpret" the "whole" society economically. Likewise, science—and within it social science, and within it, social systems theory—can look at the "whole" of society and interpret it scientifically. This is why social systems theory, being part of the social system of science, can claim to come up with a theory that is valid for society in its entirety.

In the terminology of social systems theory, function systems can be identified by their respective *codes*. The legal system, for instance, operates on the basis of the legal/illegal code. It communicates on the basis of this distinction. Every attorney, judge, or juror has to start from there. However, what specifically is legal or illegal is a matter of dispute. Function systems thus develop *programs* on the basis of their code that supply it with flesh and bone, so to speak. In the case of the legal system, such programs are the concrete laws, constitutions, norms, and so on. These programs allow the code to be applied by supplying it with certain guidelines for being processed. It is hard to argue about the legality or illegality of an action in the absence of law, be it natural, divine, or otherwise. In order to be actually communicated, a code cannot do without programs. In the system of science, to give another example, the code of true/false on which scientific communication is based, must be applied in connection with certain scientific theories, methods, and so on. Without relation to these programs you cannot argue scientifically for something to be true or false. Only in the context of, for instance, a theory or a method, can a scientific statement be called *scientifically* true or false.

Along with their specific codes and programs, the systems create their own functioning and thus their respective social *function* (*Funktion*). The science system produces (scientific) knowledge. Only science can provide society with a scientific explanation of its functioning. (This is not to say that society asked for such explanations, but once they are there, they are a social reality.) The function of the legal system, to give another example, is to establish norms for social expectations. The specific function of a social system can further be distinguished from its *efficacy* (*Leistung*). While science, for instance, has the function of producing knowledge, it also has the efficacy to make knowledge available for social purposes. Scientific knowledge can not only be known, it can also be "applied." Accordingly, the distinction between theoretical science and applied science would be a distinction between the social function of the science system and its efficacy (Luhmann 1997a, 758).

Modern function systems have developed into communicational "organisms" that communicate with more effective and diverse tools than simply language. They have developed their own *media*. A medium is, simply put, that which can take on form in communication, and in the case of many function systems these media are called by Luhmann (on the basis of Talcott Parsons's terminology) "symbolically generalized communication media" (*symbolisch generalisierte Kommunikationsmedien*). According to Luhmann, these media were developed to increase the likelihood of the successful continuation of communication. When it comes to highly functionally specialized communication (for instance, in the case of economic, legal, or scientific communication), language is a rather awkward medium. It is hard to *buy* something with language (for instance, by offering a promise in exchange for a horse), and it is equally hard to communicate a legal punishment on the basis of "plain" language without recourse to specifically legal communication media. Highly specialized communications need highly specialized media to succeed and to continue their autopoiesis. It is unlikely that economic communication would succeed and continue without a specific economic medium—and such a medium was established in money. (Today, with the economy becoming more and more complex, it seems that new economic media are gradually replacing money. Larger financial transactions are no longer made literally with money, but rather with stocks, bonds, and so forth.) In their "Luhmann Glossary" Baraldi, Corsi, and Esposito explain the need for symbolically generalized communication media in the terminology of social systems theory. Here they are referring not to money as the medium of the economy or to jurisdiction as the medium of law, but to power as the political medium and to scientific truth as the medium of science:

> Ego's motivation to accept the selection suggested by Alter becomes unlikely—and the symbolically generalized communication media respond to this problem. Ego accepts Alter's order to pay a penalty, because Alter possesses power. Ego accepts Alter's assertion that the earth circulates around the sun, because it is scientific truth. (Baraldi, Corsi, and Esposito 1997, 190)

Baraldi, Corsi, and Esposito also hasten to add that

the concepts of "acceptance" and "motivation" are used without any reference to the psychic system. Acceptance does not mean any inner agreement and motivation, not a psychic state, because one does not and cannot know anything about these matters: "acceptance" and "motivation" are only considered as conditions of success in communication. (1997, 191)

They summarize their definition of symbolically generalized communication media by stating that these are: "specific structures that secure the likelihood of communicative success because they transform the unlikelihood that Alter's selection is accepted by Ego into likelihood" (1997, 189). Luhmann remarks similarly:

> Symbolically generalized media miraculously transform a no-likelihood into a yes-likelihood—for instance, by making it possible to offer payment for goods or services one wants to have. They are symbolic insofar as they use communication in order to produce a fit that is unlikely as such. At the same time, however, they are also diabolic because by achieving this fit, they simultaneously produce new differences. (1997a, 320)

Media, such as money in economy, make the "fit" because they make transactions much more likely and easy. How difficult would it be to bring a buyer and seller together without money! Thus media are functioning *sym*bolically by fitting two pieces together. However, they also create new differences, as Luhmann (1997a, 320) adds: "Who can pay gets what he/she wants, who can't, doesn't." This is the *dia*bolic function of the media that introduces new distinctions (between the rich and the poor in the economy, between the powerful and those without power in politics, for instance).

Interestingly enough, Luhmann also remarks that highly specialized symbolically generalized communication media contribute to the growth of inequalities between the function systems. It seems that those systems, such as the economy, that have highly effective symbolic media and are, what is more, able to further refine these (money into stocks, and so on), gain some kind of evolutionary advantage over the others. For example, the "growth" of the economic system (not in terms of an increase in the GSP, of course, but in terms of an increase in social presence) as opposed to the decline of the religious system may be explained as an effect of the communicative advantage that money has over faith (being the medium of religion). Money and stocks seem to function better—both symbolically *and* diabolically—than faith. They easily bring "people" together and force them apart. Luhmann states:

> The different capabilities for system-construction of the various symbolically generalized communication media distinctively characterize the features of modern society. They lead (among other factors) to an unequal growth of the function systems, and thus to unequal applications of those functions regarding their respective communicative expenditure and visibility—without a hidden rationality or hierarchy fundamentally attached to those functions. Society does not expand like leavening; it does not symmetrically grow in size, complexity, and differentiation as supposed by the nineteenth-century theories of progress (which could suppose this because they understood society as merely an economic system). Modern society rather increases the complexity of some systems and lets others wither. (1997a, 391–92)

The different symbolically generalized communication media of the larger systems of modern society contribute to the dynamics of their respective functional "organisms." Communication systems have no intrinsic essence—as Marxists, for instance, believed. Social systems theory, on the contrary, does not assume that there is a predetermined order of society throughout history. Neither does it assume the unchanging stability of social systems. All systems continue their autopoiesis, and thus they all "develop." It seems that a central aspect of this development, especially in the conditions of modern society, is the adequacy and efficacy of a system's symbolically generalized communication medium. These media seem to be decisive factors when it comes to gaining "social space." Systems with rather "awkward" media, such as faith, will find it relatively hard to compete with systems that have more functionally capable media, such as money, power, or legislation. A symbolically generalized communication medium that is lacking in functional dynamics may contribute to the "marginalization" of the functional system that operates with it.

Functional social subsystems can be analyzed in great detail in regard to their codes, programs, functions, efficacies, media, and so on. Luhmann did this and wrote numerous articles and lengthy books on many of them, including law (1993c), the economy (1988a), politics (1975), science (1990c), religion (1977), education (Luhmann and Schorr 1988), and art (1995b). These represent the sociological heart of Luhmann's work. Given the specific characteristics of each system, however, it is difficult to do justice to each of them in a more general book on systems theory, such as the present one. I have therefore chosen to thoroughly concentrate, in the second part of this book, on only one function system, namely the mass media. Social systems theory describes all systems on the basis of the same theoretical outline and with a similar conceptual terminology, but, of course, with different concrete results in each case. The following table summarizes some of the main characteristics of function systems as they are identified and analyzed in Luhmann's extensive case studies (see Krause 1999, 36; table modified).

Figure 1.2. Social Systems

System	*Function*	*Efficacy*	*Code*	*Program*	*Medium*
Law	elimination of the contingency of norm expectations	regulation of conflicts	legal/illegal	laws, constitutions, etc.	jurisdiction
Politics	making collectively binding decisions possible	practical application of collectively binding decisions	government/ opposition	programs of political parties, ideologies	power
Science	production of knowledge	supply of knowledge	true/false	theories, methods	truth
Religion	elimination of contingency	spiritual and social services	immanence/ transcendence	holy scriptures, dogmas	faith
Economy	reduction of shortages	satisfaction of needs	payment/ nonpayment	budgets	money

While function systems are the subsystems of modern society and constitute its basic level of differentiation, or its "deep structures" (Luhmann 1998, 60), they are—as pointed out above—by no means the whole of society. One reason they are not is that not every communication can be classified as a communication within or of a functional system. A chat on the street corner, a short conversation with somebody who dialed the wrong number, a flirtation at a party, are difficult to attribute to any of the standard function systems. Social systems theory views society as systemic—but the notion of a social system is not limited to function systems alone. On a lower level, a whole range of other autopoietic communications emerge. Luhmann explains this metaphorically by saying that the larger types of social subsystems "float on a sea of small-scale systems that are continuously newly built and then dissolved" (1997a, 812). In a more analytic manner, he declares:

> On the foundations of an already existing society, a differentiation (*Ausdifferenzierung*) of autopoietic social systems can also happen without any relation to the social system or its previously established subsystems—simply through the experience of double contingency and the subsequent initiation of autopoietic system construction. Frequently very short-lived and trivial system-environment distinctions emerge in this way without any further constraints of form and without any necessity or possibility of legitimizing this distinction by relating it to society. (1997a, 812)

In the terminology of social systems theory such short-lived "anarchic" social systems that do not fit into any of the established functional realms can be called "interactions" (*Interaktionen*). Interactions typically operate on a "face-to-face" level and presuppose physical presence (see Baraldi, Corsi, and Esposito 1997, 82–85). A casual conversation in the elevator begins and ends with physical presence. Once the two people are back in their offices, they will continue to communicate in the function systems of law (if they are lawyers) or in the function systems of education or science (if they are professors). There they will communicate in a more systemic manner. The attorneys may study legal files while the professors grade papers.

As Luhmann points out in the quotation above, interactions can happen outside of function systems, or, in the words of Baraldi, Corsi, and Esposito (1997, 85), in "function-free" contexts such as standing in line for tickets, sitting on the bus, or having a drink at a bar. However, such interactive communicative *episodes* also occur within function systems. One can chat economically with a salesperson, joke legally with one's client, and even speak on friendly terms with one's students (but only if the office door is left open—otherwise this communication will be under the suspicion of no longer being educational).

While interactions are the communicational sea on which the function systems float, there is another type of social system that is more closely intertwined with the function systems. This type of social system is small-scale in comparison with social subsystems, but large-scale in comparison with interactions—it is the increasingly important "organizations" (*Organisationen*). Organizations are, according to Luhmann, a relatively new social phenomenon (specifically when compared to interactions), which have evolved along with functional differentiation, in other words, along with the establishment of the various function systems. The emergence of politics as an autopoietic system paved the way for the emergence of political parties. Similarly, the differentiation of the education system was a precondition for the emergence of educational organizations—such as schools and universities. The emergence of the economy as an autopoietic system lead to the founding of companies, firms, and corporations. The autopoietic system of medicine has hospitals and asylums as its corresponding organizations— and the establishment of the legal system has led to more and more courts and prisons.

Organizations are not necessarily confined to the communicative borders of just one function system. An organization like the IRA had *both* a political and a military side. A university is not only active in education and in science, it is, at least in North America, more often than not also playing an economic role. On the other hand, function systems do not focus on just one kind of organization. Economic transactions are not limited to companies and corporations, education does not only take place at universities, and politics does not only consist of political parties.

A central characteristic of organizations is membership. Organizations include people by accepting them into themselves. In order to enter a university, a sanatorium, or Al Qaeda one has to somehow qualify for membership, for instance, by grades, a diagnosis, or a common enemy.

Organizations can also be called "systems of decision." What an organization does depends on its decisions. Their communicative life is mainly one of decisions. If one reads about organizations such as companies or parties, one usually reads about the economical or political decisions they made. And the decisions of an organization are typically made in the context of further decisions. The autopoiesis of an organization thus becomes an autopoiesis of decisions—one decision generates endless decision-making (just think of serving on a university committee or making a managerial decision in a company). Luhmann says in regard to organizations: "As a result there comes into being an autopoietic system that is characterized by a specific form of operations: It produces decisions by decisions. Behavior is communicated as decision-making" (1997a, 831). The importance of organizations and their specific type of communicative operation—decision-making—seems to increase in modern society. Organizations (such as corporations and political parties) become more and more "powerful," in Luhmann's terms, they occupy more and more communicative space within various function systems. Functional communication is increasingly the communication of organizations. Baraldi, Corsi, and Esposito write:

> In the functionally differentiated society formal organizations gain a previously unnoted relevance. This is true not only for the economic system in which case the importance of organizations has been recognized and researched for a long time. The operational capabilities of other subsystems too are increasingly based on organized systems, such as schools in education, churches in religion, research institutions in the sciences . . . (1997, 131)

Besides function systems, interactions and organizations are two important types of autopoietic communication systems. There may well remain more such systemic types to be discovered below the level of functional subsystems. One candidate identified by Luhmann in his later writings is social movements, especially protest movements (see Luhmann 1997a, 847–65; Luhmann 1996a). Luhmann could not fully explore this interesting hypothesis because of his sickness and eventual death. Further below I will try to shed some light on this social phenomenon from a Luhmannian perspective.

The large-scale function systems of present-day society have completed their own operational closure. Just as society in general is an operationally closed system of communication shut off from the biological, mental, and technological operations of its environment, so the various function systems are operationally closed off from the other social subsystems in their intrasocial environment. Biological operations can only connect to biological operations and communicative operations can only connect to communicative operations. In a functionally differentiated society, communication cannot simply connect to *any* communication. The autopoiesis of a social subsystem can only be continued with communication of the same subsystem. Economic transactions can only be continued with further economic transactions. One cannot pay for goods with law, and one will not be taken seriously in the system of science, if one attempts to refute the truth claims of an academic publication with quotations from holy scriptures. In court, one needs lawyers to speak for oneself, because only they know how to contribute to the autopoiesis of legal communication.

By virtue of their respective codes, functions, media, and so on, the social subsystems were able to differentiate themselves in such a way that they became incompatible discourses. In the time before functional differentiation (I will discuss the historical dimensions of social systems theory in the next chapter) a quotation from the Bible *could* prove a scientific truth claim wrong, and when accused of a crime, one *could* represent oneself in court. This has thoroughly changed and the theory of functional differentiation and operational closure explains the results of this change. The highly specialized types of communication developed within the subsystems of society are no longer interconnected or interchangeable, and attempts to artificially impose one type of systemic communication on another fail. Under the conditions of functional differentiation, a fundamentalist state that is dominated by religious discourse and does not allow other function systems to operate independently will hardly be accepted as modern.

In a modern society, attempts to reject functional differentiation are not easily accepted nor are they likely to succeed. Religious politicians, for instance, will find it hard to avoid appearing too political from the perspective of the religious system and too religious (or "fundamentalist") from the perspective of the political system. The conditions of functional differentiation do not favor attempts to merge operations of different systems or attempts to steer the operations of one system by operations of another.

A well-known example of the failure of an operationally closed social function system to intervene in the operations of another is the failure of communist economy in Eastern Europe. If analyzed from the perspective of social systems theory, this failure had nothing to do with the "weakness of human nature" (regarding the unlikelihood of the establishment of an altruistic society), or with the corruption or brutality of totalitarian regimes, but rather with the impossibility of overcoming the operational closure of present-day function systems. In the communist countries of Eastern Europe, the economy was supposed to directly communicate with the political system—the economy was believed to be under immediate political control. This, however, was only a communicative construct, not a social reality. The economy still functioned economically and politics still functioned politically. In the long run, the illusion that the economy could efficiently communicate with the political system and that the political system could thus "control" the economy could not be upheld. Luhmann says:

> One of the most dramatic events of the past two or three decades was the breakdown of the socialist economy that was obviously unable to transform economic information into political information. The planning centers were in fact not informed about what was happening economically—whatever "economy" may mean in this connection—but they could only see if their plans were met or not. All those taking part in the planning processes could also see that the center saw if the plans were met or not. It was all about a political schema of goal-data that were more or less met, and the whole system focused on this. The information could be produced through factual reports or through forgeries and fictional data, and thereby the whole information processing could be continued without having any information available in the economy other than the political. (2002a, 130)

What Luhmann explains here is that in the politically planned economy of communist countries a peculiar communication about economic goal-data emerged. This communication was a central element of political communication provided by the economy. The economy was, so to speak, forced to continuously communicate politically—and not economically. The goal-data were politically, not economically produced. The economy was supposed to take part in political discourse instead of communicating by its own means. Thus, the economy lacked information about itself. Its situation can be compared to that of the political system under religious "control." Under such circumstances the political system is forced to communicate religiously and it has, while still somehow functioning politically, only religiously, not politically, valid information concerning itself. It is just as unlikely that an economic system can continue its autopoiesis well while artificially and fictitiously controlled by the political system, as it is unlikely that a political system can while artificially and fictitiously controlled by the religious system.

It may be important to note that neither social systems theory in general nor Luhmann in particular intends the theory of the operational closure of function systems to speak in support of a "market economy" or capitalist propaganda that hails the beneficial effects of a "free" economy. The theory merely observes that operationally closed function systems cannot be controlled by other function systems. It not only denies that communist governments can control the economy, it also denies this to capitalist or "democratic" ones. The economy controls itself—and no one knows if this is good or bad for the "people." Social systems theory neither believes that systemic self-control automatically leads to systemic success or to "prosperity" or "liberty." These concepts are themselves part of very specific political semantics. From the perspective of social systems theory, no function system is "good" or "bad;" it does not claim to know if it is better for a society to have an autopoietically functioning economy. It simply says that under the conditions of functional differentiation there *is* an autopoietic and operationally closed economy and that neither communist politics nor capitalist semantics can change this. Moreover, like communist politics, capitalist democracies tend to deny the systemic gap between the economy and politics. They create the illusion that political communication about economic matters actually "helps" the economy. Like communist regimes, democratic regimes counterfactually pretend that their political communication about the economy actually somehow "steers" economic development. Luhmann writes:

> I suspect that also here (in free-market economies) information that we treat as economic information—even though it may well be founded on the realities of the dispositions of companies and banks— is only produced for political purposes when it is compressed to data on joblessness, currency values, etc. Thus I suspect that politics works with data that are summaries of economic data but that have a purely political information value. On the level of the operations of companies completely different information is relevant. Companies focus on

their balances, on contracts they receive, on prices, on what competitors do, on the increase or decrease of demand and thus of possibilities of production. This information world is purely economic. It is very questionable if anybody in this world orients him/herself with statistics about joblessness. Within the economy market data count as information. (2002a, 131)

Luhmann points out that even in democratic societies with "free" markets, politics creates a pseudo-economic discourse. Political communication about joblessness, for instance, is political communication—and not economic communication. What politicians say about joblessness remains political communication. It is an illusion that political communication about joblessness can directly interfere in or even control the operationally closed economic system. Political communication about joblessness, as Luhmann says, serves political, not economic purposes. This is the case with communist and "democratic" regimes.

That function systems are operationally closed does not mean that they do not influence each other. Politics certainly influences the economy—and vice versa. All social subsystems "influence" each other in various degrees, and social systems theory provides a conceptual framework to describe and analyze this.

In a functionally differentiated society, all subsystems form the environment of the others. The economy exists in the midst of all other function systems, and the same is true for those as well. Operationally closed systems can, by virtue of their operational closure, observe and "resonate" with their environment. By closing themselves off, social systems develop a "membrane" that allows them to distinguish themselves from their environment and to relate to it. By being differentiated from their environment, social systems are not only capable of self-reference, but also of other-reference. They can—within their operational boundaries—make the environment an issue and refer to it. The law, for instance, by developing its own specific code, can relate to anything in its social environment. Anything that happens in politics, science, or religion can become a legal issue. Legal communication is specific to the legal system, but at the same time it is universally applicable to all that happens in its environment. The same is true for all other function systems. The economy can and will observe what happens in politics, in the legal system, and in science, and can deal with it economically. Religion often communicates about such issues as economic inequalities, legal decisions, or changes in the education system. Operational closure does not prevent other-reference; it is rather a condition for "making sense" of the other systems.

Within society, social subsystems not only continue their own autopoiesis by observing other systems, but function systems can also enter into "structural coupling" with each other so that their autopoiesis—though still operationally closed—is in contact with that of another system. The structural coupling between different function systems can be of varying degrees, and some systems that are tightly coupled are of great social relevance. An example of an intense structural coupling is the relation between the political and economic systems. Luhmann explains:

> The coupling between politics and economy is primarily established through taxes and tariffs. This does not alter the fact that all monetary dispositions are carried out as payments within the economy. The disposition can, however, be conditioned politically and in this case it will not be oriented to profit-making. For which purposes a nation's budget is used then becomes a political issue, and when much (or little) money is available, this will irritate the political system. Still, the spending of money itself is subject to the market rules of the economic system (nothing becomes more or less expensive because it is paid for with tax money) and it has significant consequences for the structural development of the economy when the state quota of the money flow increases. (1997a, 781)

Systems such as politics and the economy can be "connected" in such a way that the operations of one system more or less continually "aim" at the operations of the other system. The political system continuously creates communication directed at the economy. By taxes and tariffs, the political system establishes a coupling between itself and the economy that cannot be ignored by economic communication. Even though the economy cannot ignore taxes or tariffs, it still deals with these political inventions economically. Even taxes and tariffs cannot transform an economic transaction into a political one. The payment of taxes still follows the economic code and its programs and uses its medium. It does not become political communication. Structural coupling does not violate the operational closure of systems, rather it establishes specific interrelations between different autopoietic processes.

Many more structural couplings can be observed. There is a coupling between politics and law regulated by constitutions. The economy is coupled to the legal system by ownership and contracts. The coupling between the system of science and the system of education is manifested in the organization of the university. Education and the economy are coupled through academic certificates and diplomas that regulate access to jobs (Luhmann 1997a, 782–86). All of these couplings can be analyzed in detail and system-theoretical descriptions of the respective systems will have to deal extensively with them if they want to adequately portray their functioning. The functioning of the economy in our society, for example, cannot be properly understood without taking into account its couplings with politics, law, education, and so on.

Structural coupling establishes specific mechanisms of *irritation* between systems and forces different systems to continuously *resonate* with each other. The two concepts of irritation and resonance are used by social systems theory to explain how operationally closed systems "interact." Through taxes, for instance, the political system irritates the economy. The economic system resonates with these irritations by adding taxes to sales prices. Under the conditions of structural coupling, irritation and resonance gain the status of permanent influences between systems. In this way, the structural development of both systems is interrelated.

In the case of the "extra-social" coupling between communication and psychic systems, the common medium of language provides for the structural coupling between individual minds and society. This structural coupling allows for both systems to develop a higher complexity. People will accordingly develop mental structures that match the complexity of their society. The growth of social complexity is structurally coupled with the increasing mental complexity of the environment of society. The same is true for "inter-social" structural coupling. If a continuous irritation-resonance relationship between two systems is established, then increases in the structural complexity of one system will bring about increases in the structural complexity of the other. If politics irritates the economy with more complex tax regulations, the economy will "resonate" by producing more complex methods to maximize profits. This will in turn "irritate" politics, possibly resulting in the development of still more complex tax policies.

Through structural coupling, systems cannot steer other systems or directly interfere in their operations. They can, however, establish relatively stable links of irritation that force other systems to resonate with them. There are always two sides to structural coupling. A system that irritates another cannot, in turn, avoid being irritated. Through taxes, politics does not actually regulate the economy in a one-way direction. It is by the same link that the economy irritates politics. That social systems are interrelated primarily through structural coupling means that no system can dominate another; no system can exert influence without itself being influenced.

The idea that one system can dominate the rest of society is a theoretical pitfall in which many theories of society have been trapped, most prominently, probably, Marxism. This idea represents an oversimplification of social complexity and of the relation between social systems. It is easy to say that the economy rules politics. But isn't it obvious that by influencing politics—and systems theory does not deny that the economy greatly influences politics—the economy itself is influenced by politics? And isn't it also obvious that increasing economic influence does not ruin or overshadow the political system but rather stirs it into increasing complexity? The same is true for other systemic relations. As I will explain in detail in the chapter on mass media, the economy and the political system greatly influence the mass-media system, but they themselves are in turn also greatly influenced by it. Intersystemic influence is not a one-way street.

Again: this is not to say that this absence of domination is good or bad. Marxists may think that capitalist domination is bad while communist domination is good. Systems theory neither desires nor believes in such domination. But it also does not say that the lack of domination is good. It does not claim to know or to decide if societies that develop structural coupling on the basis of functional differentiation and operational closure are better or worse off than societies that do not have these characteristics. Why should a theory presume to have such knowledge? Systems theory does not agree with Marxists who say that capitalist politics is "ruled" by the capitalist economy. But it also does not agree with capitalists who say that a "free" market solves every problem and leads to a better life. Social systems theory does not even believe that a market can be "free" in the Old European sense of this word. Systems theory is a theory of contingency, not one of liberty. The economy is not freer than a biological cell. The semantics of domination and liberation that is *shared* by Marxists and liberal capitalists is utopian when it comes to coping with the complexity and contingency of a functionally differentiated society.

The complexity of a functionally differentiated society, a society in which a variety of functional subsystems and other social systems (such as interactions and organizations) co-exist, is also reflected in the fact that no system can claim to be *the* basic system. A functionally differentiated society is not fundamentally "economic" nor can a singular system, such as religion, claim that its way of observing the world encompasses all the other types of systemic observation. Systems theory describes society not on the basis of an underlying unity but on the basis of underlying *difference*. Society is not made up of small units that constitute a larger unit, it is rather based on differences that constitute more differences. Systems theory is a "theory of distinction" (see Luhmann 2002b). Luhmann says: "The thesis was that a system is not a unit, but a difference, and that one thus ends up with the problem that one has to imagine the unity of a difference" (2002a, 91). Society is not a unit—it is a difference, consisting of differences. Systems theory is, strictly speaking, not a theory of systems, but of system-environment distinctions. A system, be it biological, psychic, or social, only comes to exist by distinguishing itself from its environment. A system exists by virtue of being distinct. The introduction of a system is, more precisely, the drawing of a new distinction. Systems theory distinguishes itself from traditional ontological attempts by "orienting itself on difference rather than on unity" (see Clam 2002). Systems have no "being" as such— they are a difference, a distinction. Luhmann says: "The process does not lead from an undetermined unity towards a determined unity, if one is allowed to paraphrase Hegel in this way, but rather from a difference towards a difference" (2002a, 70). Society has no fundamental nature or "being," no final core that represents its essence. Society is not composed of social systems; it is the reality that results from systemic differentiation. Yes, differentiation produces structures, maybe even "deep structures," but these are structures of difference, not of unity. A social system is what it is, not by virtue of its inner nature, but by how it distinguishes itself from its environment.

Society emerges on the basis of contingent differences drawn by emerging systems. The economy becomes the economy by operating economically in a noneconomic environment. It starts creating an economic world by treating things and communications in its environment (the fruits on the tree, their consumption, their exchange, for instance) economically. It distinguishes itself from other communications and things outside communication and thus it establishes itself within society. It becomes another difference within the differences already made. None of these differences "have to be" made, but once they are made, they make a difference. There is no principal need for establishing a social system of economy, education, or politics. The existence of society is not by its "nature" dependent on these systems.

Modern society is a complex multiplicity without a center, an essential core, or a hierarchy. It is a complex multiplicity of a wide variety of system-environment realities. Systems change, they come and go, and the same is true for the "deep structures" of society. Functional differentiation is not the *telos* or goal of social evolution. Just as other types of differentiation preceded it, still others may follow.

(c) History

Functional differentiation is a product of the evolution of society. According to Luhmann it became the primary type of social differentiation in Europe between the sixteenth and eighteenth century and replaced "stratified differentiation." Looking back in history, and also at non-European societies, Luhmann discerns four types of social differentiation—but he does not claim that this list is complete or indicative of any general law behind social evolution. Social evolution does not "progress" to "better" kinds of differentiation; and the fact that certain types of stratification are sometimes replaced by others does not mean that the earlier types are inferior to the later ones. Systems theory does not evaluate or judge the unfolding of social evolution.

Different types of social differentiation do not exclude each other; they often co-exist at the same time and in the same society. Luhmann suggests that mixtures of various types of differentiation may be rather the rule than the exception and that such hybrids may be a necessary condition for social evolution to take place. Only when several types of differentiation compete or at least are present at the same time, can one type outplay another. Social evolution in the strict sense takes place, according to Luhmann, when a new type of differentiation becomes dominant. He defines this dominance or primacy in the following way: "We speak of the primacy of a type of differentiation (and such primacy is not a systemic necessity) when one type can be identified as regulating the applicability of others" (1997a, 612). Luhmann further explains this by adding:

> In this sense, aristocratic societies are primarily differentiated into strata, but they still preserve a segmentary differentiation into households or families so that endogamy is made possible for the aristocracy and that aristocratic families can be distinguished from other families. Under the conditions of functional differentiation one can find even today stratification in the form of social classes, and also center/periphery distinctions—but these are now byproducts of the function systems' own dynamics. (1997a, 612)

This passage makes reference to all four types of differentiation discussed by Luhmann: segmentary differentiation, center/periphery differentiation, stratified differentiation, and functional differentiation.

Segmentary differentiation is defined as the equal differentiation of social subsystems "on the basis of descent, of communal living, or by a combination of these two criteria" (1997a, 613). Many societies that were formerly called "archaic" or "primitive" were based on segmentary differentiation. They were also sometimes called tribal societies. Luhmann points out that such societies cannot be assumed to be primordial, because they seem to be the product of systemic evolution: in these societies one type of differentiation has obviously already gained primacy. Native American or pre-historic Chinese societies may be examples of segmentary differentiation. A social group or segment defines itself through kinship and communal living—and in such a society the very same can be expected from the neighboring group or segment. In a society strictly based on segmentary differentiation, there is no center of social power—no tribe or segment is generally perceived to be the core—and there is also no established social hierarchy that has gained primacy over these structures. A person is primarily identified by the segment he/she belongs to, and not by the social stratum. One would, for instance, be perceived as a member of the Ojibwa prior to being perceived as a chief. The community of the Ojibwa has more structural value than the community of chiefs. The subsystems in these societies would not be groups of chiefs and groups of warriors but rather the segments that define themselves by common descent or communal living.

As noted above, different types of differentiation normally coexist, and thus living in a society that is based on segmentary differentiation does not mean that there is a total absence of social strata or center/periphery distinctions, it only means that this differentiation "outweighs" other types. A society based purely on segmentary differentiation will hardly ever be found.

In contrast to segmentary differentiation, center/periphery differentiation is not based on the structural equality of social subsystems (even in a tribal society some tribes are likely to be more powerful that others, but this does not make these tribes more "tribal" than the others, and it does not turn them into the commonly recognized social core), but on structural inequality. Luhmann defines the center/periphery differentiation as such:

> Here, a kind of inequality is tolerated that transcends the principle of segmentation, and thus allows for a multiplicity of segments (households) on both sides of the new form. (This is not yet the case, but practically prepared for when there are centers within a tribal structure that can only be occupied by one prominent kinship group, such as the "strongholds" of the Scottish clans.) (1997a, 613)

As in the case of the Scottish clans, a society based on segmentary differentiation may well have some center/periphery features that will eventually become the primary social divide. Relating to the works of Immanuel Wallerstein (see Luhmann 1997a, 612) and other research on center/periphery differentiation (Rowlands, Larsen, and Kristiansen 1987, Champion 1989, Chase-Dunn and Hall 1991), Luhmann says:

> Traits of the center/periphery differentiation can already be found in segmentary societies, especially when one of these societies takes on a dominant role in external trade. Still, it does not yet challenge the segmentary differentiation. This only happens when the dominant status

of the center is used to establish another kind of differentiation and particularly stronger role-differentiations (division of labor). The center/periphery differentiation results from the differentiation of the center. It is, so to speak, at home at the center. (1997a, 663)

The increasing power and wealth of one social segment can lead to an overturning of segmentary differentiation. One segment may become so dominant that it establishes the difference between itself and the other segments as the new primary difference of this society. In this case, a center/periphery differentiation would be born—and it would be born by the center itself. The center makes itself the center. An example of a society with a significant center/periphery distinction would be ancient Rome.

Like the center/periphery differentiation, stratified differentiation is also based on inequality. It is a second type of hierarchical differentiation. Unlike the center/periphery differentiation, stratified differentiation is not as strongly intertwined with aspects of location and it usually comprises more than two basic subsystems. (A center in the strict sense of the term is only one and has only one periphery.) The inequality involved in stratified differentiation is one of *rank*. Luhmann explains stratified differentiation in comparison with the center/periphery differentiation as follows:

> The foundational structure of this form is also a dual distinction, namely the distinction between the aristocracy and the common people. In this way it would be, however, relatively unstable, because the hierarchy could be easily converted. Stable hierarchies such as the Indian caste system or the order of ranks in the late Middle Ages construe—no matter how artificially—at least three levels in order to produce an impression of stability. (1997a, 613)

Stratified differentiation, as pointed out in the above quotation, characterizes medieval Europe and the Indian caste system. Its definition is rather clear-cut: "We only want to speak of stratification when society is represented as an order of rank and when order without differences of rank can no longer be imagined" (1997a, 679). In a society based on stratified differentiation, social order is perceived to be a direct outcome of distinctions in social status. The subsystems of a stratified society are the different "classes" that constitute the social hierarchy. Communal living or common descent does not primarily distinguish the strata—even though one achieves one's status, of course, by birth, members of different families can nevertheless belong to the same stratum. This distinguishes stratified societies from segmentary societies in which one is more defined by the segment one belongs to than by the stratum. In a tribal society, the primary distinction is between tribes, and the hierarchical distinctions within the tribes are secondary. In a stratified society a family is first of all distinguished by its social rank.

The social order within a stratified society is regulated through ranks, and households or families distribute ranks. The household one is born into decides the rank one has. These households regulate social inclusion and exclusion, one is born into a particular family and is thus given a particular rank and excluded from all others: "One can only belong to one stratum, and exactly thereby one is excluded from all other strata" (Luhmann 1997a, 688). Because of this, Luhmann says: "The importance of households for stratified societies can hardly be over-estimated. Households, not individuals, are the units to which stratification is related" (1997a, 697). In a segmentary society, the segments (based on descent and locality) are structurally equal to one another. In a stratified society, the strata provide for a structure of inequality in which each household is assigned a certain rank.

Luhmann is more interested in stratified differentiation—particularly, that of medieval Europe—than in segmentary or center/periphery differentiation, because he identifies it as the immediate predecessor of functional differentiation which is the main focus of his theory. Contemporary society, as he sees it, is basically the outcome of the replacement of medieval European stratified differentiation with functional differentiation between the sixteenth and eighteenth century. For Luhmann this is the period in which modernity was born. The decisive characteristic of modernity is functional differentiation. It can be defined in comparison with the previously dominant types of differentiation described above as a form of differentiation that is based on *both* the equality and inequality of its social subsystems: "Function systems are equal in regard to their inequality" (Luhmann 1997a, 613). Social function systems (politics, economy, education, and so on) are all "equally" different—they all have different codes, programs, media, and so on but their functional inequality does not go along with a hierarchical inequality. Like the segments of a segmentary society, function systems are neither ranked nor oriented towards one central core. But, like the strata of a stratified society, function systems have separate and mutually exclusive characteristics. While segmentary differentiation is based on the structural equality of its subsystems and center/periphery and stratified differentiations are based on the structural inequality of their subsystems, the subsystems of functional differentiation are equally unequal. Luhmann states:

> Along with the transition to functional differentiation society refrains from imposing a common pattern of difference on the subsystems. Whereas in the case of stratified differentiation every subsystem defines itself through the difference in rank in relation to the others and only thereby achieves an identity, in the case of functional differentiation every function system determines its own identity. (1997a, 745)

Under the conditions of stratified differentiation, the social strata are all part of one hierarchy and an aristocrat is what he is by being distinctly different from his vassal—and vice versa. Under the conditions of functional differentiation, there is no overarching hierarchy that unites the function systems. The economy is not what it is because of a certain relation to education or any other system. The function systems are what they are by being "equally" distinct from one another. Of course, this does not mean that subsystems are totally "independent" of each other. Structural couplings still tie systems together, but the function systems do not gain their identity by being a certain element within an established order of rank.

The transition from stratified to functional differentiation has severe consequences for people. While social strata included a person wholly and exclusively—one's social existence was totally determined by one's status and one could not simultaneously be an aristocrat and a commoner—function systems do not simply divide the population into groups:

> When society changes from stratification to functional differentiation, it has to dispense with the demographic correlates of its internal pattern of differentiation. It can no longer distribute the human beings who contribute to the communication of its subsystems as it had been possible with the schema of stratification or with center/periphery

differentiations. Human beings cannot be distributed to the function systems in such a way that everybody would only belong to one system so that one would, for instance only take part in the legal system, but not in the economy, only in politics, but not in education, etc. This leads finally to the consequence that one can no longer claim that society consists of human beings, since human beings can obviously not be located in any social subsystem, and thus nowhere in society. (1997a, 744)

In a society based on functional differentiation human beings can no longer be identified in reference to a singular subsystem. An aristocrat could still basically identify himself as an aristocrat, regardless of whether he was dealing with law, politics, or education. He was primarily an aristocrat at all times. Under the conditions of functional differentiation this is no longer the case. An aristocrat cannot win a court decision simply by behaving and speaking aristocratically; and he will not succeed as a politician simply by reminding voters of the superior dignity of his status. Time travel movies display the absurdity and grotesqueness of such attempts in both directions. When, in a fictional story, a modern man returns to a medieval society, his political or economic skills count for little when he has to compete with inherited rank and status.

In a functionally differentiated society human beings are not only unable to locate themselves "wholly" in one social subsystem—they cannot even identify themselves "primarily" with one system. A good lawyer can excel in the legal system—but this expertise is of little help when she invests her money in stocks. There is no hierarchy among the systems that would allow one systemic "identity" to determine others. When at home, the lawyer has to be a wife, and if in politics she has to be politician. She cannot carry one systemic identity into another:

The differentiation of one subsystem into one particular function means that this function has priority for this system (and only for this system) and gains precedence over all other functions for it. Only in this sense, one can speak of functional primacy. For the political system, for instance, political success (no matter how it is operationalized) is more important than anything else so that economic success is only important for it as a condition for political success. This means also: On the level of the larger system of society no generally valid and encompassing mandatory ranking order of functions can be established—and no ranking order also means: no stratification. (1997a, 747–48)

The absence of an all-encompassing hierarchy does not mean that each system has the same opportunity to develop—it only means that from the perspective of each system, its own function is primary, and that there is no Archimedean Point from which one could establish a function of all functions (see Luhmann 1997a, 770). Some systems, such as the religious one, seem to have more difficulty surviving than others, such as the economy, but the economy still cannot replace or immediately interfere in religious operations. Social evolution may let some systems grow at the expense of others—but under the condition of functional differentiation no subsystem can directly take control of another. Every subsystem can only operate on the basis of its own function:

> Every function system can only perform its own function. No one can in the event of a crisis or on a continuing or supplementary basis sit in for another one. When there is a government crisis, science cannot help out with truths. Politics does not have its own means to create economic success—as much as it may be politically dependent on it and as much as it pretends to be able to do so. The economy can let science take part in the conditioning of money payments, but it cannot produce truth with all the world's money. Through financing one can attract, one can irritate, but one cannot prove anything. Science honors financing with "acknowledgments," not with provable argumentation. (Luhmann 1997a, 763)

The replacement of stratification by functional differentiation also does not mean that social ranks have disappeared leaving everyone "equal." The opposite is the case:

> Along with the switch from stratification to functional differentiation the form of social differentiation is altered, but this by no means eliminates social strata. There are still immense differences between the rich and the poor, and these differences still have an effect on lifestyles and on access to social opportunities. What has changed is that this is no longer the visible social order as such, that it is no longer the order without which no order would be possible at all. (Luhmann 1997a, 772)

Functional differentiation does not mean that society is free of class-distinctions (and neither that society is without center/periphery distinctions), it simply means that class (or center/periphery) distinctions are no longer equivalent with social order. In a society of functional differentiation it is assumed that we are all somehow equal and that there is no generally affirmed order that would exclude the poor from casting a vote or buying certain things—if a poor woman has registered, she has the same voting rights as a rich man, and if she has money, she can buy the same goods as he can. Again: this does not mean that the poor are factually any more equal in a functionally differentiated society. There is—most obviously—no more "social justice" in a functionally differentiated society than in a stratified society. Humans are no more equal today than they were in the Middle Ages—but social systems are. Since society does not consist of human beings but of social systems, an absence of a systemic hierarchy cannot be equated with an absence of a hierarchy among people.

Under the conditions of functional differentiation the inequality among people no longer corresponds to the inequality of social strata. This is why leftist theory fails to properly analyze today's inequalities—if it does not accept the fact that we no longer live in a society of stratification. Inequalities and social inclusion and exclusion in modern society have to be analyzed with more adequate and less anachronistic theoretical means. Luhmann's article on barbarism, included in the appendix, is one attempt at this. The following chapter on globalization will also address this issue.

According to social systems theory, at least in Luhmann's version, the last decisive "paradigm shift" of social differentiation occurred in Europe between the sixteenth and the eighteenth century. During these centuries functional differentiation gained primacy over structural differentiation and thus created "modernity." Modern society can be defined as a society based on functional differentiation. If one accepts this definition, then the various attempts to distinguish a "postmodern" society or "postmodern conditions" from modern ones become problematic. Functional differentiation still rules, so that, sociologically speaking, there is no such thing as postmodernity. Luhmann concludes an article in which he summarizes his analysis of the functional differentiation of contemporary society by saying:

> If we take a broad look at these considerations, they pull the rug out from under the contrast of modern and postmodern. It is impossible to speak of such a division on a structural level. At most we can say that the evolutionary gains distinguishing contemporary society from all its predecessors, namely fully developed communication media and functional differentiation, have grown from humble beginnings to dimensions that have made the course of contemporary society irreversible. (1998, 17)

From the perspective of Luhmann's theory, although modernity began about four centuries ago it is still quite alive. The structures that characterize contemporary society have only become more dominant and obvious during the past few decades. Functional differentiation has developed from humble beginnings into a grand structure, a giant social "organism" of global scale and extreme functional intensity. "Postmodern" theory thus appears as a theoretical reaction to social change that took place *within* modernity, not after it. Postmodern theory is a first attempt at describing a more mature modernity. It actually refers to, if one takes a closer historical look, still-growing developments that began centuries ago.[8]

The emergence of so-called postmodern descriptions of a still modern world signals "a need to catch up on a semantic level" (Luhmann 1998, 18). The structures of modernity have so far been described with premodern semantics. Postmodern thought represents an attempt to catch up with the structural changes that have taken place. This is an attempt to develop a new semantics for an already established social structure. Social structures and semantics—especially the semantics of the self-descriptions of society—do not necessarily develop in parallel. Semantic changes may well lag behind structural changes. In any case, there seems to be *some* connection between the structures and the semantics of a society, and Luhmann published a serious of four books (Luhmann 1980, 1981, 1989, 1999) that present a wide variety of case-studies on these developments (discussing, for instance, the semantics of time, social order, and individuality). Perhaps his best-known work is dedicated to the exploration of a specific semantic issue: the modern European discourse of "love as passion" (Luhmann 1982a).

Luhmann technically defines his usage of the notion "semantics" as the "socially available sense that is generalized on a higher level and relatively independent of specific situations" (Luhmann 1980, 19). Semantics is the general understanding of "things" or the "world"—including itself—that a society has and uses in communication. It comprises both "common semantics"—such as the semantics of the "swearing of the rowers in the galleys"—and the "cultivated semantics" developed in science or religion that enables the "take-off of a specific revolution of ideas" (Luhmann 1980, 19). The jargons of both academic and common speech are expressions of the semantics of a society. Both represent the "sense" a society ascribes to itself and to the issues it deals with. Obviously, these semantics change. Today it is, for instance, no longer acceptable to use the word "Negro." That we speak now of "African Americans" does not only signal a change of terminology, but also a change of sense. The word "Negro" suggests the social acceptance of racial profiling and separation, while the term "African American" suggests the nonacceptance of such things. This lexical change also represents a semantic change. A semantic change, needless to say, does not necessarily adequately reflect corresponding changes in social structure. The semantic change from "Negro" to "African American" has no immediate correspondence to the social structures that pertain to the people who were/are designated by these terms.

Social semantics and social structures resonate with each other, but in various ways semantics can be more or less faithful to social structures. Luhmann explains that there is no strict causal relation observable between semantics and structure, rather:

> smoother mixtures between continuities and discontinuities, another rhythm of time, is possible. In some cases, semantics dare innovations that are not yet built into the patterns of the functions supporting the present structures. (I demonstrated this in *Love as Passion* in regard to the semantics of love before it was actually applied as motivation for marriage.) In other cases it constitutes ideas, concepts, or words that became obsolete a long time ago and thus it obscures the radicalism of a structural change (for instance, the continuation of the concept of *societas civilis* or civil society until the end of the eighteenth century, or, if one should take this semantics seriously, until today). . . . These and other tricks can lead to an overestimation of continuity and

to an underestimation of change, especially in regard to the eighteenth century. (1989, 7–8)

There are cases in which the semantics are more "progressive" than structure. The semantics of passionate love was created before it was translated into the modern form of marriage. There emerged first (specifically in novels) a revolutionary semantics regarding love outside of the traditional social structures of marriage—which then were transformed to match that semantics. On the other hand, concepts of a "civil society" enjoy a much longer life than the corresponding structures. Even today, when functional differentiation is so dominant, this semantics is still commonly used—especially in North America.

Social systems theory can historically analyze the relation between social structures and the semantics of a time. With each instance the results will vary, some semantics will turn out to be ahead of their times, some (and probably most) semantics will turn out not to be. Social theory has, of course, a semantics too—a semantics that describes society and its structures. This semantics tends to be retrospective: "The structural change of society is beyond the observation and description of its contemporaries. Only after it has been completed and when it becomes practically irreversible, semantics takes on the task to describe what now becomes visible" (Luhmann 1989, 8). It is exactly this task that social systems theory takes on.

(d) Globalization

With functional differentiation as its main structural characteristic, society is no longer primarily divided by regional borders—society is now world-society (Luhmann 1997a, 1084). From a systemic point of view, the term "globalization" designates the fact that function systems transcend geography. Function systems are no longer confined to specific localities. Society has become a world society, and therefore the social system is a world system. Luhmann explains:

> Basing itself on this form of functional differentiation, modern society has become a completely new type of system, building up an unprecedented degree of complexity. The boundaries of its subsys-

tems can no longer be integrated by common territorial frontiers. Only the political subsystem continues to use such frontiers, because segmentation into "states" appears to be the best way to organize its own function. But other subsystems like science or the economy spread over the globe. It therefore has become impossible to limit society as a whole by territorial boundaries, and consequently it no longer makes sense to speak of "modern societies" in the plural. . . . Neither the different ways of reproducing capital nor the degrees of development in different countries provide convincing grounds for distinguishing different societies. The inclusion of all communicative behavior into one societal system is the unavoidable consequence of functional differentiation. Using this form of differentiation, society becomes a global system. For structural reasons there is no other choice. (1982b, 178)

Only the political system still uses regional frontiers to operate— the political authority of the nation-state ends at its borders. But even this is much less the case today than it was a hundred years ago (or a quarter of a century ago, when the above lines were writ- ten). The European Union, for instance, has since grown into a political entity that transcends national borders. The traditional concept of the nation-state hardly applies to the complexity of the political reality in Europe. The political system also seems to be unable to avoid the "globalizing" effects of functional differentia- tion. Other systems, such as the economy and science, have already stepped beyond geographical borders. Economic communication is global communication. This, once again, by no means implies that there are no economic differences between regions—but a poor region still operates in the same systems as a rich region. Cheap labor in a poor country and low prices in a rich country make up one system, not two. Science is also a global endeavor. The truth or falsity of a scientific claim does not depend on the sci- entist's geographical location. Of course, one will have better resources and a wider audience in some countries, but this does not divide science into different regional enterprises—it does not split the scientific code, its function, or its medium.

On the basis of functional differentiation, society is a "global system." The fact that functional differentiation goes along with "globalization" does *not* imply that social *homogeneity* necessary follows. The global society of functional differentiation is *not a harmonious whole*. It is not a thing-like aggregate, with a singular "being" or body. Luhmann says that the last chance for keeping such a concept of the world was lost with the demise of the all-encompassing concept of "God" (Luhmann 1997a, 147). When God lost His sociological and philosophical primacy—as had already been observed by Sartre—the foundation for an essentially definable world as a whole was irreversibly lost. Global society is a complex multiplicity of subsystems, which are not integrated into an overarching global unity. Function systems operate beyond geographical borders; in this sense they are universal. There is no geographical space where they cannot go, but at the same time they are all functionally particular. They are bound by their function, not by space. Global society consists of a plurality of systems that are both universal and particular (Luhmann 1997a, 930–31).

Global society exists as a multiplicity of functional subsystems, but it does not exist as a multiplicity of societies. The latter would mean that there would be completely different communication systems that lack communicative links (Luhmann 1997a, 78). The global economy and global science, for instance, are each other's intrasocial environments. They are functional subsystems of one global system. There is no second global system—and if there was, it could not be communicated with. The global system is *one* system but, again, it is not a harmonious whole.

The global system is not a simple enlargement of the nineteenth-century nation-state. It is not just a more geographically encompassing form of the so-called civil society (Luhmann 1997a, 31). The nation-state was conceived of as representing the individuals that constitute it. This is not the case with the global system. The global system consists of subsystems of communication, not of people. Taking part in its operations provides inclusion in a system. One acts in the global economy by spending money, for instance. By buying an American soft drink in a little street parlor, a Chinese peasant becomes, economically, a little "global player"—but not a "world citizen." Those that buy products do not constitute the global economy; it is constituted by the economic communication that occurs.

Global society, as an effect of the globalization of functional differentiation, can neither be essentially defined in terms of one particular fundament (for instance, "materialistically" as an economic whole, or "humanistically" as one large community of human individuals) nor can it be properly analyzed with the traditional recourse to geographic notions. Luhmann therefore criticizes Immanuel Wallerstein's concept of a world-system as being too rooted in Old European concepts. An exclusive focus on the center/periphery distinction and, along with it, on the economy will, according to Luhmann, not lead to an adequate social theory of globalization, but rather to "blockades of understanding" (Luhmann 1997a, 159). Luhmann says:

> Immanuel Wallerstein's much discussed concept of a capitalist world system is based on the primacy of the capitalist economy and it thus underestimates the contributions of other function systems, especially those of science and mass media communication. . . . Only when one brings to light in synopsis the very different tendencies of the globalization of specific function systems, can one realize the level of change in comparison to all traditional societies. (1997a, 171)

To reduce a society to the economy or to explain it on the basis of regional differentiation means to tackle the problem of modernity with too traditional tools and to overlook the structural differences that separate traditional societies from the era of globalization. Today, a "society cannot be characterized by its most important part, be it a religious commitment, the political state, or a certain mode of economic production. Replacing all this, we define a specific type of societal system by its primary mode of internal differentiation" (Luhmann 1982b, 177).

That globalization is not *only* an economic phenomenon certainly does not imply that it is not an economic phenomenon. But globalization is not restricted to the economy; it is something that happens likewise in the mass media, in law, and so on. There is no systemic hierarchy of globalization.

That neither the economy nor the economy in combination with regional differences (center/periphery) is the central aspect of globalization certainly does not imply that economic differences and center/periphery distinctions do not exist. Luhmann does not mean to deny or downplay gross differences in economic wealth between different regions of the world: "This fact is evidently not to be denied nor is its importance to be diminished" (1997a, 161). Likewise, Luhmann by no means intends to underestimate other regional or "cultural" differences. Social systems theory does not say, as many apologists and critics of globalization do, that a functionally differentiated society will become more and more homogenous. It "does not claim (because there are hardly any indicators for this) that regional differences will gradually disappear" (Luhmann 1997a, 161). Luhmann rather stresses the opposite: "The argument from inequality is not an argument against but for the existence of a world society" (1997a, 162). Functional differentiation operates worldwide and "is a starting point for the production of differences" (1997a, 810). Globalization is a worldwide process of differentiation, producing functional equalities (each place has the same economy, the same mass media system) and inequalities (each place has the same structural differences between rich and poor, and so on) at the same time. Regional differences are not a competing type of differentiation; they rather gain new significance on the basis of functional differentiation. The theory of functional differentiation does not aim at explaining regional differences away, it simply aims at explaining regional differences with functional means: "Obviously the effects of different function systems are combined, amplified, or obstructed by conditions of regional provenance so that they produce various patterns. No one will deny these facts. The question is: Which theory can do justice to them?" (Luhmann 1997a, 807). Systemic differences are not equivalent to regional differences. Regional differences have an effect on systemic realities—the economy in Saint Petersburg will produce different data than the economy in San Francisco—but it is still the same economy that produces these differences. Once more:

> Only by supposing a unitary world-wide social system can it be explained that even, and especially, today (on a much larger scale than during the times of archaic tribal societies) there are regional differences that do not take on the form of systemic differences. These differences are to be explained by different participations in and reactions to dominant structures of the global social system. (Luhmann 1997a, 167)

Regional differences established on the basis of functional differences are, for instance, differences regarding production, consumption, labor, and financial credit in the economy. Some regions produce more; others consume more. Some regions have cheap loans; others do not. Such differences are differences within a single system that are amplified by regional inequalities. The same economy produces different situations under different local conditions. The same is true in regard to politics:

> The autopoietic system of this society can be described without any reference to regional particularities. This certainly does not mean that these differences are of minor importance. But a sociological theory that wants to explain these differences should not introduce them as givens, that is, as independent variables; it should rather start with the assumption of a world society and then investigate how and why this society tends to maintain or even increase regional inequalities. It is not very helpful to say that the Serbs are Serbs and, therefore, they make war. The relevant question is rather whether or not the form of the political state forced upon all regions on earth fits with all local and ethnic conditions, or whether or not the general condition, not of exploitation or suppression, but of global neglect, stimulates the search for personal and social, ethnic or religious identities. (Luhmann 1997b, 9)

The emergence of all kinds of regional separatism and "fundamentalism" can well be explained as an effect of the globalization of functional differentiation. The expansion of political, economic, and other social structures meets with all kinds of regional peculiarities and resistance. Function systems "neglect" regional, religious, or cultural identities. This neglect does not mean that these identities are not tolerated by the global function systems that world society has become. Of course, the global system equally tolerates every region, religion, or race—as long as they do not obstruct functionalism. There is a total *indifference* towards these older "identities"—that only become "identities" once they are overrun by functional differentiation. Under the conditions of functional differentiation it does not matter which region, religion, or race functions—as long as it functions. Muslims or Serbs are perfectly fine, as long as they function "democratically" with "free markets"—to use the euphemistic Old European designations for today's global systems of economy and politics. Obviously, there are some regions and religions, for instance, which are not happy with the indifference imposed on them by functional globalization. Some become violent, turn into saboteurs, and desperately try to be taken seriously—not indifferently. The survival of ethnic and religious fundamentalism can be understood as a "process of insulation" that provides possibilities for "identity certainty" that are incongruent with the function systems and their codes and efficacies (Luhmann 1997a, 796).

Globalization and regionalization—for instance, in the radical form of ethnic fundamentalism—are parallel phenomena. From the perspective of social systems theory, they can neither be explained by a sole or primary focus on culture, religion, or the economy, nor can they be understood psychologically. First, fundamentalism is an effect of the globalization of function systems as such—not simply an effect of the globalization of one system. Secondly, from a systemic point of view, that which goes on in the mind of the individual fundamentalist is totally irrelevant for the emergence of fundamentalism. Fundamentalism or regionalism is not to be explained by a specific mind-set that all fundamentalists share. It is highly unlikely that all radical Muslims or radical Serbs have similar thoughts and feelings. Violence is a social phenomenon, an extreme act of communication. It is not a specific mental operation.

According to Luhmann, violent religious fundamentalism, racial extremism, and regional separatism can be interpreted as "demonstrations of non-irritability" (1997a, 797). These movements display a pose of immunity against the effects of functional globalization. They attempt to withstand the systemic irritation they are exposed to and resonate with sheer resistance. They make it socially known that they prefer a more radical and singular kind of social identity than those offered by global function systems. Rather than identifying themselves as members of democratic parties or with certain roles within the economic system, some Muslims and Serbs choose to identify themselves first of all as Muslims or Serbs—and this is where the tolerance of functional differentiation ends, because these identifications have no place within function systems. Once more—functional globalization allows every Muslim to be a Muslim and every Serb to be a Serb, but only as long as they accept that their religion or ethnicity is ultimately *neglected* by the function systems.

Luhmann asks:

And what can we expect when we know that the very success of the function systems depends upon neglect? When evolution has differentiated systems whose very complexity depends upon operational closure (and the paradigmatic case is, of course, the brain), how can we expect to include all kinds of concerns into the system? (Luhmann 1997b, 10)

How are we to expect that function systems can "fundamentally" operate on the basis of such "essentials" as religion, ethnicity, or locality? The function systems have completed their operational closure by establishing totally different distinctions: legal/illegal (law), spending/earning (economy), and good grades/bad grades (education). The new functional distinctions have to neglect such distinctions as Muslim/heathen or Serb/Albanian. Global function systems do not grant Muslims more legality than heathens, and they do not grant Serbs better educational success than Albanians. They have replaced religious and ethnic differences with functional differences. Some Serbs or Muslims, however, try to protect or preserve or regain certain nonfunctional distinctions and corresponding identities. It seems that one of the few ways they can demonstrate this socially is by using violence. How could it be done legally or politically if the primacy of the "global" legal or political system is exactly what they demonstrate against? On the one hand, one can ask: how do you expect operationally closed function systems not to neglect race, religion, and region? And, on the other hand, one can ask: how do you expect "fundamentalists" not to neglect the systems of law, politics, and education? And: how else can their neglect be demonstrated than by sabotaging the function systems? Sabotage is the neglect practiced by those neglected by "globalization."

The globalization of functional differentiation not only produces neglect and counter-neglect, it also produces a new type of social *exclusion*—and the social effects of this might be even more devastating than those which result from neglect. Luhmann states:

The worst imaginable scenario might be that the society of the next century will have to accept the metacode of inclusion/exclusion. And this would mean that some human beings will be persons and others only individuals; that some are included into function systems for (successful or unsuccessful) careers and others are excluded from these systems, remaining bodies that try to survive the next day. . . . (Luhmann 1997b, 12, see also his text on Barbarianism in the appendix)

On principle, global function systems are open to everyone. They do not discriminate because they do not operate on the basis of race, religion, or ethnicity. The codes of the economy, of law, and education are purely functional. And even if older types of discriminations still exist in various degrees (some countries still have no voting rights for women, for instance), it is, for example, not the code of the economy that would exclude any particular group from buying or selling. Under the global economy, the only condition for being able to spend money is to have some. And, functionally speaking, no one per se is excluded from doing this. The same is the case with all other systems. There is nothing in the code of politics or education that essentially excludes any particular group from being political or from receiving an education.

Function systems aim at all-inclusion. Ideally, the economy and politics will include everyone. This is also what the propagandists of a "free market" economy and its counterpart, "free" democracy, say: with free markets and free elections, economic backwardness disappears and political liberation takes place. Function systems do not only not recognize geographical boundaries, they are also blind to color, gender, and sexual orientation. The globalization of the function system—according to many of those who interpret this process in terms of the traditional "emancipatory" enlightenment vocabulary—will eventually establish a global village of free citizens, who pursue happiness and live together in solidarity along the lines of rational and fair rules and regulations. Even exploitation and suppression may finally be minimalized, or vanish, if we only establish a truly good and just version of a global society. This is, at least, what rational universalists or "globalists" like Habermas or Rawls and their followers suppose. Unfortunately, there is no empirical support for this interpretation:

> We have to come to terms, once and for all, with a society without human happiness and, of course, without taste, without solidarity, without similarity of living conditions. It makes no sense to insist on these aspirations, to revitalize or supplement the list by renewing old names such as civil society or community. This can only mean dreaming up new utopias and generating new disappointments in the narrow span of political possibilities. These desirabilites serve as a central phantom that seems to guarantee the unity of the system. . . . If we look at the huge masses of starving people, deprived of all necessities

for a decent human life, without access to any of the function systems, or if we consider all the human bodies, struggling to survive the next day, neither "exploitation" nor "suppression"—terms that refer again to stratification—are adequate descriptions. It is only by habit and by ideological distortion that we use these terms. But there is nothing to exploit in the favelas; nor are there, at the higher levels of society, actors or dominant groups that use their power to suppress these people. (There are, of course, individuals, families, or groups which, like everyone else, use their networks to their own advantage.) "Exploitation" and "suppression" are outdated mythologies, negative utopias suggesting an easy way out of this situation, e.g. by revolution. The predominant relation is no longer a hierarchical one, but one of inclusion and exclusion; and this relates not to stratification but to functional differentiation.

Traditional societies included and excluded persons by accepting or not accepting them in family households, and families (not individuals) were ordered by stratification. Modern society includes and excludes persons via function systems, but in a much more paradoxical way. Function systems presuppose the inclusion of every human being, but, in fact, they exclude persons that do not meet their requirements. Many individuals have to live without certified birth and identity cards, without any school education and without regular work, without access to courts and without the capacity to call the police. . . . And modern values, such as equality and freedom, serve as cover terms to preserve an illusion of innocence—equality as equal opportunity and freedom as allowing for individual (and not societal) attribution. (Luhmann 1997b, 4–5)

While the function systems are, in principle, all-inclusive—and while this all-inclusiveness of globalization is celebrated by "rightist" propagandists and demanded by "leftist" critics (who are not against globalization as such, but only an evil and unjust globalization)—they produce, in fact, mass exclusion. In the *favelas* of Latin America, the ghettos of North America, in Africa, and in war-torn countries like Afghanistan and Iraq, functional differentiation ends—and with it inclusion. The exclusion from one system, for instance, the exclusion from the economy because of a lack of money, easily leads to exclusion from other systems. It is not easy to take part in politics or the healthcare system, or education, sports, the arts, or the legal system, if one leads an existence completely outside of the economic system. The same is true for someone who is totally excluded from other systems, and has, for instance, no passport or no access to legal procedures. The problem cannot simply be solved in one system alone. If somebody who grew up in the *favelas* is given $100,000—is that proper compensation for his or her exclusion from education? And if so, what about the others who live there?

The people who live in the *favelas* are not exploited by capitalists—there is no money to be taken from them and they do not work or produce. Their exclusion from the function systems puts them beyond exploitation and suppression. It seems to be a simple empirical fact that the globalization of function systems not only goes along with mass inclusion, but also with mass exclusion. This is the "paradox" of the all-inclusiveness of functional differentiation. By being able, on principle, to include everyone (regardless of race, gender, religion, and so on) in the economy—if only he or she has money to spend—the economy in fact excludes all who have none. By being able, on principle, to educate everyone, the education system in fact excludes all those who happen to not go to school. By being able to include anyone with an identity card as a voter, the political system in fact excludes all those who do not have one. Maybe this must not be the case. Maybe, as the rightist advocates of globalization and the leftist advocates of a better one, would say—the function systems can include everybody. But again: this is simply not the case. True, there is nothing that *in principle* prevents anyone from having money. But, *in fact*, there are probably more people prevented from having money than ever before—and there is no indication that this will change, despite all the free markets and all the Habermasians and Rawlsians at American universities.

It seems as if functional differentiation produces massive social exclusion that reduces the lives of many people to a purely bodily existence that is primarily concerned with bare physical survival. Under the conditions of functional differentiation, these "inequalities" can neither be sufficiently analyzed with the traditional vocabulary of exploitation and suppression that was based on stratified differentiation nor with simplified concepts of society that are based on only one system, be it politics or the economy. They can also not be credibly explained as only an early effect of functional differentiation that will be solved once we learn to introduce more rationality or fairness. Functional differentiation cannot simply be steered or changed by good intentions. Society is much too complex and polycentric for such illusions. No person can steer a society of autopoietic function systems. Systems steer themselves (Luhmann 1997c).

Of course, politicians of various ideologies, ads from the multinational companies, and the global mass media still vehemently cling to this illusion. They provide a soothing and comforting semantics that helps us to cope with a core paradox of functional differentiation: in principle it is all-inclusive, but in fact it is not. And they continue the Old European myth that people will finally get things right, if only they assume responsibility and do things "rationally." From the perspective of systems theory this myth is a self-administered ideological opium for the gratification of human(ist) vanity.

2

What Is Real?

(a) Making Sense, Making Reality

Social systems and psychic systems do not only share language as a common medium,[9] they also share the "universal medium" (*Universalmedium*) "sense" (or *Sinn*[10]). Society and minds are continuously "making sense"—they are "sense-constituting systems" (*sinnkonstituierende Systeme*). Minds make sense of the world and themselves, and so do social systems. What we think and perceive has a certain sense—and even if it is nonsense, it is not non-sense. Making nonsense is also making sense. We cannot think or perceive without operating on the basis of sense. We may think or perceive nonlinguistically, but even if we think pictorially, these images make sense. In an analogous fashion, communication makes sense, too. If communication takes place—as the unity of announcement, information, and understanding—then sense is produced. As with minds, even nonsensical communication makes some sense. If it does not make sense, communication ceases to be communication.

Making sense couples minds and communication at an even more general or "universal" level: communication makes sense, and this sense irritates minds and makes them think. Conversely, what we think makes sense, and communication resonates with the sense produced in our minds. If communication processes complex sense, our minds will be forced to cope with this complexity and to therefore increase the complexity of their sense-making.

The meaning that Luhmann ascribes to sense (*Sinn*) goes back to Husserl's phenomenology.[11] In a certain manner, Luhmann's adaptation of Husserl's philosophy is similar to his adaptation of

Hegel—and of Matruana and Varela. He makes use of basic theoretical models that explain the operations of consciousness (or, in Maturana's and Varela's case, of life) and integrates them into a theory of communication. In contrast to Husserl, for Luhmann it is not only the mind that can be understood as an intentional system, but also communication. Both create their reality by relating to an outside world or to an "environment." Mental and communication systems create a reality by locating themselves within a "horizon of sense" (*Sinnhorizont*).

Sense, and the sense-horizon, is the "product of the operations that use sense—and by no means a quality of the world thanks to a creation, a donation, or an origin" (Luhmann 1997a, 44, referring to Deleuze 1969). Through their operations with the medium of sense, both psychic and social systems produce a framework in which they locate themselves. By making sense of the world, we also make sense of ourselves—and so does communication. This is similar to a ship that finds its position and direction by locating itself within the horizon of the sea. Of course, this horizon continuously changes. Through its motion, the ship continuously relocates itself within a horizon and thus has the horizon change with it. The horizon—the ship's environment—is a direct product of the ship's own operations, of its own movements. Sense is therefore technically defined by Luhmann (again in connection to Husserl) first as the "unity of the difference between the actual and the possible" (see Baraldi, Corsi, Esposito 1997, 170–73). Or, more extensively:

> The phenomenon of sense appears as a surplus of references to other possibilities of experience and action. Something stands in the focal point, at the center of intention, and all else is indicated marginally as the horizon of an "and so forth" of experience and action. In this form, everything that is intended holds open to itself the world as a whole, thus guaranteeing the actuality of the world in the form of accessibility. Reference actualizes itself as the standpoint of reality. It refers, however, not only to what is real (or presumably real), but also to what is possible (conditionally real) and what is negative (unreal, impossible). The totality of the references presented by a sense-making intended object offers more to hand than can in fact be actualized at any moment. (Luhmann 1995a, 60; translation modified)

A ship locates itself within its horizon—but thereby realizes that it can move. The ship is not bound only by its actual location; its horizon is a horizon of possibilities. It could also be elsewhere. Sense-making is this interplay between the actual and possible. What we think makes sense within a horizon of possibilities. Without a context of sense, thoughts cannot make sense. Similarly, communication without a context of sense cannot make sense. Our minds and communications operate within a sense-horizon like a ship operates on a body of water. These operations take place on the basis of a distinction between what is actual and what is possible.

Secondly, and in connection with the previous definition, sense can also be defined in terms of the distinction self-reference/other-reference:

> Systems operating within the medium of sense can and must distinguish between self-reference and other-reference, and this has to be done so that the actualization of self-reference also implies other-reference, and that the actualization of other-reference also implies self-reference as the respective other side of the distinction. (Luhmann 1997a, 51)

Making sense within a horizon constituted of actuality and possibility implies the distinction between the sense maker and that which makes sense for the sense maker—the distinction between the ship and its horizon. A mind that makes sense can distinguish between itself and what it intends. Similarly, communication can distinguish between itself and its context. The expression "to make sense" has a double meaning and always introduces two elements at the same time: this makes sense to me. It makes sense, and I make it make sense. The form of sense therefore goes along with two basic and interconnected structural distinctions: the actuality/possibility distinction and the self-reference/other-reference distinction.

By making sense, sense-processing systems like psychic and communication systems distinguish between themselves and the world they are in—they distinguish between system and environment. And this distinction is somehow "reflected" within the system itself. Sense-making systems make sense by making sense of the difference between themselves and their environment, by making sense of the difference between the "it" that makes sense and this "I" that makes that sense. By making this distinction the sense-making system performs a *re-entry*. It re-enters the distinction it just made. The system not only makes sense by introducing the distinction between itself and its environment, it also "reflects" on this distinction by reintroducing the distinction into itself. It can also make sense of it-self: the self becomes an it and a self! The system can make sense of making sense—in other words, it can "know" or ascribe to itself (as to one side of the initial distinction) the making of that distinction. First, a system can observe an environment and make sense of it by producing the distinction between system and environment. Then, secondly, it can also perform a re-entry by relating that distinction to itself and, so to speak, be self-referential in the way it used to be other-referential. It can refer to "it-self" just as it used to refer to something else. Or: "The problem of re-entry is nothing else but the "otherness of the same" (Baraldi, Corsi, and Esposito 1997, 152). Or, in Luhmann's words: "The difference system/environment occurs twice: as the difference *produced by* the system, and as the difference *observed within* the system" (1997a, 45). Autopoietic and sense-constituting systems construct themselves and their horizon through their own operations. Making sense is equivalent to making reality, both self-referential and other-referential. By distinguishing itself from its environment a system establishes itself and the world around it. The reality of systems theory is a constructivist one:

> If one accepts this theoretical disposition, one can neither assume that there exists a world at hand (*vorhanden*) consisting of things, substances, and ideas, nor can one designate their entirety (*universitas rerum*) with the concept of a "world." For sense-systems the world is not a giant mechanism that produces states out of states and thus determines the systems themselves. The world is rather an immeasurable potential for surprises, it is virtual information that needs systems to produce information, or more precisely; to ascribe to selected information the sense of being information. (Luhmann 1997a, 46)

This passage sums up quite nicely Luhmann's constructivist theory of reality. The world and its reality are not a given—there is no ontological "being" already there; nothing is simply "at hand" (*vorhanden*, a very common German word that became philosophically prominent through Heidegger's *Being and Time*). The world is not the totality of things and ideas, somehow created as a unit and waiting to be explored. According to systems theory, the sense and essence of the world do not precede the being of systems: the being of systems rather precedes the sense and essence of the world—to put it in Sartrean terms. The world's sense and essence is what autopoietic, sense-processing systems make it to be. The world is nothing specific as such. It only becomes something that makes sense by being observed as such by systemic operations. It is not the world that determines the sense that systems make, it is rather the systems that determine the sense the world makes—and thereby its reality.

Sense can only be processed when the world is regarded as information. Systems are able to perceive something as information; they are able to let themselves be surprised or irritated; they can observe. Sense-making, observation, and the production of information are related terms, they are the "cognitive" tools of systems—and systems theory does not limit cognition to psychic systems. It also describes the observations and the sense-making of communication systems as "cognition." To observe is to produce cognition, and to produce cognition is to construct reality. That reality results from cognitive construction, that it results from observation, does, of course, not make it less real—a reality constructed by observation is not less real than one that is "at hand" prior to observation. It just makes reality different, more complex and plural.

Modern physics has also discovered this complex aspect of a reality that is not simply "at hand." A new observation of physical reality results in a new physical reality. To observe physical realities with new instruments of observation produces new realities. By introducing the observer as an integral element of reality, this concept becomes a constructivist one.

To observe reality is to construct reality, and observation is performed as the making of a distinction. By observing something, the observer has to distinguish the observed from the unobserved. The observer has to focus on something and not focus on something else. Observation is therefore "the handling of a distinction to indicate its one side and not the other" (Luhmann 2002a, 143).[12] Observation is performed as the drawing of a distinction— a distinction between what is observed and the "unmarked space" of what is not. This operation is the observation of something as distinguished from something else. The operation of observation not only distinguishes the observed from the unobserved, it also distinguishes the observed from the observer. Through continuous operations of observation, a system constructs what it observes— and it constructs itself as an observation system.

By observing the visual data provided by the brain, the mind observes, for instance, colors. It selects colors as information in a particular way and thus constructs a world of color. The colors perceived by an individual human mind differ from those perceived by another human mind, and even more from those observed by the mind of a horse or—if there is one—the mind of a fly. Every color-observing system establishes its own color spectrum, its own color-distinctions and thus its own color-world. But by observing colors and by observing colors through the establishing of distinctions, the observing system also continues its own operational autopoiesis. The cognition of the world not only constructs the observed, it also constructs the observer. The observer may observe operations—but at the same time is also an operation: "other than as an observation the observer cannot exist. The observer is a formation that constitutes itself by linking operations to each other" (Luhmann 2002a, 143).

From the constructivist perspective of systems theory, reality is not something given, but an effect of cognitive construction. There is not "one" reality, no one realm of "being," as in the traditional Old European ontology—but rather a plurality of realities created through cognition. Cognition produces reality by producing system/environment distinctions. Reality thus emerges as an effect of the operational closure of systems. Once systems are able to link their observational operations, they establish their own operational closure, their autopoiesis, and themselves. Cognition produces operational closure and thus systemic autopoiesis, and systemic autopoiesis produces cognition. In this way a complex constructivist reality, not based on singular "being," but on multiple differences emerges.

Luhmann probably most comprehensively summarized his general epistemological theory of reality-construction in the essay "Cognition as Construction" (included in the appendix of the present book).[13] In this essay Luhmann points out that cognition, and thus the production of a reality that makes sense, does not happen despite, but because of, the operational closure of the observer of reality—and the observer may observe biologically (the brain), communicatively (the social systems), or consciously (the mind). The cognition is in each case "indifferent" to the reality it observes—it does not matter what kind of reality there is. For cognition what matters is how it manages to establish itself as an observing system. And it can do this only by itself and by linking its own cognitive operations to another's. It is by the "self-isolation of a cognizing system—a cell, an immune system, a brain, a consciousness, a communication system" (1988b, 13) that a system/environment distinction emerges and thus a reality. Luhmann explains: "The question how systems are able to produce cognition within an environment can then be reformulated as the question how systems can uncouple themselves from their environment" (1988b, 13). The uncoupling of a system from its environment establishes a system/environment distinction and thereby constitutes the condition for the possibility of cognition, and thereby the condition for the possibility of reality. Once more: reality is a product of (cognitive-constructive-observational) differentiation—not of a singular world that is given "at hand."

(b) Second-Order Cybernetics

If reality is conceived as a cognitive construct, as an effect or correlate of observation, then descriptions of reality become descriptions of observation. When observation becomes an integral part of reality, it can no longer be understood as a kind of Archimedean Point—such as the one Descartes claimed to have found in his *Meditations*. There is no one place where all that is certainly real can be grounded. Observation loses its simplicity—an observer can no longer observe reality without taking into account its very observation as a generating element of reality. A constructivist view of reality directs the attention of observation to the observation, so that the observation of reality becomes an observation of the observation of reality. It becomes second-order observation—and the theory of second-order observation is called second-order cybernetics. Second-order cybernetics is concerned with the reality-construction of observing systems—and here the expression "observing systems" has a double meaning: second-order cybernetics observes systems that are themselves systems of observation, it is observing systems that are observing systems. When second-order cybernetics uses the expression "observing systems," the term "systems" is grammatically both an object and a subject.[14]

Second-order observation paradoxically or "autologically" includes itself in its theory. The subjective and objective sides of observation become equally valid and mutually constitutive.

Luhmann explains the epistemological turn of second-order cyber-netics with the following example: "In this way, the epistemologist becomes him/herself a rat in the labyrinth and has to reflect on the position from which he/she observes the other rats" (Luhmann 1988b, 24). Such a theoretical turn may have its philosophical predecessors,[15] but it is quite revolutionary for a theory of society. For Luhmann, observation becomes a truly formal term that gen-erally designates the making of a distinction and is not limited to one specific type of observation: "First of all, something that causes problems over and over again has to be pointed out. One can say it a hundred times without avail. The observer is not nec-essarily a psychic system, not necessarily consciousness. The observer is defined purely formally: to distinguish and to indicate. A communication can do this too" (2002a, 147). As a sociologist, Luhmann is most concerned with observing communication—again in the double sense of this expression. While Luhmann bor-rows the general theory of second-order cybernetics, he applies it primarily to social theory.

Before we take a closer look at the application of second-order cybernetics to social theory, let me clarify two further aspects of the general theory. *First of all, second-order observation neither observes "better" or "more clearly" than first-order does nor can it be overcome by third- or other higher-order observations.* Observations of any order can do no more than observe. They all observe what they observe—but they observe, so to speak, under different conditions. Second-order observation is also a kind of first-order observation, but one that has to pay for its increase in complexity with the loss of the ontological certainty of data, essentials, or contents (Luhmann 2002a 157). A first-order observation can simply observe something and, on the basis of this, establish that thing's factuality: I see that this book is black—thus the book is black. Second-order observation observes how the eye of an observer constructs the color of this book as black. Thus, the simple "is" of the expression "the book is black" becomes more complex—it is not black in itself but as seen by the eyes of its observer. The ontological simplicity is lost and the notion of "being" becomes more complex. What is lost is the certainty about the "essential" color of this book. While second-order observation arrives at more complex notions of reality or being, it still only observes—it is a second-order observation, because it observes as a first-order observation another first-order observation. It is, so to speak, the result of two simultaneous first-order observations. A third-order observation cannot transcend this pattern—for it is still the first-order observation of a first-order observation of a first-order observation.

Second-order observation does not "see through" the world any more than first-order observation. The relation between them is not parallel to the Old European distinction between truth and appearance—this is exactly the semantics of first-order observation. On the level of first-order observation, observations can compete for being more correct: if you only look closely enough, you will see that this book is not black, but navy blue. Two first-order observations can compete with one another, so to speak, in a Platonic style. Second-order observation—in a more Nietzschean manner—can observe that the distinction between truth and appearance is "merely" an effect of competing first-order observations, but of course it cannot see the "essential" truth. In a way, second-order observation sees less truly than first-order observation.

No higher-order observation—not even a third-order observation—can observe more "essentially" than a lower-order observation. A third-order observation is still an observation of an observation and thus nothing more than a second-order observation. There is no Platonic climb towards higher and higher realities—no observation brings us closer to the single light of truth.

This leads directly to the second aspect of general second-order cybernetics that I would like to highlight: *every observation, regardless of order, has its so-called blind spot*:[16]

When handling a distinction you always have a blind spot or invisibility in your back. You cannot observe yourself as the one who handles a distinction, instead you have to make yourself invisible when you want to observe. Or, to put it differently: While you have to be able to make the distinction between the observer and the observed—i.e. you have to know that you observe something that is not yourself—you still cannot reflect this distinction once more. . . . All observations therefore simultaneously produce something invisible. The observer has to make him/herself invisible as the element of the distinction between the observer and the observed. Therefore . . . there is no enlightenment or scientific clarification of the world as an entirety of things or forms or essences that one could work through time after time (even if conceived of as an infinite task). In classical theory, there was still the impression that one could collect more and more knowledge and that one would not always simultaneously have to leave something in the dark when one wants to indicate something particular. (Luhmann 2002a, 147)

On the level of second-order observation, the second-order observer can observe that the first-order observer cannot observe him/herself as the second observer does. The first-order observer can only observe something from a certain perspective and, in order to take on this perspective, cannot turn around and see what is behind his/her back. The second-order observer can then autologically realize that the same is true for him/herself: Second-order observation is also first-order observation in the sense that it observes something from a certain perspective and that while observing this something (in this case: a first-order observer) it cannot simultaneously "turn around" and observe from where it observes. This is likewise true for all higher-order observations: there is no observation that does not create a blind spot by being an observation—that can be observed by an observation that creates another blind spot, and so on. With second-order cybernetics it becomes evident that no observer can see what he/she cannot see. Any observation can only observe something at the expense of creating a blind spot. Reality depends on blind spots.

Modern theories have realized that this problem haunted Old European metaphysics and ontologies. Luhmann describes this traditional philosophical "flaw":

> This is the decisive point. One sees what one sees and is so fascinated by it that one cannot simultaneously see the nonseeing of everything else as the condition of seeing, or as I nearly want to say: as the transcendental condition of seeing. There is, by the way, an old metaphor: the eye that cannot see its seeing, and then Fichte's reversal: the eye sees its seeing, and thus the subject lights up internally. (2002a, 159)

Old European philosophies were "so fascinated" by their findings that they did not see the darkness on which their insights were based (and it was probably Nietzsche who most thoroughly "deconstructed" this pattern). While some philosophers like Fichte tried to annihilate the blind spot by a total "lighting up" of an ultimately self-observing subjectivity[17] (previous philosophers such as

Nicolaus Cusanus only allowed for such a subjectivity in the case of God), more modern thinkers tried to find "therapeutic" solutions. Luhmann mentions Marx and Freud as two examples:

> There are theories that have a sort of therapeutic intention and attempt, so to speak, to cure the blind spot: the capitalists cannot see that they are effecting their own downfall, and thus the problem arises if one should try to assist a bit in helping it come or if one should rather wait until it happens by itself. In the Freudian theory you find the same pattern in the realm of a theory of consciousness. The unconscious is an unconscious that marks the blind spot of a person's consciousness that can only become conscious to someone who deals with this person. (2002a, 158–59)

Marx and Freud claimed to make some of the blind spots of others (capitalists, psychopaths) visible. One can do this. Second-order cybernetics, however, does not attempt to therapeutically clear away all the blind spots, it rather attempts to integrate them into a new theory. It does not aim at ultimately unmasking blind spots, but at taking them seriously as a condition of systemic reality and complexity.

Social systems theory describes modern society as a reality that is constituted by second-order observation systems—and acknowledges that it is itself taking part in the autopoiesis of one of those subsystems, namely, the system of science. The function systems of modern society are observing systems, and they usually observe the observations of others. In modern society,

> the observation of observers, the change of the consciousness of reality towards the description of descriptions, towards the perception of what others say or what others do not say, has become the advanced way of perceiving the world. And this is the case in all important function areas, in science as well as in the economy, in art as well as in politics. . . . We no longer need to know how the world is if we know how it is observed and if we can orient ourselves within the realm of second-order observation. . . . We . . . follow the legitimizing systems such as science, economy, politics, or mass media of which we are not independent but who themselves are also only observing observations. (2002a, 140–41)

The virtuality-effect of the social reality in which we currently live and in which the social subsystems exist can be explained by second-order observation. Social systems observe—and thereby, of course, construct reality—by observing how others observe. Functional differentiation plus second-order observations are two main characteristics of the present.

A prime example of the interplay between functional differentiation and second-order observation is the relation between politics and the mass media (to be discussed in more detail in part 2). It has become a central focus of politics to deal with its observation by the mass media. The mass media create a so-called public opinion. (This is a somewhat obsolete term because it counterfactually suggests the existence of a sum of individual opinions—a concept that is similar to, but even more obscure than, that of society as a community of individual citizens. How can one compare and present the average of certain mental contents of a group of people?) This "public opinion" is a mass media observation that observes the observations of politics. "Public opinion" might, for instance, agree or disagree to a certain extent with the observations of the government. In turn, the government has to continuously observe how it is observed by the mass media. Political communication observes not simply "facts," but also how facts are observed. The competition between political parties or personalities can well be described as a competition for being more favorably observed for their observations. And, in order to win this competition, political organizations and personalities have to develop an expertise in observing how they are observed—for instance, by the mass media and thus by public opinion.

Practically all modern function systems "observe their own operations on the level of second-order observation" (Luhmann 1997a, 766). Science, for instance, has developed the medium of academic publication for processing its second-order observations. What primarily counts for these publications is not to come forward with a completely new first-order observation—this would hardly be understood, and even less likely accepted—but to show one's familiarity with the publications of others (as I do in the present book in regard to Luhmann's publications). The researcher must "demonstrate in the medium of publications that he has considered the state of research, that is, that he has observed what others have observed. He must show that he has put his own presentation together with a care that enables others to observe how and what he has observed" (Luhmann 1998, 58). The ability to follow this system-ically legitimizing pattern of scientific second-order observation (that is, the ability to write something that can be published) is what students are primarily taught once they reach the level of grad-uate studies—because here education basically becomes systematic training for the pursuit of an academic career. In a systemically hybrid organization like a university, the switch from the education to the science system takes place when it is no longer grades but publications that matter. In the humanities and the social sciences, this usually happens somewhere around the Ph.D. level.

In the art system, representational first-order observation, for instance, of nature, vanished with the nineteenth century. Art observes other art or other types of observations (again, mass media observations are becoming an increasing focus of the obser-vations in art) with the systemic means of art. Thereby art proves to be art today.

The economic system "looks at market prices and registers whether the competition is offering other prices and what trends can be deduced from these price changes" (Luhmann 1998, 59). Probably even more importantly, large-scale economic transactions are no longer directly related to goods and traditional markets, but take place in the form of the trading of financial assets that can be defined as a new generalized medium for the observation of finan-cial observations. The stock and bonds market is, so to speak, a second-order observation that observes first-order markets. It has long surpassed the first-order markets in economical capacity and importance.

Regarding the legal system, Luhmann explains,

> the critical development lies in the full positivization of law, that is, practically, in the replacement of the distinction between natural and positive law with the distinction between constitutional and normal law made at the end of the 18th century. This leads to a situation where law is observed with a view to the question of how something was or will be decided. Interpretation and prognosis are forms of the production of texts from texts and therefore forms of second order observation. (Luhmann 1998, 59)

Today, legal communication has to observe "facts" by observing how these facts have been and will be legally observed. Legal communication judges cases not simply by virtue of their nature but rather by relating them to previous or possible future legal observations. In order to legally observe an incident, legal communication observes how it was or could be observed by other legal observations. Shifts from first-order to second-order observation have taken place even in the function systems of intimacy and education. "The medium of love, used in communication for the making of families (whatever is thought of psychic realizations) leads to a situation where every member must consider how he or she is observed by others" (Luhmann 1998, 60). And while prior to the seventeenth- or eighteenth-century education looked at the child "as a natural phenomenon of the species of humankind, as a small, not yet finished person, and education was tasked with guiding this development, enhancing it, or preventing corruption, now the observation of the child is observed in order to gain insight into an appropriate education for children" (Luhmann 1998, 60). In the family and in the school, we now tend to observe how and what others observe—and accordingly also observe ourselves as lovers or teachers in reaction to how our spouses or students observe us. I think Luhmann is correct about the increasing importance of second-order observation even in these function systems. It seems that teaching-evaluation forms would have appeared entirely outlandish in the educational organizations and institutions of the seventeenth or eighteenth century. Students were not granted the status of qualified observers, so there was no basis for second-order observation. Nowadays student teacher-evaluation is an accepted tool in the education system. By observing these evaluations we as teachers observe how the students observe our observing of them.

3

What Happens to the
Human Being?

(a) Beyond Humanism

Michel Foucault ended his book *Le mots et les choses* ("words and things," published in English as *The Order of Things*) with the famous wager that man—or the "humanist" concept of the human being—will vanish like a face drawn in the sand at the seashore. In that same final paragraph he pointed out that the human being is neither the oldest nor the most constant issue that human knowledge has dealt with. One only has to look at the ancient Greek Presocratics or, on the other side of the globe, at ancient Chinese philosophy, to verify Foucault's assertion. Anthropocentrism is by no means a given in the enterprise of understanding and cognition. Contemporary or postmodern thought—like contemporary or postmodern art—re-connected to pre-modern and ancient non-anthropocentrisms (once more Friedrich Nietzsche may be named as an important forerunner—one who took a great step backwards in order to make a great leap forward[18]) to come up with a new kind of non-anthropocentrism. Niklas Luhmann's version of social systems theory and his "treatment" of the human being can certainly be understood in the context of this quite recent development in intellectual history.

To be sure, social systems theory does not attempt to merely "erase" the human being as Foucault's image might suggest. In a probably more Nietzschean spirit, it rather finally (after a couple of centuries of humanism) tries to step beyond the conceptual limits of the "human, all-too-human." Traditional humanist notions are too simple to explain the complexity of reality—this is why there needs to be a new theory. As discussed in the first chapter of this book, Luhmann replaces the notion of a singular and integrated human being with the assumption of at least three autopoietic systemic realms: body, consciousness, and communication. "We" are a complex assembly of bodily functions, psychic operations, and social performances. Human beings are not "one-dimensional," but at least three-dimensional—and the three dimensions are by no means in perfect harmony.[19] We cannot exactly translate our mental contents into communication, and neither can the thoughts of our mind translate the exact physical processes of the brain. The Aristotelian concept that mental contents are the same for all human beings (*De Interpretatione*, 16a) has become obsolete. And it is not only the belief in a common human "mindset" that has waned—the corresponding conception of the human being as a singular entity is also beginning to fade.

Traditional Old European philosophies—probably with Plato and Descartes as the most famous representatives—were often ready to concede that human beings are not simply made of a "soul," but also of a body. However, these traditional views, as was the case with the authors I mentioned above, tended to look at the soul as the seat of human "individuality" and thus as the essential element that defined the human being (this is still very obvious in regard to Western, especially North American, religious arguments against abortion). The soul was the essential element within the human body, and the body was acknowledged to be a more or less integral part of actual human existence. On the basis of this idea, the human being was conceived of as a singular compound of mind and body. Various traditional philosophies then discussed the so-called mind-body problem—how a singular entity could consist of two parts. Social systems theory does not offer a new and easy solution to this old problem, it rather suggests that "human reality" is even more complex: we do not only have to deal with the mind and the body—we also have to take into account communication. And in the face of such multiplicity it might be wise to give up the attempt still to "singularize" the human being.

There is no scientific evidence or any ultimately convincing philosophical or theological argument that forces us to ascribe dominance to one of these three systemic realms. Why should we claim that the human being is essentially spiritual, bodily, or social at the expense of the other two systems? Social systems theory, even though it is explicitly a social theory, does not suggest any kind of "centrism" or "essentialism" in regard to the human being. There is no substantial essence on the basis of which *the* human being can be defined. And since the human being cannot be essentially defined, it does not make a lot of sense to use it as the starting point of a theory. This is the reason social systems theory tries to wipe out the humanists' one-dimensional portrayal of the human being and replace it with a more complex model of reality.

As discussed in the first chapter, Luhmann's systems theory conceives of the relation between the three autopoietic and operationally closed systemic realms of body, mind, and society—to put it simply—in such a way that the mind functions as a kind of filter between communication and the world (Luhmann 2002a, 272). No "outside" information can enter communication without first being processed by the mind. Whatever happens in the body, for instance, must first pass through the mental operations before it can appear in communication. A pain in the body must first be *felt* before it can be talked about. Of course, we can also talk about pain that is not really felt—but if an actual pain is to enter communication, it can only do so by being "filtered" through the system of consciousness. This configuration, once more, does not imply any hierarchy among the systems (bodily pain does not have a more primary or essential status than communicated pain), but it highlights a specific structural coupling, namely, that between the mind and communication. By conceiving of the mind as a filter for communication, the "mind-communication problem" is of more direct concern for a theory of society than the "body-communication problem." The problem of the "human being"—when viewed from the perspective of social theory (and not from the equally valid perspective of biology)—does not therefore primarily appear in the form of the "mind-body-problem," but rather in the question: "How does the mind participate in communication?"—to use the title of an article by Luhmann (1994a).

The "mind-communication problem" is addressed in at least three different ways by social systems theory. The first perspective could be called a structural one. Here, the question would be: what are the basic structures of the mind-communication relation? The second perspective is historical. One can ask: what shapes can the mind-communication relation take on under different social conditions? Or, more precisely: which options for dealing with this problem arise under different types of social differentiation? Or, more concretely: how did the change from stratified to functional differentiation affect this problem? This question leads to the third perspective, which has to do with the present relevance of the mind-communication relation. It can be asked: What does it now mean to be a social agent? What are the current conditions for "personhood?"

Answers to the "structural" question have already been given. The structural relation is a structural coupling; psychic and social systems "interpenetrate" one another. This structural coupling described above can be summarized once more in Luhmann's own words:

> We are dealing with an exclusion of nearly everything that happens to be in the world, and with a compensation of this exclusion through a total dependency of communication. Communication is dependent on consciousness that in turn is dependent on its own brain that in turn depends on the organism being alive because it can survive the death of its organism for a few seconds at best.[20] (2002a, 273)

Minds and society are both totally dependent on *and* independent of each other. They are totally dependent on the other's existence for the continuation of their own autopoiesis. At the same time, on the basis of their operational closure, they are both totally independent for no direct determination or interference is possible. Their operational closure and a certain openness of the mind and communication correspond to their respective independence-dependence:

> Systems of the mind and systems of communication exist completely independently of each other. At the same time, however, they form a relationship of structural complementarity. They can only actualize and specify their own structures and thus can only change themselves. They use each other for reciprocal irritation of these structural changes. Systems of communication can only be stimulated by systems of the mind, and these in turn are extremely attracted to what is conspicuously communicated by language. My argument is as follows: the independence of each closed system is a requirement for structural complementarity, that is, for the reciprocal initiation (but not determination) of the actualized choice of structure. (Luhmann 1994a, 380)

(b) Problems of Identity

As explained above, the structural coupling of the systems of mind and society leads to the emergence of the co-evolution of minds and society, primarily furthered by their common media of language and sense (*Sinn*). This basic structural framework for describing the mind-communication relation leads to specific conceptions of human "individuality" or "identity." The process of attaining an individual identity can now be understood as co-evolutionary, involving both mental and communicative operations. Therefore, the process can be described from two perspectives: from that of the autopoiesis of both psychic systems as well as that of social systems. Just as the human being is not a singular thing, so also "individuality" and "identity" are not simply singular objects. They have no singular "home." Individuality and identity have a place in both consciousness and communication. In the case of the mental systems, individual identity emerges as a result of *self-socialization*; in the case of social systems, individuality, and identity are part of an important semantics of the self-description of society and are connected to the *inclusion* of "persons" in society. Expressed in the technical language of social systems theory, this is to say: self-socialization means that "the autopoietic system of society that operates on the basis of communication makes its own complexity available for the construction of psychic systems"; and, conversely, inclusion means that "an autopoietic psychic system that operates on the basis of consciousness makes its own complexity available for the construction of social systems" (Luhmann 1989, 162). Each mind is an individual psychic system, and therefore each will develop individual structures that resonate with its environment—especially, of course, with its social environment with which it is structurally coupled (or, in the older Parsonian terminology: is in "interpenetration"). Luhmann says: "Systems of the mind are socialized by interpenetrations with social systems. This concept requires a fundamental rethinking of the classical sociological theory of socialization, all the way from external socialization to self-socialization" (1994a, 386; translation modified). Mental systems autopoietically develop themselves and can only develop an understanding or consciousness of themselves by way of self-socialization. Society cannot "socialize" a mind— socialization is a "do-it-yourself" project as far as consciousness is concerned. No parent, teacher, preacher, or government can directly interfere in the mental operations of the systems of consciousness. In this respect, mental individualization is totally independent of society. How we structure our own consciousness is ultimately decided by our own consciousness; mental structures are "the result of an individual system history" of the mind (Luhmann 2002a, 137).

On the basis of structural coupling, however, the total operational independency of the individual mental systems always goes along with total "cognitive" dependency. The framework for mentally conceiving of ourselves as individuals is ultimately dependent on the semantics of individuality made available by our social environment. The language and the sense (*Sinn*) of individuality link or couple our perceptions of our individualities to society. Each individual consciousness has its own particular systemic history, its own individual mindset—but in each case this history and resulting mindset are informed by the available "cultural supply" (Luhmann 2002a, 137).

On the other hand, communication systems ascribe individuality to "persons." This is how they are able to resonate with the psychic complexity in their environment. Social systems develop notions or a semantics of "persons" or "individuals" so that communication can be properly addressed and can form proper conceptions of "entities" that correspond to ongoing activities of consciousness that irritate communication. Inclusion is the term for the manner in which social systems can recognize persons. By inclusion, social systems assign persons with a social position so that there is a framework "in which they can act in conformity with expectations, or, to put it more romantically: in which they can feel at home as individuals" (Luhmann 1997a, 621). Successful inclusion takes place when society is able to prepare molds for "individuals" to fit in.

The features of social inclusion, the shapes of the social molds for persons change with social change; and this means, of course, that they most significantly change when the primary type of social differentiation changes. Along with social evolution, along with the unfolding of history, the "cultural supply" varies. The social semantics of individuality that link or couple social inclusion and mental self-socialization change with time. Therefore, from the perspective of social systems theory, to describe or analyze human individuality basically means to describe or analyze the semantic changes of individuality that took place along with structural changes in society. The issue of the human individual is therefore an issue to be investigated by comparing "social structures and semantics"—and thus Luhmann's most systematic treatment of this issue is to be found in one of the volumes of the book series on *Gesellschaftsstruktur und Semantik* ("Social Structure and Semantics") (1989, 149–258; see also Luhmann 1986b).

"Human" individuality—as distinguished from the general, literal meaning of individuality that simply designates a "singular entity" and according to which every autopoietic system, be it psychic, social, or biological could be called an individual—is a product of the semantics and language that couple psychic and social systems. It is a historical communication phenomenon that cannot be understood essentially. "Individuality" is a word with varying senses and not a substantial quality of human existence: "Everyone knows, of course, that the word 'human being' is not a human being. We must also learn that there is no such thing as an objective unit that corresponds to this word. Words such as 'human being,' 'soul,' 'person,' 'subject,' and 'individual' are nothing more than what they effect in communication" (Luhmann 1994a, 387; translation modified).

If one accepts that there are no individual human beings as such (or as "objective units"), but only historically contingent semantic constructs that emerge from the structural coupling of psychic and social systems, then one has already arrived at the second possible question mentioned at the beginning of this chapter: which shapes can the mind-communication relation take on under different social conditions? Or, more precisely: which options for dealing with the mind-communication problem arise under different types of social differentiation? Or, more concretely: how did the change from stratified to functional differentiation affect the mind-communication problem?

As outlined in chapter 1, section c above, Luhmann distinguishes among four types of social differentiation (segmentary, center/periphery, stratified, and functional) and describes the historical evolution of society as a sequence of their respective primacies. The most decisive change for our present society took place in sixteenth- to eighteenth-century Europe when stratified differentiation was gradually replaced by functional differentiation. In accordance with this scheme, Luhmann also focuses on this transitional period in his analysis of the semantics of individuality.

The basic structuring principle within a stratified society is social rank, and it is consequently primarily divided into a hierarchy of social strata. Within such a society the stratum, and, more concretely, the family or, even more concretely, the household, is the social locality where an individual becomes an individual. The family and the household are, so to speak, the germ-cells of the dominating social order and supply the individual with a rank and respective attributes. By being born into a family and into a household within a stratified society, the individual gains its individuality "in the sense of its socially respected characteristics" (1989, 166).

Individual identity is granted by social "placement," by being assigned a specific place within the pattern of social strata. Individuality in the sense of an indivisible identity is attributed to each single person within the family. The family automatically provides each member with a social position and with the social relations and responsibilities connected to this position. Or, as Luhmann says: "One was socialized where one had to lead one's social life: within the house" (1989, 167). In this context, individuality means—in accordance with its literal meaning—"indivisibility," and thus it does not yet mean "uniqueness" or "singularity." The individual is not yet characterized by its specific peculiarity, but rather by possessing—through birth, rank, and family-status—a specific indestructible and unchangeable identity. The social positioning grants an inviolable individuality in the sense of a fixed social status.

In addition to this secular type of individuality, the semantics of individuality in Old European stratified societies could also grant a second kind of indivisibility: namely a religious indestructibility. By being indivisible, the individual could be assured of its immortality: "The individuality of the soul guaranteed its indestructibility, thus its immortality, and this explained why human beings had to answer for themselves at the Last Judgment"(1995a, 257). Since individuality was literally understood as the substantial indivisibility of the soul, an eternal life was to be expected: "That which cannot be taken apart cannot perish. Only the complex, not the singular is transitory" (1989, 172). In this way, the individual was neither socially nor religiously "characterized by the peculiarity of its (coincidental) characteristics," but rather shaped by birth and divine creation as an "indivisible unit" (1989, 176). The individual was still far from being something "original," it was, on the contrary, something quite uniform. The individual was fixed to a position within a world whose order "resided in the more general references of genera and specia"(1995a, 258). The individual became an individual by being placed on an individual spot within a general frame; it became an individual, so to speak, by "direct" inclusion.

When the Old European society based on "stratified differentiation" was replaced by a social structure based on "functional differentiation," the definition of individuality through "direct" inclusion was replaced by a paradoxical inclusion through a distinctive form of *exclusion*—not, of course, the total exclusion from functionality of those living in the *favelas*, but rather the exclusion of the "extramundane position of the transcendental subject" (Luhmann 1986b, 319). When the established social strata started to dissolve and society lost its hierarchical stability, both the established social and religious order eroded. The "general" was no longer outside of the individual and inside society and religion, but was moved into the individual itself. Luhmann says that then "precisely individuality is universal, because it applies to everyone without exception" (1995a, 259). Individuality no longer means indivisibility, but uniqueness. The individual is now supposed to be individual by being different from all others—by being a "subject." In the nineteenth century, the notions of individuality and subjectivity became semantically similar, and both were designations of modern "uniqueness": "It is now expected from the individual to identify itself in regard to its individuality, and this can only mean: in regard to that which distinguishes itself from everybody else. Self-observations and self-descriptions can no longer (and if still, then only externally) rely on social positions, affiliations, inclusions" (Luhmann 1989, 215). Functional differentiation in modern societies means differentiation into the multiple functional subsystems of society, such as law, economy, politics, and so on. The boundaries between these systems now mark the primary social differentiations—and no longer the boundaries between social strata. The newly emerged individual as "subject" cannot be entirely at home within any of these function systems. Specifically, German Idealism contributed to this semantic shift of individuality that followed the structural change of society. In this philosophy the individual is understood as a singular, unique world-relation (*Weltverhältnis*) that becomes conscious by its own self and that is realized as human existence. Since then it has become impossible (even though many do not recognize this!) to conceive of the individual as a part of a whole, as a part of society. Whatever the individual makes of himself and however society contributes to this: it has its standpoint in itself and outside of society. The formula "subject" symbolizes nothing else. Thereby the individual is external to all function systems. It can no longer participate. (Luhmann 1989, 212)

The shift from the individual as indivisible to unique is nothing else than the shift of the semantics of individuality from social inclusion to the peculiar social exclusion-inclusion of the "subject."

Under the conditions of stratified differentiation it was exactly his or her individuality that included the individual in society. And this individuality was "pure:" one member of one family belonged to one social stratum. A mixed individuality was inconceivable. Under the conditions of functional differentiation, however, such an integral placement is impossible, since social positions can no longer exhaustively determine one's place in society. Integration has to be found outside the multiplicity of social functions, and the new semantics of subjectivity provide a basis for the re-integration of the individual outside of society. At the same time, the functionally differentiated society also provides roles to *partially* re-include individuals that constitute themselves as subjects outside of society. One can re-enter society "as a voter, as a patient, as a reader, as connoisseur etc." (Luhmann 1989, 160). While the individual gains his or her identity as a subject outside of social roles, the multiple functions provided by society allow for a variety of new partial inclusions.

This new situation is not without problems. First, individuality based on *uniqueness* is supposed to be the *common* characteristics of all individuals. Thus, the individual is unique, but by being unique, isn't. Secondly, while the individual is supposed to constitute him- or herself "uniquely," the criteria for his or her uniqueness are still supplied by society. Out of sheer uniqueness he or she cannot build a positive identity: "The individual can describe and know itself as a Bavarian and yet know that this excludes being a Prussian. But can an individual describe itself as individual?" (Luhmann 1995a, 266). I can describe myself as different from the Prussians, by knowing that I am Bavarian, but can

I ever positively describe myself "only" as an individual? The characteristics that distinguish me from others always have to be socially available. I have to be something else in order not to be a Prussian. Thus, I always have to accept something general to signify my individual uniqueness. Society offers quite a few options for my exclusive self-inclusion. I may describe myself as belonging to a specific party that most others do not vote for, as a reader of specific books that many others don't read, as a connoisseur of "unique" wines, and so on. I exclude myself from others by doing this, but I must always include myself somewhere else. Thirdly, the individual can no longer be an *in-dividual* in the traditional sense of indivisibility. In order to exist as a social being, he or she has to divide him- or herself: "He or she is in need of a musical self for the opera, a diligent self for the job, a patient self for the family. What is left for him- or herself is the problem of his or her identity" (Luhmann 1989, 223). Exclusive individuality confronts the individual with the problem of multiple selves as soon as he or she becomes socially active. Or, to put it more dramatically: the individual is torn apart as a social being—as Luhmann writes, "in any case, the unity of the multiplicity of possible self-identifications becomes the greatest individual problem that everyone has to resolve for him/herself and that is no longer resolvable by conformity to morality and consciousness, by repressing the worse ego" (1989, 225). The father confessor who had to take care of the sanity of the individual souls of Old European individuals is replaced by New European psychiatrists and therapists who now look after the multiple selves.

Instead of falling apart into multiple selves the subjective individual has another choice that is, according to Luhmann, preferred by most as a reaction against these individuals' paradoxical situations. It can become, in Luhmann's terminology, an *homme copie*, an "imitational person." "This means: to admit from the first the failure of the programme of individuality and to establish one's principle of life on the opposite. To be able to be different then means: to be just like someone else" (1989, 221). In living a "copied existence," one borrows one's originality from others. Just like in the world of fashion, one becomes special by copying what others present as being special.

The subjectivity-based semantics of individuality in a functionally differentiated society is lead astray in two ways—it may either lead to a multiple self or to an *imitational person*. The paradoxes (or parodies) of subjective individuality may lead, according to Luhmann, to the impression "that the rise of the individual was a decline and that the expectation that the individual describes itself as an individual leads to meaninglessness" (1995a, 267). The human subject so grandiloquently introduced by the great philosophies of early modernity (one may think of Kant, Hegel, and also of Kierkegaard) turned out to be unable to fulfill the high expectations connected to it. The breakdown of stratified differentiation seemed to set subjectivity and true human individuality free at last. But as it turns out from the perspective of today (and perhaps it was once more Nietzsche who first anticipated this somewhat surprising turn), subjective individuality was no more than a semantic hoax connected to the shift towards functional differentiation. Set free from the constraints and fixtures of stratification, individuality felt quite elevated for some time and became fascinated by its new emancipation from social "placement." But subjectivity was never free—the semantics of freedom was rather a development in accordance with social change. It is now more or less obvious that even subjectivity is not the essential core of human existence, but rather a semantics tightly connected with a type of social differentiation, namely, functional differentiation. The problems of subjective individuality diagnosed above—showing themselves in the symptoms of the *imitational person* and the multiple self—result from functional differentiation. The problem of the multiple self arises with a nonhierarchical multiplicity of options for socialization with which the contemporary mind is confronted: Which self shall we choose to accept as the essential one, as our "true identity?" Are we first of all a husband, and then and only secondarily a professor? Or are we substantially a free citizen, and then and only secondarily a sexual being? And how can we claim to be original when we have to copy a pattern of originality in order to be discernible as original?

If one accepts the suggestion that the modern semantics of subjectivity is once more a semantics of individuality developed in accord with a type of social differentiation, then one will view it as a contemporary way of dealing with the mind-communication problem—and not as a human condition. Thus, one has already arrived at the third possible question I mentioned at the beginning of this chapter: what does it mean to be a social agent today? In other words, what now are the conditions for personhood? If, in accordance with the semantics of modern society we become persons by being *subjects* that take on a *variety of functions*, what does this mean in "real life?"

In real life, this means that we become persons by going through *careers* (that can be, of course, more or less successful) within the various function systems. But, while we differ regarding our individual careers, we all have the universal qualities of being free and equal human beings with the corresponding rights and dignities. Once more, this was not always the case. This new type of social inclusion represents a "dramatic change in regard to the self-conceptions of the individuals" (Luhmann 1997a, 626). Under conditions of stratification one was born into an identity. One could identify oneself simply with a name and a position. To have a social identity it was enough to have a name and a home. When you identified yourself to someone as the daughter of a poor Norman peasant, there were few other questions that you could be asked. The same, of course, was true if you said: "I am Count Montgomery." In neither case, would you have had to indicate your hobbies, your favorite authors, or the college you graduated from. This is obviously no longer the case:

> Today the more typical situation is that one has to explain who one is, that one has to send out test signals in order to see how far others are capable of rightly evaluating with whom they are dealing. Therefore, one needs an "education," or signals that indicate the properties one possesses. Therefore, identity becomes a problem. . . . Therefore, one cannot essentially know who one is, but has to find out if one's projections receive recognition. (Luhmann 1997a, 627)

In a stratified society you could essentially know who you were by knowing that you were Count Montgomery. Today, even for Count Montgomery this would no longer be enough. Even he would have to explain what else he is: he would have to say that he graduated from Oxford, that he went to law school, that he has been married twice and has kids from both marriages, and that he likes football. By making these and other social features known, one can expect to be recognized as a specific person—to be ascribed an individual identity. One will know who one is by finding out which social features—which "projections of oneself"—are socially recognized as one's identifications. By teaching at a university one will be recognized as a "professor," by further being a man who has various intimate relationships, one can be recognized as a "polygamous professor," and by further being a Republican senator from Alabama, one can be recognized as "that polygamous professor who is a Republican senator from Alabama." Such specifications make for unique identities that allow persons to know who they are.

On the basis of functional differentiation, social identities are—partially—acquired in function systems. Within a function system one makes a "career": "And what is above all decisive is that in modern society the career (...) has advanced to become the most important mechanism for the integration of individuals and society" (Luhmann 1997a, 742). By having a career within a function system, one is included in society. As indicated above, careers can be successful or unsuccessful, but an unsuccessful career still provides one with no less of an identity. To be a criminal with four children out of wedlock and no college education is, technically speaking, no less a career pattern than being a Methodist preacher, a major shareholder, or a painter of North American landscapes.

Careers usually change with time, and so do our identities. Whereas Count Montgomery could be a count for an entire lifetime, today we have to work continuously on our identities, and, basically, renew them day by day. This is one reason individual identities became "a problem." Careers put us under identity stress. We cannot avoid having an identity, and we cannot avoid having it through a career—because even failure will count as *career*-failure. Even if one quits Wall Street for sheep farming in Australia this is merely a switch in careers, and such switches, on smaller scales, happen on a quite regular basis in most people's lives.

Since the intimacy system is also a system, being a "loving husband" or a "depressed single mother" can also be counted as career features. To have personal attributes such as "loving" or "depressed" attached to one's functional indicators does not take away the career focus of our social identity. One can, of course, be a loving person, but in order to be this, one has to be "loving" *as* a mother or *as* a nurse or *as* a captain in the army. One cannot simply be "loving" outside of all systems. If one were to be loving only outside of social systems one would cease to be loving in society. If society consists of systems (such as function systems, interactions, and organizations), then one's social identity is also systemic. There may well be individual psychic qualities that influence our social identity, but this identity is social, not psychic. Careers cause us to be included in society, and our social identity cannot be disconnected from them.

As pointed out earlier, social inclusion on the basis of functional differentiation is principally all-inclusion. Nobody is on principle excluded from having a career, be it a successful or unsuccessful one. However, it has to be noted that in fact many have no access whatsoever to careers and are reduced to a bodily existence without social identity—or with a strictly negative one. Children born in the *favelas* of Central America have no careers, not even unsuccessful ones, to identify themselves with. They often do not even have the chance *not* to graduate or have a low income or to lose an election. Social inclusion through careers only includes those with access to function systems.

On top of our career-identities, we still have our universal "subjectivity." In present-day society, this supposed subjectivity is compensation for our composite career-patchwork identities that emerge in the form of the semantics of freedom, equality, and human rights. Functional differentiation is laid out for all-inclusion. That nobody is in principle disqualified from being "functionalized" means that everybody is in principle somehow "okay:" I'm okay—you're okay. But how can society explain this universal assumption that everyone can be included?

In earlier societies, it was assumed that some, or, in most cases, most, could not be included. One traditional semantic distinction that expressed this division was the Greek/Barbarian distinction.[21] Barbarians were believed to be entirely different from Greeks and therefore it made no sense to socially include them. In a society of functional differentiation we all become principally Greeks, so to speak. But while the old Greeks could describe and identify themselves by distinguishing themselves from the Barbarians, this possibility is eliminated once all are Greeks. The leading modern semantics of all-inclusion, the totalitarian semantics of our time that makes us all Greeks (or should I say Americans?) is the result of the semantics of human rights, equality, and freedom. Today, we become social individuals not only through individual career identities, but also by accepting the

social self-description of the "universal subject" as the free and
equal human being that has certain human rights:

> The function of a semantics of inclusion is taken over in the eigh-
> teenth century by the postulate of human rights. It is directed against
> the old differentiations and simultaneously it summarizes the condi-
> tions of inclusion of all function systems so that a difference-neutral
> "human" principle is advocated. Freedom and equality are now
> (semantically established) because all limitations and inequalities are
> set up only by the codes and programs of the individual function sys-
> tems since general directives for the whole of society no longer exist—
> and probably also since no one can tell someone else what his or her
> actions are ultimately good for. (Luhmann 1997a, 628)

All-inclusion cannot go along with the older semantics of differentiation. We cannot define "humanity" on the basis of the nobility of
one ethnicity as opposed to others, or of the distinction between
those to whom God revealed himself and those to whom he did
not. We can no longer primarily distinguish between Greeks and
Barbarians, Christians and Heathens. Individual function systems
cannot provide a semantics that can be valid for others and so the
"universal human being" has to be a "difference-neutral" one.
Before we enter the function systems and our careers, we are all the
same. Universal freedom and equality, as the basic content of
human rights, are the semantic counterweight to the factual
restraints and inequalities produced by the function systems. In fact,
some are poor and some are rich, some get good grades, other bad
ones, and some are in the government while others are in the opposition. Still, on principle, we are all "subjects," we all have "human
rights," and we are free and equal. General social directives are not
available—we cannot determine, for instance, the general primacy
of one religion over another—and we also cannot give any ultimate
reasons why careers and function systems are good. But we can
establish a semantics that is emptier than such content-based directives or "meanings": Freedom and equality are perfectly suited for
providing such an empty semantics of universality. You are free—
choose your path into the function systems for yourself; there is no
ultimate guideline that forces you into a particular one. Which job
you get, with whom you have sex, and which hobbies you may like,
all this depends on free choices. We are all equal—do not assume
that anybody has the authority to impose a certain way of life on

you. You can compete with anyone for a job; you can sue anyone; and you can even try to be elected. Choose for yourself; create your own personal identity. Be a free and equal human being with an individual career and individual beliefs.

The difference-neutral semantics of human rights, freedom, and equality is the "true" fundamentalism of our time (see Luhmann 1997a, 1022). The traditional fundamentalisms of various religious or ethnic groups are desperate attempts to replace a career identity with an "against identity" (Luhmann 1997b, 9), desperate attempts to disrupt functional differentiation and to perform inclusion or to attain an identity outside of it. These fundamentalisms are in fact not at all fundamental—they are acts of sabotage performed on the fringes of society. The *real*, literal fundamentalism that semantically grounds the *fundamental* structures of contemporary society is the (relatively) new ideology of human rights.

The present-day semantics of universal subjectivity and human dignity sounds pretty good. It has a soothing effect and has "the rhetoric function to protect the individual against the insight into its own meaninglessness as one among many billions: It is, after all, a subject (and not merely an object) and has the right to be treated accordingly. No wonder that it is especially intellectuals who do not want to let go of this word" (Luhmann 1997a, 1027). The semantics of subjectivity—that flourished after the American and French Revolutions—allows the retaining of some self-respect. It is a fine addition to the structural reality of functional differentiation and supplies us with dignity. It makes us feel more important on an individual level, and it can supply professional intellectuals with some impressive phrases. To speak of ourselves as free and equal subjects is rather comforting on the personal level and also enhances the aura of academic talk.

Human rights, freedom, and equality are ideas that transcend our functional existence, but they do not hinder it. They rather provide a fundamental level of sense on the basis of which functional differentiation also makes sense. They help us to make sense of our social existence—as meaningless as they may factually be. In the following passage, Luhmann summarizes his analysis of this new ideology:

> The old society had regulated inclusion through the assignment of fixed positions to families or corporations (and thus indirectly: to

persons). This simple solution has to be abolished along with the transition to functional differentiation, because families cannot be distributed to function systems. Instead, new principles of inclusion are sought and found that are given the names of freedom and equality and that take on the form of civil or even human rights. Freedom means that the distribution of persons (no longer: families) to society is no longer determined by social structures, but based on a combination of self-selection and external selection. Equality means that no other principles of inclusion are accepted besides those determined by the function systems themselves. Or, put differently: only the function systems have the right to produce inequalities on the basis of system-internal (and thus for them rational) reasons. All issues have to be presented under the aspect of equality, i.e. unstructured, to the system, for instance; equality of all before the law with the exception of the distinctions established in the law system itself. The latent function of these human rights therefore lies exactly not in honoring and ratifying essentials that are given with the "nature of man." They rather lie in the principal impossibility to predict in modern society who has to say what, or contribute otherwise, in which social contexts. It lies in keeping open the future against all a priori determinations that could result from a distribution or classification of human beings (for instance, into higher and lower ones) and particularly from political sorting. (1997a, 1075–76)

Careers and the semantics of subjectivity focus on human rights. Freedom and equality are the cornerstones of contemporary self-socialization and social inclusion and thus they significantly contribute to how we attain personhood and individuality today. This process can be described in far more detail, especially when one looks at a concrete function system. I will return to this issue in connection with the discussion of the mass media system.

In social theory, particularly in sociology, the semantics of the subject has survived in the form of "theories of action" (*Handlungstheorien*). Such theories, with Talcott Parsons and Jürgen Habermas as two quite different representatives, try to describe society as being constituted by the actions of its individual members. Thus, in the final analysis, these theories re-introduce the individual or the subject as a basic constituent of society. To Habermas, for instance, society should be a community of rational beings who realize "communicative action." From a Luhmannian perspective, this is a self-contradictory notion. There is nothing like "communicative action" that can be traced back to rational individuals. Communication systems are autopoietic and operationally closed and only have individual, "rational" minds (among other things) as their environment. Communication does not emerge from "human action." The structures of communication are communicative structures, not structures of action.

According to the constructivist view of social systems theory, "action" is a communicative construct, or more precisely, the construct of a self-observing communication system that identifies a communicative announcement (*Mitteilung*—one of the three elements of communication) as an "action" and ascribes it to an "agent" or "actor" (Luhmann 1997a, 86). That we speak of communication as an action is due to a semantic construction within communication. If a "selection" is ascribed by the system to itself, it is understood as "active" and thus as an action. If the selection is attributed to its environment, the communication system will perceive it passively and thus as "experience." Action and experience are, so to speak, the active and passive modes of communication systems. Corresponding to those modes, actions and experiences can be distinguished (see Luhmann 1997a, 335–36).

Being a constructivist theory, social systems theory does not conceive of communication as a result of human action, but rather views the concept of human action as a result of communication. As a nonhumanist theory, it does not locate human beings within communication but within communication's environment; and it describes "human action" as designated by communication systems. As stated above, this is what the "scandal" of systems theory amounts to when humanists and "action theoreticians" evaluate it. The expulsion of the human being from society may be perceived both as an insult to human dignity and as counterintuitive. But is it really so bad if we position ourselves, at least as far as our psychic individuality is concerned, outside of society? And is it really so counterintuitive to state that in this dimension we can finally operate outside the frames and structures of functional differentiation? Luhmann says:

> I, for one, would in any case feel more comfortable in the environment of society than within a society in which other people could think my thoughts and in which other biological or chemical reactions

could move my body with which I had intended to do something else. This is to say that the difference between system and environment also offers a possibility to conceive of a radical individualism in the environment of the system, and to conceive of it in a way that could not be attained if the human being would be seen as a part of society and if one would thus adopt a humanist idea that would turn the human being either into an element or into the purpose of society itself. (2002a, 256–57)

It is somewhat ironic that the expulsion of the human being from society offers it a more radical "emancipation" than theorists of social action could have ever imagined. If, as Sartre famously put it, "hell is other people," then the only way to escape this hell is to radically separate the realms of society and individuality. Social systems theory allows for this without having to imagine some otherworldly transcendence or dubious dignity of the human soul. It simply distinguishes between bodily, psychic, and communicative processes and gives up the illusionary notion that the human being has to be, in the final analysis, a singular and fully integrated entity.

4

What Can Be Done?

(a) Limits of Activism and the Conformism of Protest

The great philosophies of early modernity tended to claim to be "groundworks" (with Kant as a prime example) for all sciences and to be able to explain *the* fundamental features of *all* that we can know. This kind of claim could well be accompanied by the belief that philosophy could also outline the best, or at least a good, way to behave and thus provide for a better—if not the best possible—future for humankind. Such "epistemological optimism" (to use a term coined by the Sinologist Thomas Metzger) paired with a corresponding *ethical* one is still very much part of North American philosophical life, especially among pragmatists and political theorists. Social systems theory is much more skeptical about the powers of philosophical or academic discourse to come up with guidelines for a progressive future society.

One of the most influential epistemological and ethical optimisms of recent intellectual history was probably Marxism. Marx famously demanded (in the eleventh thesis on Feuerbach) that philosophers should finally stop interpreting the world and begin to change it. This demand did not remain unheard. However, the concrete social results of the attempt to materialize Marxist thought did not necessarily match the expectations of its inventor. Today "rightist" thinkers can gloatingly point to the downfall of the Soviet Union to substantiate the assertion that Marxism simply does not work, that it was nothing but a great failure. But one could also—and this is not mentioned very often—point to the People's Republic of China and observe quite different results. Besides the atrocities of recent Chinese history (that happened, for instance, during the Great Leap Forward and the Cultural Revolution), the Communist rule of more than half a century transformed China from an extremely poor and backwards country that was exploited and militarily suppressed by imperialist countries into a politically independent and economically successful neo-capitalist state of more than a billion people. Interestingly enough, the Chinese economy seems to be much healthier than, for instance, the post-Communist Russian "free market" or the economy of India—that is often praised as the "largest democracy of the world."

The quite contradictory examples of Russia and China demonstrate that Marxism cannot be simply characterized as a monumental failure of the application of a social theory to politics and the economy. In Russia, Marxist rule eventually led to political collapse and an economic catastrophe; in China it lead at the same time to a transition from a poor agricultural society to a modern economy that bears hardly any traces of Communism. Thus, the example of Marxism rather seems to demonstrate that while a social theory can have an extreme political and economic impact, it is almost impossible to predict what this impact will be. The impact Marxist theory has had on the politics and economies of various countries cannot be described by simple causal relations. Rather, it seems that what happened in the respective political systems or economies was not "caused" by the political theory or ideology that the organizations that governed these states adopted. Instead—to use the terminology of social systems theory—it seems that in each case the economic and the political realities developed their own *resonance* with the "academic" or ideological *irritations*. It seems that under the condition of functional differentiation function systems cannot be steered or controlled externally—not even by theories that claim to understand how society works and how it can be improved.

"Activist" social theories tend to share the epistemological optimism of Marxism that *humankind* can *rationally* plan or at least decide on its own future. Social systems theory is nonhumanist and does not presuppose the existence of any transcendent rationality that underlies humankind, history, or society. It therefore is more of an epistemological pessimism and particularly doubts the capability of humans and their theoretical activisms to steer change. It does not contend that "we" can do much to actively change a functionally differentiated society in any "organized" manner. Social activisms and social theories that put forth their "practical" relevance have to at least implicitly assume that society has a center or a "head" and that it can thus be somehow directed. They must assume that if society can be "led," there is a place within society where this leadership can establish itself. Again: on the basis of its noncentrist, "polycontextural," and nonhierarchic view of social complexity, social systems theory cannot share such a conception of contemporary society.

It is important to stress once more that social systems theory by no means denies the impact of social theory and social activism. This impact, as in the case of Marxism, can be immense. But it does not believe that such an impact can be predicted or decided by a theory or the political groups that claim to represent it. In a society based on functional differentiation, social developments cannot be imposed by one system on another. Society as a whole cannot be directed. Function systems are operationally closed and function autopoietically. No human being and no academic theory can guide them. Thus social systems theory does not claim to know how to make the world better—and it does not claim to be able to predict the future shape of society. It can hardly be translated into any kind of immediate activism—but it can give an explanation of how activisms communicatively function within a society of functional differentiation.

Luhmann devoted an entire book to the analysis of one particular activism, namely, the politically highly successful "Green" movement in Germany. In *Ecological Communication*, he presents an in-depth analysis of "engaged" communication that aims at changing the world for the better.[22] The Green movement of ecological activism was, of course, not a strictly academic or theoretical phenomenon. It was rather a more encompassing social movement that brought Luhmann to consider identifying "movements" as one more type of social system (in addition to function systems, interactions, organizations[23]). Luhmann's study of ecological communication, however, can also be read as a case study on the limits and possibilities of activisms in general, including those of the academic, theoretical, or ideological variety.

Activisms typically declare an intention to change the world—and consequently complain about its present state. Activisms can thus be described as movements of complaint that ask for interventions in order to change the circumstances they complain about. The area of complaint and the demand for intervention can be rather encompassing, as is or was the case with the Green movement in Germany that addressed both society and the environment as a whole. The generality of their complaints and demands makes it more or less impossible to acknowledge the systemic structures of society: Society is addressed "as if it was not a system" (Luhmann 1986a, 20[24]), as if it could be generally changed if only people would start to think and act better. Luhmann sees a role of systems theory in "disciplining the accusations towards the address of society" (Luhmann 1986a, 20[25]). The accusations against society are, according to Luhmann, based on an inadequate understanding of how society functions, of how society can change itself, and of the own social nature of the activist movement itself.

Activisms such as the ecological movement tend to overlook the complexity of society and the accordingly limited possibilities for social resonance with problems that occur in the environment of society. Systems theory, of course, does not claim that environmental concerns are unfounded nor does it claim that the demands for a cleaner environment are unjustified. It only tries to point out that such observations are themselves social and that good will itself cannot overturn social realities. If society is indeed differentiated into a multiplicity of function systems, then the possible resonance with environmental problems will have to take functional differentiation into account. Thus, the core issue for Luhmann regarding ecological activism is, "How can environmental problems find resonance in social communication if society is differentiated into function systems and can react to events and changes in the environment only through these?" (Luhmann 1986a, 75[26]). Luhmann then goes on to analyze how different function systems—economy, law, science, politics, religion, and education—can actually resonate with ecological problems. The economy, for example, will only be able to respond through financial operations and by means of prices; law can come up with certain regulations; and politics can develop certain political programs. In any case, all this resonance will immediately affect the function systems—and not the environment. Economic resonance with ecological problems will first and foremost change the economy before it irritates the environment—that can only change itself. The same is true for legal or political resonance. More ecological regulations will profoundly change certain areas of the law—but its effect on the environment remains to be seen. Likewise, the transformation of the ecological movement into a political party had immense effects on the political landscape in Germany. New governments and new oppositions—and particularly new career opportunities for activist politicians, journalists, lawyers—were established. Still, environmental changes could not immediately follow these social changes.

Even if not discussed in detail by Luhmann, the issue of nuclear power generation demonstrates the preceding point quite well. The complete termination of nuclear power generation was one, if not the core concern of the ecological movement in Germany. About three decades after the beginning of this movement and after about a decade of Green Party participation in government, nuclear power plants still operate and will continue to operate in Germany for at least two more decades—not to mention, of course, the nuclear power plants elsewhere in the world. Politically, the Green movement was a great success. It led several Green politicians into the most powerful positions and firmly established itself as a new political party in Germany. But because of functional differentiation, the economy and the law system, to name only two other systems, did not change in the same way as politics changed. They changed by their own means. The political system cannot, by itself, close down a nuclear power plant. Other systems, such as the legal one and the economy, are also involved. Under the conditions of nonhierarchical functional differentiation, systems will all do "what they want." Political changes will irritate the economy and the law, but these will produce their own resonance with those political irritations. There can be no general "social change" that overarches or even transcends the function systems. The immense political success of the Green Party did not translate into the elimination of nuclear power plants—and even if it does eventually eliminate them in Germany (maybe around 2030) this will have only a very minor and insignificant effect on nuclear power generation worldwide. Luhmann says, not in regard to nuclear power generation, but generally in regard to the effects of ecological communication: "As one can see readily, this produces internal systemic effects that bear no similarities at all to the changes in the environment that originally triggered them. These internal effects are to be observed with respect to their own dangers and may need control" (Luhmann 1986a, 100[27]). The existence of nuclear power plants in the environment of society affected ecological communication about such plants that resulted in various changes in politics, the economy, and law. As Luhmann rightly points out, there is no direct relation between the existence of nuclear power generation and these social effects—the effects are purely socially constructed—and in turn there will be no immediate effects of these social changes on the environment. There is no operational continuity or causality between society and its environment.

All function systems operate autopoietically and cannot be steered. It is not only impossible to orchestrate, plan, or direct changes in the function systems, but it is also, and maybe even more importantly, totally impossible to calculate the environmental resonance with social irritations. Who can predict how the environment will react to the termination of nuclear power generation in Germany in the year 2030?

Once again: systems theory does not want to say that all ecological communication is futile and should be given up—it does not suggest, for instance, that the Kyoto Accord (the international treaty aimed at reducing air pollution in the form of greenhouse gases) makes no sense and should not be ratified. It only wants to point out that the Kyoto Accord is an event in politics, and that it has first and foremost political effects—not environmental ones. Under the conditions of functional differentiation we cannot do more than develop resonance with the environment within systemic boundaries. Society has no choice other than to come up with the Kyoto Accord and similar agreements to cope with ecological problems in its environment.

Systems theory therefore does not say that activism has no impact or that environmental problems do not really exist. But it does say that to demand that society "as such" should change or to imply that "we" can immediately intervene in environmental problems signifies not so much an "ecological consciousness," as a misunderstanding of how contemporary society works.

The success of the Green Party was much more a political than an environmental success. It is very doubtful that the environment would be any different without the Green Party in the German government—but German politics would be. Society can only react to ecological problems with ecological *communication*—this is Luhmann's main point, as is reflected in the title of his study. Society is a communication system; it can only communicate about its environment. Society cannot *act* more or less ecologically—it can only have a more or less ecologically communicating politics, law, economy, and so forth (Luhmann 1986a, 218). Today, movements, protests, and activisms are, after all, communications within a functionally differentiated society and can never be immediate "action."

Luhmann's main concern with the ecological movement is therefore its presumptuousness—its lack of a theoretical analysis of society compared with its claim to know exactly what is wrong and what should be done. Ecological communication does not see itself as just another communication, but as something more than mere communication, as a better way of dealing with and understanding the whole world: "In the new order there are no natural primacies, no privileged positions within the whole system and therefore no position in the system that could manifest the unity of the system in relation to its environment" (Luhmann 1986a, 229[28]). The problem with ecological communication is that it produces a lot of social irritation without being able to directly connect this communication to the issues that it addresses. Ecological communication, like other kinds of social activism, produces both too little and too much resonance at the same time. Luhmann says:

> . . . there is no guarantee that society as a whole will in any case prevent or at least be able to tackle possible ecological dangers. On the contrary, society can react only in exceptional cases. This implies that it brings too little resonance into play in the face of ecological dangers. . . . So social communication alarms and stimulates itself to more activity without, however, being able to translate these demands into the language of the function systems. But this is only half the problem. The other half is more difficult to discern and at present is overlooked to a great extent. There can also be too much resonance and the system, without being destroyed from the outside, can burst apart from internal demands that cannot be met. (1986a, 220[29])

As opposed to its general claims, ecological communication is hardly able to produce enough resonance to effectively change the environment. Even the outstanding political success of the Green

Party could not put an end to nuclear power production in Germany. Functional differentiation seems to offer few possibilities for truly significant resonance in regard to environmental problems. On the other hand, heated communication may well produce too much resonance within function systems. Luhmann further explains:

> Through resonance small changes in one system can trigger great changes in another. Payments of money to a politician that play no role in the economic process—measured by the hundreds of billions of dollars that are transferred back and forth daily—can become a political scandal. Theoretically insignificant scientific discoveries can result in medical torment. Legal decisions that hardly have any effect on other decisions in the legal system itself can form road-blocks for entire political spheres. (1986a, 222[30])

The problem of both too much and too little resonance is a characteristic of social activism and leads us back to Luhmann's main criticism of it: it pretends to address "trans-communicational" issues, but in fact it functions basically within the structures of functional differentiation. Activism in the Green Party does not so much lead to a better environment as to careers in politics, and activism in ecological literary criticism does not so much lead to cleaner lakes as to careers in universities. Activism, no matter what issue it pretends to deal with, is first and foremost a communicative phenomenon within social systems and its effects are mainly effects within these systems. Activisms can "make a difference"—but there is no empirical or theoretical reason to believe that this difference is likely to be the one that activism intended.

If Luhmann would have looked at North America, he might have observed new types of activism that seem to be much more "conscious" of functional differentiation and the limits it imposes. In this respect, North American activisms or protest movements seem to be significantly more modern than Old European ones. Movements for minority rights, for women's rights, or, more recently, for the rights of homosexuals, tend to be very functionally oriented—more often than not their main focus is to demand better access to function systems. They demand more representation in the political and legal systems (more female politicians, more African American judges and jurors), equal treatment in education and the economy (equal access to universities for visible minorities, the same pay for the same work, regardless of gender), and equal status in the intimacy system (gay marriage). These kinds of activism seem to much more readily accept functional differentiation than, for instance, the ecological movement in Germany. They have harmonized their aims and their semantics with a "principal" goal of functional differentiation: all-inclusion.

The social adaptation of these activisms seems to grant them much greater or at least more immediate success than old-fashioned activisms such as Marxism or the ecological movement. Their demands can actually be met by the function systems—they can be directly translated into the function systems. It is much easier for the education system, for instance, to allow a certain percentage of African Americans access to universities than to save the environment or to abolish class differences. Universities can simply accept a higher number of African American students—and thus meet a core demand of the minority rights movement. They also can introduce classes on environmental ethics to please the ecology movement—but it is very doubtful that this will bring about clean lakes. Movements such as those for women's or gay rights have obviously learned to demand changes that can be fulfilled by function systems. There is, of course, no guarantee that these demands will be fulfilled, but at least there is a reasonable chance that they may.

Socially-adapted activism basically speaks the language of functional differentiation and asks for the same thing that the function systems do: for all-inclusion. (As pointed out earlier, all-inclusion, of course, does not happen in reality; neither gay marriage nor gender equality in salary means anything to the millions or billions living in the *favelas* or in Africa who have access neither to the economic and legal benefits of marriage nor even to paid work—or to the tens of thousands of African Americans whose main access to social inclusion is provided by one social institution only: the prison.) In this way, these movements cooperate with functional differentiation and help to stabilize and perpetuate it. This means that they are by no means "revolutionary." They are rather "conservative" in their adaptation to functional differentiation. They get easy access to political platforms, to the mass media, and even to religious communication. Political communication will happily address gender equality, the mass media will happily show African American politicians, and (some) courts will—probably less happily—grant marriage rights to homosexuals.

Such human rights movements are not antagonistic to society, they are in more or less perfect accord with functional differentiation. It is no wonder that their semantics are shared by most politicians, by the mass media, and even by the economy. They might even turn into a new type of social system itself. In *The Society of Society* (1997a, 847–65) and in the volume *Protest*, Luhmann reflects extensively on this possibility. It is highly questionable, though, whether one should still call these movements "protests." They do not oppose society and do not change it—they contribute to functional differentiation and represent a further increase of its complexity. Modern "protest" movements are possibly among the best adapted and systemically conformist developments in society.

(b) Negative Ethics

Theoretical activism and protest movements make frequent use of a specific type of communication: moral discourse. They share this propensity with many function systems, particularly with politics and the mass media. A recent turn in international politics is an increased use of moral language, for which the famous phrase "axis of evil" is probably the most notorious example. Following a certain tendency to justify or at least sanction military interventions on the basis of international law or in accordance with international treaties, the Iraq War of 2003 was explicitly communicated as a moral necessity. Moral obligations were deemed to overrule political institutions like the UN and were, of course, also portrayed as more important than economic or religious considerations.

Moral communication often indicates social conflict, and it often increases in the case of social confrontations. Most social systems do not need to communicate morally to function well, because moral distinctions do not correspond to any of the basic codes of the various function systems. Neither true/false, nor immanent/transcendent, nor legal/illegal are necessary parallel to the good/evil distinction. When, however, systemic communication (in politics or religion, for instance) becomes increasingly moral, then this can well indicate—as in cases of war—that tensions increase or that something is going wrong. Luhmann says,

"In normal everyday interaction, after all, morality is not needed anyway; it is always a symptom of the occurrence of pathologies" (2000a, 79). Luhmann's evaluation of morality as being indicative of pathological states is grounded on the observation of a certain "problem of morality": "Whenever the catchword "morality" appears, the experiences Europe has had with morality since the Middle Ages should actually demonstrate this problem well: religiously adorned upheavals and suppressions, the horrors of inquisition, wars all about morally binding truths and revolt arising in indignation" (1989, 370). Given this "problem" of morality, or, more precisely, of moral communication, Luhmann is interested in tracing this problem historically and systemically—it becomes another issue in his research on semantics and social structures. How does moral discourse change with changes of social differentiations and how did it come to be what it is? Such an enquiry is for Luhmann an "ethical" task—and ethics for him means: reflection on morality (as a phenomenon of communication). Luhmann's ethics does not aim at the formulation of some basic moral rules or "imperatives" or at judging morality as morally "good" or "bad." It aims, instead, at explaining morality from the nonmoral perspective of a theory of society—and thus it may be called "negative ethics."[31]

Historically speaking, Luhmann points out that in the stratified Old European society moral rules were largely set up in the form of *manners* (1997a, 1038). Social agents or persons were born into a certain stratum and obtained an identity by being placed in a certain position within this stratum. Manners were connected to every social position or placement, and a person could gain social esteem by acting in accordance with the manners connected with his or her position. Moreover, there existed a single source that provided the semantics of morality in medieval Europe: Christian religion. In this way, medieval society was highly integrated: People were fixed to a single social position and identity adorned with a specific set of manners or rules of morality. And there was only one unchallenged authority that morally integrated society—the church.

In early modernity this situation changed dramatically. Unlike life in a stratified society, social agents were no longer restricted to a single, multi-functional social unit—to their family and its stratum. In modernity, social life requires one to act within many different function systems: one has to earn money in the economy system, one is a citizen within the political system, and one has to arrange a significant part of one's social activities within the limits of legal procedures. Along with this functional diversification and de-integration of social life, morality can no longer be measured by manners, and, in addition, this disintegration of society and moral standards is accompanied by the church's loss of an unrivaled supremacy concerning the vocabulary of morality.

What happens then to morality in modern times and under the condition of a functionally differentiated society? Luhmann suggests that, given the fact of the breakdown of the older social distinctions and boundaries, and taking into account the decline of Christianity, there "emerges the ambition for a universal and yet socially practicable morality on an individual basis deeper than all social divisions, and even religions" (1997d, 18). But where was one to discover such a new foundation for morality if it could not be found within the social reality or religious dogma at hand? Morality had lost its social and religious "anchorage" (*Verankerung*, Luhmann 1989, 416), and thus there appeared the need for a new theoretical endeavor that aimed at founding morality on itself, on its own inherent principles. Now the time for a philosophical "ethics" in a strict sense had come. Ethics became, according to Luhmann, for the first time in history a truly "reflective theory of morality" (*Reflexionstheorie der Moral*). This "new type of ethics" tried to discover the universal *reasons* inherent in morality. Luhmann names two main representatives of this theoretical awakening: Kant and Bentham. These two philosophers—each in his own way, of course—did not merely state what moral behavior was, their ethics were intended to be a reflective description of the grounds of morality. Luhmann says: "The ethics of utilitarianism and of transcendental theory both aimed at a rational or (in the exceptional German case) a reasonable justification of moral judgments" (1990b, 21). In this way—or in these ways— ethics was established as a philosophical discipline of a different kind and under new conditions. Luhmann praises the theoretical achievements of philosophers like Kant and Bentham who were able to establish a new kind of ethical thought and thereby to react to social change. However, he thinks that such ethics do not provide a suitable description of the function of morality in our present society. And it is rather obvious, in retrospect, that their epistemological optimism regarding the possibility of constructing a universally valid ethics proved to be unwarranted. Empirically speaking, Luhmann says, academic ethics have failed (1997d, 17). No philosophical ethics was able to provide generally accepted "reasons" for morality. Unlike in medieval Europe, there exists no single source in our time for moral semantics: "Paradigm Lost" is the title of one of Luhmann's essays on morality and ethics (Luhmann 1990b).

So what can be done? Can the lost paradigm be regained? Luhmann is skeptical about this possibility and quite frankly states that he does not believe in a paradigmatic ethics for our society. He argues—somewhat similarly to the American neo-pragmatist Richard Rorty—that contemporary ethics should refrain from attempting to find "the" reasons for ethics. He says: "Ethics can't provide reasons for morality. It finds morality to be there, and then it is confronted with the problems that result from this finding" (1989, 360). But even if a contemporary ethics has to give up trying to provide definite reasons for morality, it can still—in the tradition of early modern ethics—be a *reflective theory of morality*. It can provide a theory of how morality functions within a functionally differentiated society. In this way, ethics is a kind of theoretical reflection that emerges from the simple fact that morality exists and that it is possible to comment on this fact.

From the point of view of such a systemic approach, all social operations are communicative operations, and, consequently, the phenomenon of morality also has to be understood in connection with the operations of the communication systems. In this vein, Luhmann defines morality as the specific type of communication for processing information on esteem or disesteem. Morality means, so to speak, the conditions in the market of social esteem (Luhmann 1990b, 19). Luhmann distinguishes between "approval" and "esteem" by following Talcott Parsons's usage of these terms. While approval is distributed according to achievements in limited contexts (such as good results in sports, arts, or education), esteem concerns the acceptance of the whole person as a communicative agent (Luhmann 1990b, 17–18).

Morality as the species of communication that distributes esteem or disesteem among ascribed agents of communication—that is, among "persons" in the sense of systems theory—is not confined to a single social system. It can be used in such diverse systems as science, politics, and law. All these different function systems operate on the basis of their own codes: the code of science is true/false, the code of politics is government/opposition, and the code of law is legal/illegal. The code of morality (good/bad) that is applied to social agents is *not* a code in the sense of a foundation of a single and autonomous social subsystem. It is instead a specific code that is "universally" applicable within all social systems. While the fundamental codes of the different function systems are in themselves "amoral," all systems can, nevertheless, add moral communication to their code.

In politics, for example, the difference between the government and the opposition is not initially equated with the difference between good and evil or social esteem and disesteem (Luhmann 1990b, 24). The same is true for law, education, economics, and even for science. A poor philosopher, for instance, may be so totally *disapproved of* by his colleagues that they deny him certain positions and refuse to give him publication space. Though proven to be a total failure in his field of research, he is not necessarily *disesteemed* as a person and his friends would continue to send him Christmas cards. (At least one should hope so.)

Despite the fact—or maybe because of it—that morality is not a basic code of any social subsystem, it can be applied within every one of them. Though in itself amoral, political, educational, or scientific communication can become, so to speak, morally "loaded." A political system that leans towards totalitarianism may tend to equate the distinction government/opposition with the distinction good/bad—just like a tyrannical teacher will equate good and bad grades with the good/bad-person-distinction, or a Calvinist economist will equate the distinction between the rich and the poor with the distinction of being good or bad in the eyes of God.

This is the reason why Luhmann points out that, empirically speaking, moral communication is closely related to conflict and force: it polarizes. Communication on the esteem or disesteem of social agents leads to a sort of "over-engagement" (*Überengagement*) (Luhmann 1990b, 26), to a kind of communicational fundamentalism.

One aspect of this inherent tendency of moral discourse is that moral communication is based on the "interdiction of self-exemption" (Luhmann 1996c, 29). Once engaged in moral discourse, one cannot but identify oneself with the positive side of the esteem/disesteem distinction. As soon as one starts to argue morally—by holding others in disesteem—one brings one's own self-esteem into play. One exposes oneself through morality, one connects one's viewpoints with moral conditions, one introduces self-esteem and the estimation of others into social discourse, and once this has happened, it is hard to step back. "In this way," Luhmann says, "wildfires can be started" (1989, 370). History attests to the fact that wars and crimes against humanity were often accompanied by moral communication.

An analysis of moral communication shows that it leads "to a rapid fixation of positions, to intolerance, and to conflict" (Luhmann 1987, 92). It considerably increases the risks of communication; it is a risk in itself. Moral communication is *risky* communication.

Discovering the risks of morality, Luhmann suggests a different kind of ethics for our current times of "functional differentiation." He advocates an ethical theory that would "warn of morality" (1987, 94). This may be the main function of an ethics that reaches beyond the textual traditions of a past society.

From the point of view of this projected ethics, morality is, as quoted above, a "symptom of the occurrence of pathologies." Using one of Luhmann's metaphors, it infects social discourse like bacteria infect the human body. He concedes that just as bacteria have a certain function in the human body, so too does morality in society. However, ethical philosophy, like medical science, should always keep an eye on these "bacteria" to prevent them from causing inordinate sickness and pain. One should, Luhmann says, be very cautious with morality and "only touch it with the most sterile instruments," since it is a "highly contagious substance" that easily infects communication (1989, 359).

It should be pointed out that, being a "reflective theory of morality," Luhmann's ethics is unable and does not intend to provide guidelines for a practical morality. It is not immediately concerned with specific moral or immoral "acts." It conceives of morality as a *communicative* phenomenon. As a theory of moral communication, it is also unable, and does not intend, to offer definite advice to people confronted with "actual" moral crises. Systems theory acknowledges its limits—it is theory and therefore cannot be moral practice. It would not and could not be of any help, for instance, to a woman having to decide for or against an abortion. If a systems theoretician wants to give advice in such a situation, he/she will have to rely on other means. Systems theory does not share the Platonic idea that a good philosopher is necessarily a good person who always knows what is right.

In loose connection with Ludwig Wittgenstein, systems theory can say: there can be no ethical propositions.[32] A positive ethics cannot be expressed. What is good *shows* itself as good in practice, and there is no direct correspondence between good theory and good practice. Therefore, systems theory does not share the presumption that a philosophy can provide someone facing a moral dilemma, such as whether to have an abortion, with ultimate guidelines. However, it claims to be able to explain why, for instance, moral communication on such an issue as abortion has led to an "overengaged" discourse that has resulted in defamation and even assassination.

Luhmann's analysis is not "against" morality; it concedes that morality is a part of society and cannot and should not be eliminated. However, since it turned out to be impossible to find the "principal" guidelines for a universal morality that is rationally applicable at all times to all of society, theory should give up the futile and presumptuous search for "positive" ethics. Ethics could rather concentrate on studying the empirical communicative effects of moral discourse in society under the conditions of functional differentiation. It can realize that moral discourse tends to increase tensions and antagonisms. Again, we cannot simply do without morality—but it might be advisable to use it with caution.[33]

If, taking into account the above deliberations, one could imagine that if Luhmannian theoreticians were invited to take part in the now popular deliberations on Applied or Professional Ethics, they might come up with a suggestion like the following. Public broadcasts and performances that contain a high dose of morality—for instance, many movies, journalistic commentaries, and not a few televised political speeches—must be supplemented with an obligatory warning, just like the ones we find on cigarette packs: "This product is full of morality and may therefore lead to unwanted communicative overengagement, possibly resulting in damage to both personal and social health."

(c) Subtle Subversions

So what can be done? Obviously, under the conditions of functional differentiation the possibilities for human interference, for the human steering of society or the world are rather limited. And moral discourse does not seem to make the world much better. Empirically speaking, it rather turns out to be an indicator of social dysfunctionality. We cannot change society—society changes itself through the autopoiesis of its function systems. And to talk of the "good" does not seem to improve society either.

Being a theory about social systems, social systems theory realizes, by way of an "autological" conclusion, that what it has to say about communication systems is also true in regard to itself. It is a theory that includes itself, and thus it acknowledges that it is only a theory—nothing more. Like any other scientific theory, social systems theory also somehow "makes a difference" but it can only do so immediately within science because it has to wait for this irritation to change the science system and its social environment, namely, the other function systems. With social systems theory, like with all other communication, society is no longer exactly what it was before, but *how* society resonates with social systems theory is eventually up to society—and not to this theory.

Social systems theory is a sociological interpretation of the world, and it can only make its interpretation, and not the world, better. This is why Luhmann states: "If this diagnosis is only roughly correct, society can neither expect advice nor help from sociology. But it could make sense to search for theories that do more justice to the facts than the optimistic-critical traditional ways of thought within our discipline—justice to those facts with which society constructs itself" (1999, 150). Social systems theory is very skeptical about the potential of theories to "help" society—but at least it can help theory understand these limitations and explain them systematically. This is what social systems theory tries to do. It tries to enlighten society—not about the slumbering potentials of rationality—but about the limits of rationality in a society of function systems. Seen in this way, the claims of systems theory are very modest or, at most, rather subtle: we cannot do much, but at least we can know why the opposite claim is presumptuous.

Still, I would say that there is more to Luhmann's systems theory than this skeptical modesty, more than this subtle critique of critical theory. In an interview, Luhmann abandoned his usual restraint and ironical distance from all claims that social theory can actually "do" something. He stated, "It had always been clear to me that a thoroughly constructed conceptual theory of society would be much more radical and much more discomforting in its effects than narrowly focused criticisms—criticisms of capitalism, for instance— could ever imagine" (1996a, 200). Luhmann here admits a kind of hidden "subversive" agenda to his theory; he does not simply distance it from all hopes for a theoretical "activism," but expresses the confidence that his theory will in fact have some thoroughly disruptive effects. I think the subversive effects Luhmann hints at in the quotation above are related to the blind trust that the humanist semantics still often enjoys in our nonhumanist society. Unlike some postmodernist thinkers, Luhmann's radical departure from a humanist semantics does not merely "deconstruct" traditional self-descriptions of society, it offers alternative descriptions and reasons why the traditional descriptions have become obsolete. Thus the theory might help to shatter some rather prestigious social beliefs and values that still dominate "popular" semantics.

Society tends to comfort itself—and this self-comfort is supported by critical theories and protest movements—that while some aspects are not "humanist" enough, it could make itself more human, if only, for instance, the right policies were adopted. Sure, there are problems with democracy even in the most democratic countries—but with the help of critical thinkers, media, and politicians we might actually make our society more and more democratic. Even the present anti-globalization protest movement shares this "grammar." Like the protestant critics of the Catholic Church during the reformation, the present criticisms do not criticize the fundamental self-descriptions of the leading semantics (today notions like "democracy," "liberty," and "human rights" are central elements of these semantics), but rather fully embrace them. Anti-globalization activists share their values and vocabulary with those they criticize, just as the protestant reformation shared the values and vocabulary of the Pope. Anti-globalization protesters (again, similar to the activists of the reformation) claim that the leading powers and institutions use those values and vocabularies hypocritically whereas they themselves are the true protectors of these semantics.

I think Luhmann is right in pointing out that his theory is "much more radical and much more discomforting in its effects" than those protests that eventually conserve and perpetuate an outdated semantics. Social protests that focus on demands for more democracy, liberation, and human rights do not truly challenge the leading self-descriptions employed by powerful institutions and organizations—they rather legitimate the semantics employed by those institutions and organizations and thus assist them in their claim for credibility. Social systems theory is more radical than, for instance, the anti-globalization movement, for it doubts that terms such as "democracy" or "liberty" can claim any kind of accuracy when it comes to describing "post-industrial" societies. Yes, powerful institutions and organizations might be corrupt and hypocritical, but not because they are not democratic or liberal *enough*—rather because they still market themselves on the basis of such euphemistic semantics. Society cannot be more democratic or free—because under the conditions of functional differentiation self-descriptions such as "democracy" (in the sense of "rule of the people") or "liberty" (the right to realize an individual lifestyle) are meaningless. The people cannot rule when society is primarily structured along the divisions of function systems.

Yes, a certain number of people from time to time are allowed to vote for a president or a prime minister—but does this vote express "the people's intentions" and does the outcome of the vote actually steer society? Can people steer society by casting votes? Similarly, social systems theory can ask: what does individuality or liberty mean under the conditions of functional differentiation? To what extent do career options and the options for social inclusion provided by functional differentiation correspond to the humanist semantics of individuality? Systems theory is quite radical in its distrust of these traditional semantics that are shared by the political system, by the mass media, by education, by protest movements, and so on. And its effects will be discomforting if it is able to irritate society so much that these semantics lose their credibility. It is potentially more subversive than many of the current protest or human rights movements regarding the distrust it has of the currently dominant social self-descriptions. Therefore it may have the potential to influence protests to go beyond the imagination of current or recent social criticisms.

PART II

Mass Media

5

The Mass Media as a System

The mass media system was among the last of the social systems "discovered" by Niklas Luhmann. In his earlier works, he focused exclusively on more traditional objects of sociological attention such as politics, the economy, and law. In the later writings, Luhmann became somewhat more experimental, more openly provocative, and also more interested in current issues. His books *Ecological Communication* (1986) and *Protest* (1996) can be named along with his study *The Reality of the Mass Media* (1995, 2nd ed. 1996) as representatives of these more contemporary interests that hardly played a role in the works published up to and including his first magnum opus *Social Systems* (1984).

I have chosen to concentrate on Luhmann's analysis of the mass media as an example of his in-depth studies of particular social systems not so much because we are dealing here with the "mature" or even the "final" Luhmann, but more because I think that the less traditional subjects of his theory better exemplify the general nontraditional and "radical" character of his thought. Moreover, while Luhmann insists that there is no hierarchy or domination among social systems—there is no fundamental system on which all others depend, there is no system that essentially characterizes society—he still admits an "unequal growth of function systems" (1997a, 391). This seems to suggest that systems can be of different importance at different times and that in the course of social evolution some systems, so to speak, gain ground while others lose their relevance and may eventually fade. The mass media system is obviously among the rising stars of social systems. It certainly has

a long history, going back to the early period of functional differentiation (when the printing press was the main means of producing mass media communication), but there was a kind of explosion
in the twentieth century when a series of new technological inventions (radio, TV, computers) established new dimensions for the
distribution of mass communication. In a certain sense, the mass
media are among the most "modern" of all modern function systems. Therefore, they may be especially well suited for demon-
strating the decisively modern aspects of Luhmann's theory of
modern society: its nonhuman, global, polycontextural, and radically constructivist features. In addition to this, the mass media
may demonstrate more drastically than other systems a certain
facet of the meaninglessness of contemporary sense-production.

In this part of the book, I will loosely follow the structure of
part 1. In the present and the following chapter I will describe how
Luhmann analyzed the mass media system with the conceptual
tools of social systems theory. We will take a look at the code, the
programs, the function, the medium, and its various other systemic
particularities. In chapter 6, we will look at one specific characteristic of the mass media system—its structural coupling with other
social systems—so as to tackle the subject of "manipulation" of
and by the mass media. In chapter 7 we will make the reality of the
mass media our focus. In chapter 8 we will discuss how the mass
media contribute to our socialization and individualization.

Luhmann defines the mass media as follows: "the term 'mass
media' includes all those institutions of society which make use
of copying technologies to disseminate communication" (2000a,
2). Thus defined, the mass media basically go back to the invention of the printing press.[34] In early modernity, mass media products were "printed matter," including religious materials, books,
and newspapers. In the twentieth century, new electronic "copying technologies" profoundly widened the possibilities for the
dissemination of the mass media: radio, film, TV, and now computer technology.

For Luhmann, the decisive difference between mass media
communication based on technology and nontechnological mass
communication (such as public speeches, concerts, or other public
events) is that "no interaction among those co-present can take

place between sender and receivers. Interaction is ruled out by the interposition of technology, and this has far-reaching consequences which define for us the concept of mass media" (2000a, 2). Technology rules out immediate interaction in the mass media. (See ch. 1, sec. b for Luhmann's concept of "interaction.") The author and the reader of a book do not engage in a real dialogue; the audience of a movie does not directly communicate with the people on the screen; and if we look at a Web site on the Internet, we do not respond in real time to real people. (It should be noted that not all communication performed with the help of computers is mass media communication: private email exchange in the intimacy system or the [economic] purchase of an airline ticket is not, whereas logging on to cnn.com or the *Playboy* Web site is.) Of course, as Luhmann admits, there are exceptions to the rule of "no immediate interaction," but these usually "come across as staged and are indeed handled as such in broadcasting studios" (2000a, 2). Sometimes the audience of a TV talk show takes part in the "discussions" that take place—or radio broadcasts have listeners call in, or "reality" TV turns "common people" into protagonists. I think it is obvious that such "exceptions" are not really exceptions. They turn interaction with a few listeners or with a selected audience into elements of the mass media programs. And these in turn cannot be directly interacted with. Even the now popular polls on all kinds of issues (like: Do you think this person is hot or not?) are not immediate interaction; they are just another staged program that presents numbers and percentages.

Technology separates senders and receivers, but this is for Luhmann, unlike for Heidegger or Baudrillard, not reason enough to decry the inauthenticity of this type of communication. It is just a defining characteristic of a rather peculiar type of communication that only becomes possible with the existence of certain technologies. Only with mass copying technologies—and the invention of writing, as such, does not count—can there be mass communication that has no need for spatial or temporal contact. The separation of sender and receiver in space and time makes it impossible to centrally coordinate the transmission and the "tuning in"—newspaper editors or movie producers have no direct control over their audience. When I speak to a group of people in person, I can always leave something out that I did not want to tell a specific person—and tell the rest of them later when that person is not present. As an immediate listener, I can make someone shut up by speaking louder than him/her, by embarrassing him/her, or by shooting him/her. This is impossible in the mass media: a writer cannot make sure that some people will not read his or her book— even totalitarian regimes were unable to prevent this—and I cannot shoot the Terminator.

It is important to note that Luhmann—unlike many contemporary theorists of communication, particularly of electronic media communication (with Marshall McLuhan as their theoretical ancestor)—does not ascribe any structural importance to the specific type of technology that is used for mass media communication.[35] This is not to say that books are more or less the same as films or as Web sites, but rather that mass media technology only constitutes the *environment* of mass media communication, not the communicative operations themselves. Computers and televisions can no more communicate than human beings or human minds or human bodies can. Only communication can communicate. The operational structures that emerge in mass media communication are of course continuously "irritated" and also limited by the technological environment (when there is a blackout, you cannot turn on your TV), but technology does not operationally connect to communication. Just as you cannot communicate with brainwaves, you also cannot communicate with what goes on in a microchip.

Technological developments therefore cannot produce revolutions in communication. They can only produce revolutions in technology. How communication reacts to technological developments is decided by and in communication alone. Strictly speaking, the Internet does not change society—society (not only the mass media, but also the economy, politics, and so forth) changes itself by resonating with changes in its technological environment. The predictable unpredictability of the social impact of technological innovations proves this point. Hardly any of the predictions—neither the enthusiastic nor the gloomy—of the technology prophets ever came true. One can find in the *Communist Manifesto* the belief that the newspaper would finally emancipate the masses and liberate the workers. Similar predictions were made in regard to television and the Internet.[36] On the other hand, practically all new communication technology was initially also greeted by a deep pessimism that equated them with the final demise of civilization.

From the point of view of social systems theory, the impact of technology on society cannot be predicted because technology cannot directly cause social change. Structural changes in communication are made by communication itself. Yes, technology made society change—but it made society change itself. Mass media communication is not a technological issue. The communicative structures of mass media communication have no equivalents or correspondences in mass media technology. You cannot expect to find analogies to the codes, the medium, or the function of mass media communication by thoroughly investigating computer hardware or software. Or, as Luhmann puts it, "we do not want to regard the work of these machines, nor indeed their mechanical or electronic internal workings, as an operation within the system of the mass media" (2000a, 3). While new technologies cannot directly take part in mass media communication, and only appear in its environment, they certainly do provide for or enhance a characteristic of the mass media system that makes it particularly modern. Technological developments make the mass media—more obviously than any of the other function systems—a truly global system. You hear the same news everywhere on the planet—who has not heard about 9/11? And who did not hear about it from the mass media? The same movies and the same Web sites are available around the globe. Of course, such things as censorship, an unequal distribution of computer technology and television sets, and regional and cultural differences do exist that prevent many people from hearing news and seeing films—but this is due to the problem of the *exclusion* that goes along with functional differentiation. This problem was discussed in detail above (ch. 1, sec. d). Like all other function systems—but even more noticeably—the mass media system is, in principle, laid out for all-inclusion and does not recognize geographical borders. It is everywhere at all times. On principle, it includes everybody (but, in fact, also excludes many) on a global scale.

If the mass media can be understood as an operationally closed system, it must have a specific *code*. Without operational closure, there cannot be systemic autopoiesis, and without its own code, a system cannot differentiate itself from its environment and close itself off. Luhmann identifies the distinction information/noninformation as the basic code of the mass media system. The mass media system observes its environment, in particular its intrasocial environment, and thus it selects and produces—or constructs—information. This is what mass media communication is occupied with: the "selective production of information" (*selektives Erarbeiten von Information,* Luhmann 2000, 19, translation modified). Mass media information is, of course, general information, not private information. It is information for "everyone." (Of course, there are again exceptions. Just think of age restrictions for movies and "adult" programs—but still, adult movies are, in principle, addressed or open to *all* adults.) Information is what the mass media system selects and thus broadcasts or prints. Noninformation is what it doesn't. This is, as pointed out above, a constructivist process. That someone has extramarital sex is not yet "essentially" information. Like every piece of information it becomes information (or more precisely: *general* information) only by being selected by the mass media as information rather than as noninformation. If it is the American president in question, it is likely to become information; if it is you and I, it is not. The code of the mass media operates by making these distinctions.

Mass media information is not private or professional information, it is not what we as married persons know about our spouses or, we as mechanics know about the motor of a car. It is rather about that "which is known to be known," it is about that which "one has to assume that everyone knows (or that not knowing would entail loss of face and is therefore not admitted to)" (Luhmann 2000a, 20). Mass media information thus constitutes in a general sense "what we know about our society, or indeed about the world in which we live" (Luhmann 2000a, 1; translation modified). It is that knowledge about society and the world that we potentially share with those around us—at least with all those of who are included in the masses addressed by the *mass* media. Or, to put it differently: it is the kind of knowledge of the world that is tested in the *Trivial Pursuit* game. If we had only private or professional knowledge, it would be difficult to talk to a stranger about our common reality. Thanks to the mass media, we share a world. We can talk with practically anyone about the wars shown on the news and the stars shown in entertainment programs. We can even talk to a stranger about the current human rights situation in China—if the stranger happens to have seen the same TV program that we watched just the other night. This is information.

In order to further define what mass media information is, Luhmann points out its particular connection with time as "perhaps its most important characteristic":

> Information cannot be repeated; as soon as it becomes an event, it becomes non-information. A news item run twice might still have its sense, but it loses its information value. If information is used as a code, this means that the operations in the system are constantly and inevitably transforming information into non-information. The crossing of the boundary from value to opposing value occurs automatically with the very autopoiesis of the system. (2000a, 19–20; translation modified)

That one side of the code is constantly transformed into its opposite is quite peculiar for a communication system: In the legal system, something does not become illegal by being officially announced as legal. The mass media code puts the system under the constant pressure of time: by declaring something as information, the information becomes noninformation, and a need for new information arises. Some topical references in this book will be no longer topical once the book comes out. This exactly points out this specific characteristic of the mass media: by turning information into noninformation very quickly, they operate at a much faster pace than other systems, such as, for instance, science or education. "Anachronisms" are therefore structurally unavoidable when academically writing on the mass media. As a result of different systemic time constructions, academic writing on the mass media is always belated and out of date—from the perspective of the "general reality" created by the mass media.

Once the information that the American president has extramarital sex is constructed, we want to know: with whom? Once we know this, we want to know: what kind of sex? And how often? This is an operational consequence of mass media communication. Information ceases to be information when it is communicated and must be replaced by new information. Mass media information is a temporary thing. It has its time and creates the time of the mass media. The mass media system is speedy, and this is because its code is temporal: "fresh money and new information are two central motives of modern social dynamics" (Luhmann 2000a,

21). Luhmann explains, "The system is constantly feeding its own output, that is, knowledge of certain facts, back into the system on the negative side of the code, as non-information; and in doing so it forces itself constantly to provide new information" (2000a, 20). Once something is known to be known, we have to know even more about it, so that it keeps on being information. Mass media personalities have to be refreshed again and again. Again: exceptions can be made. The body parts of Pamela Anderson can be displayed more than once, so there is "the possibility of repetition." This is especially the case in mass media advertising (Luhmann 2000a, 20). Still, Luhmann says, this can be well interpreted in accordance with the code information/noninformation: "The same advertisement is repeated several times in order thus to inform the reader, who notices the repetition, of the value of the product" (2000a, 20). Repeated advertisement and continuous display of the same body parts only state: Okay, this is not new information, but you should understand that the presented information is something you cannot get enough of.

Like the codes of all other function systems, the mass media code needs programs. The code legal/illegal needs concrete laws, and the code information/noninformation needs concrete "fields of selection such as sports or astrophysics, politics or modern art, accidents or catastrophes" (Luhmann 2000a, 18). Fields of selection, like the subject categories in *Trivial Pursuit*, categorize information. They transform chaotic multiplicity into ordered contingency. They provide a framework in which information can actually be presented. Without actual laws, it is hard to distinguish what is legal from what is not. Without the programs of the mass media, it is hard to know what can and cannot be information. For something to become information, there has to be a "field of selection" in which it can actually appear as information.

Regarding its programs, the mass media system can further be divided into "program strands" or "areas of programming" (*Programmbereiche*). Luhmann names *news* (and documentary reports), *advertising*, and *entertainment* as the three program strands that again each have a variety of programs or "fields of selection." While all three program strands share the information/noninformation code, they use different criteria for selecting information. They are all part of the mass media because of their common code—and therefore they are *not* differentiated as independent social subsystems—but they can be distinguished in regard to the different kinds of programs they make use of.

The first program strand, news, most obviously produces "information" in the sense explained above. A variety of selectors for producing news information can be identified. Typically, one or more of the following selectors will be applied to produce news information (see Luhmann 2000a, 28–35): *surprise* (for an event to become news it is beneficial if there is something unexpected about it), *conflict* (antagonisms typically include "self-induced uncertainty"—so with conflicts there are good prospects for connectivity, we can always expect a new development on the next day), *quantities* (numbers allow for distinctions and for comparisons—even to people who do not exactly know what a gross national product is, it is still information to say that it shrank about 1 percent), and *norm violations* or *scandals* (they intensify resonance, "liven up the scene," and generate feelings "of common concern and outrage," and thus receive particular attention, see 2000a, 29). Other selectors are *local relevance, moral judgments, the focus on personalities,* and *key events* (such as earthquakes, accidents, and murders).

The second major program strand identified by Luhmann, advertising, also obviously produces information, even though this information is largely restricted to products available for purchase. Still, like news, advertising provides the masses with general knowledge. We do not only know about 9/11 through the mass media, we also know about Coca-Cola and Pepsi.

As is sometimes the case in Luhmann's writings (especially his later ones), in his treatment of advertisement he switches to a satirical tone while maintaining his "technical" language. This results in a good dose of irony regarding both his subject and his own theory. In this section, I will let Luhmann mainly speak for himself—for irony is better presented than represented.

Luhmann defines advertising as the "self-organization of folly": "How can well-to-do members of society be so stupid as to spend large amounts of money on advertising in order to confirm their belief in the stupidity of others? It is hard not to sing the praise of folly here, but it obviously works" (2000a, 44). Advertising fools us—we all know this, both the advertiser and the consumer, but no one cares. Advertising "seeks to manipulate, it works insincerely and assumes that that is taken for granted. It takes, as it were, the deadly sin of the mass media upon itself—as if in so doing all other programs might be saved" (Luhmann 2000a, 44). Advertising is the Jesus Christ of the mass media—by its humility and its willing acceptance of being looked down upon, it grants salvation to the other program strands. Okay, we all know this is just a stupid commercial—thus it is not real and not even very entertaining (we have already seen it a hundred times), but if this is so, then the previous news was really real and the following movie will be truly entertaining.

Luhmann grants advertising another merciful feature. Among its most important functions is one of well-needed charity: it provides "people who have no taste with taste" (Luhmann 2000a, 46). This can once more be explained in reference to the historical switch from stratified to functional differentiation:

> This function, which substitutes for taste, is all the more important in that the old connection of social status and taste, taken for granted in the eighteenth century, has today been broken and in the upper social strata in particular there is a need for supplementation due to rapid upward social mobility and unregulated marriage practices. (Luhmann 2000a, 47; translation modified)

The nouveau riche and the parvenus who climbed the social ladder in an instant—thanks to our liberal democracy, free economy, and loose partnership regulations—desperately need the assistance of advertising to know what is "classy," unlike the Old European aristocrats who were classy from birth.

As to the communicative structure of advertising, its most important schema "lies in the relationship of surface and depth": "As the divination techniques of wisdom once used to, it uses the lineations of the surface in order to suggest depth" (Luhmann 2000a, 48). Like the ancient men of wisdom, advertising always shows only the surface, but by showing it, suggests a vast depth. We only see a short commercial for a new car on TV. The new car appears more or less in a flash and then disappears as abruptly as it came, but the commercial inevitably hints at the immense strength and speed hidden in this car and at the great prestige with which it will not fail to supply its lucky owner.

Another decisively useful social function of advertising is "the stabilization of a relationship of redundancy and variety in every-day culture" (Luhmann 2000a, 50). Luhmann explains:

> Under the conditions of industrial production it is surely more of an act of desperation than reason to buy the same thing once again. Therefore, additional support for motives is needed, and this is best done through generating the illusion that the same is not the same, but rather something new. Given this, one of advertising's main problems is in continuously introducing new things and at the same time having to generate brand loyalty, in other words, variety and redundancy. A BMW is still a BMW, but it gets better and better from one model to the next, and even the disposal of the object, the so-called recycling can be improved. (2000a, 50; translation modified)

Advertisements help society to stabilize variety and redundancy. Too much variety would lead to chaos, too much redundancy to stagnation. By semantically establishing a nice blend of variety and redundancy, advertising makes it rational to buy more of the same thing (such as another BMW) in relatively short intervals of time, and much earlier as required. And, what is new is not only new, it is also better than what we had before, even if its only advantage is that it makes for better garbage.

Advertising is thus crucial for establishing our society as "a kind of best of all possible worlds with as much order as necessary and as much freedom as possible. Advertising makes this order known and enforces it" (Luhmann 2000a, 50). By supplying society with a harmonious blend of variety and redundancy we have both order (not a chaotic plurality of soft drinks that would make life too complicated) and freedom (we can freely choose between Coca-Cola and Pepsi). Advertising is the "enforcer" of this much-appreciated social stability. Luhmann concludes the chapter on advertising in *The Reality of the Mass Media* with a nice example taken from real life in what is for most people the "best of all possible worlds":

> In any typical American restaurant you can choose between salad dressings (French or Italian), but you cannot ask for olive oil and lemon juice and then decide yourself on an appropriate mixture. And obviously only a few people take the escape route of going—under these conditions—without salad altogether. (2000a, 50; translation modified)

Like advertising, entertainment can also take on very useful social functions, for instance, as "a component of modern leisure culture" it is very good at "destroying superfluous time" (Luhmann 2000a, 51). Still, in the chapter on entertainment in *The Reality of the Mass Media*, Luhmann soon returns to a more serious tone. He first tries to explain why the program strand of entertainment can also be explained on the basis of the code information/noninformation. While this code obviously underlies the production of news and advertising, it is not so evident why entertainment should also use it.

Luhmann explains entertainment on the basis of the model of a game. He defines this model in the following way: "A game . . . is a kind of doubling of reality, where the reality perceived as the game is separated off from normal reality without having to negate the latter. A second reality is created which conforms to certain conditions and from which perspective the usual ways of life appear as real reality" (2000a, 51). Entertainment—a movie, a TV quiz, a novel—functions like a game because it inserts a second reality into the "usual" reality for a certain time period that is identified by a more or less clear beginning and end. The common reality is not denied through entertainment or a game but is temporally kept in the background. The second temporal, or "leisure" reality needs its own structures to be discernible as a specific reality. In the case of a game, the rules of the game provide such a structure. In "real" life the rules of life apply, but, when playing a game, they are temporally replaced by the rules of the game.

Luhmann also conceives of mass media entertainment as such a second reality, but one that is—unlike games—not structured by specific game rules. He explains that entertainment:

> does not assume complementary behavior on the part of a partner, nor any rules agreed prior to it. Instead, the excerpt from reality in which the second world is constituted is marked visually or acoustically—as a book, as a screen, as a striking sequence of specially prepared noises which are perceived as "sounds" in this condition. This external frame then releases a world in which a fictional reality of its own applies. A world!—and not merely, as in social games, a socially agreed sequence of behavior. (2000a, 52)

Instead of rules, the second reality created by entertainment makes use of *information*. A film, a song, or a novel is a second reality that is constituted by a sequence of information that creates a "world." A film or a novel begins with information—in Luhmann's and Spencer Brown's technical language: with the drawing of a distinction. It then goes on from there. It may begin with the distinction between the woman in love and the man who does not love her—and then a whole world is constructed by a sequence of further information.

Entertainment, especially in the form of novels and movies (but also in the form of talk shows and pop music) has an important function, and perhaps its most important one, in regard to the structural coupling of the psychic system with society. It thus plays an important role in self-socialization and social inclusion: it is crucial for the construction of identity in our present society. Entertainment enables "self-localization" in the world. I will discuss this in more detail in chapter 8 below.

The three different program strands of the mass media system produce and process information with different selectors. They have the same code, but apply it in their respective manners. The possible distinction between these program strands does not prevent them from overlapping. "Mutual borrowings" (Luhmann 2000a, 63) among the program strands seem to be increasingly important for recent mass media developments. Luhmann did not explicitly address these recent trends in his 1996 study, but I think they are quite obvious.

Advertising and entertainment cross over and mix in many ways. Product placement integrates advertisements into movies, while, on the other hand, TV commercials and, especially, the ads shown in movie theaters before the feature presentation adopt the structures and techniques of the movies themselves. They more and more resemble short movies or movie trailers.

Another phenomenon is the crossover between movies and news. Movies deliberately connect to events in world news. An Oscar-winning film like *Gladiator* pretends to be historical, but in fact alludes to contemporary political conflicts (between democracies and dictatorships). The film and its semantics, I believe, could hardly be understood by someone who actually lived in late Roman antiquity—but it can well be understood by millions of viewers today if only they have been sufficiently exposed to political news. Conversely, news also copies the form of movies. CNN labeled its coverage of 9/11 and the Iraq War with action movie–like headlines (like "America under Attack") and jingles. A particularly interesting example of this kind of "mutual borrowing" was the staging of "saving Private Jessica Lynch" during the 2003 Iraq War in the fashion of a Hollywood movie. (As pointed out above, it is unavoidable and an effect of the structural-temporal characteristics of the mass media that topical references like this may well be no longer topical when this book is published.)

Advertising also frequently connects to news topics and traditionally adopted the form of reports—but today it seems more promising to design an ad in accordance with the patterns of entertainment rather than those of reporting. An attention-gripping spectacle is more important than the pretense of factual veracity. The time for commercials featuring a man who looks and speaks like a newsperson seems to be gone. As to a crossover in the other direction, the extensive placement of products in the news may not be far away, given the dimensions it has already reached in entertainment.

The social *function* of the mass media system is a rather complex issue. Some functional aspects have already been addressed. Not without irony, Luhmann ascribed to advertising the function of "the stabilization of a relationship of redundancy and variety in everyday culture." In a more general way, this may be a function of all mass media communication. Not only advertising, but also the news and entertainment supply society with norms and choices. We are presented with a variety of political viewpoints—and with the respective choices. We can not only choose between salad dressings and kinds of pop, we can also choose between major parties and their candidates, and they are introduced to us by the mass media. Entertainment presents us with structurally similar choices: we can prefer one actor over another; we can even vote for this or that contestant on *American Idol;* and we can choose which baseball team we will cheer for.

Another function that has already been mentioned was the impact on social dynamics, the speeding up of time. Luhmann says:

> It might be said, then, that the mass media keep society on its toes. They generate a constantly renewed willingness to be prepared for surprises, disruptions even. In this respect, the mass media "fit" the

accelerated auto-dynamic of other function systems such as the econ-omy, science and politics, which constantly confront society with new problems. (Luhmann 2000a, 22)

The mass media system accelerates the speed of society by continu-ously providing new irritations. It produces new information—and then converts the same information into noninformation. Its pro-cessing of time is twofold. It produces two parallel timelines: one that runs into the future and presents us with novelty on a day-to-day basis. Simultaneously another timeline runs in the opposite direction and continuously produces antiquity or obsoleteness. By producing new information, the mass media system also produces old noninformation. The other function systems cannot ignore this production of time. Politics, for instance, has to constantly watch what is new and what is old. Political organizations and can-didates have to meet this challenge and present themselves anew from day to day. "Time for a change" already suffices as a political slogan. The economy, on the other hand, cannot trust that the current million-dollar advertising campaign will help next year's sales. Advertising money has to be spent on a continuous basis and new ads have to be developed speedily to outplay the competitors. The mass media fuel social dynamics by the constant irritation of society. They inject speed into society.

In an attempt to summarize the various functional aspects of the mass media—such as the two just mentioned—Luhmann sug-gests that the mass media can be ascribed the general function of providing society with a universally available *memory*. And by memory he means, more specifically, the generation of familiarity and its variation from moment to moment (Luhmann 2000a, 101). The mass media provide society with that which is known to be known—and they provide it not as something essentially given, but rather as a highly dynamic process. The memory is for Luhmann *never a storehouse or stock*, it is, quite to the contrary, a *continuously operating production of actuality*.

The memory function of the mass media by no means implies any kind of large-scale social "recollection." It implies the contin-uous production of general self-descriptions of the social reality. And for this production *forgetting* is even more important than recollecting. The mass media have to be highly selective and not only forget about that what they did not select in the first place, but also transform what they do select into that which they no longer select in order to provide social space and time for new selections. The mass media system constructs memory mainly through forgetting, not through recollection! In this way, it incessantly presents society with some selected self-descriptions so that we always know—and know anew—about the shared knowledge of our society. Luhmann says:

> The function of the mass media lies after all in the directing of the self-observation of the social system. . . . What is involved is a universal, not an object-specific observation. We have already spoken . . . of the function of the system's memory which provides a background reality for all further communication which is constantly reimpregnated by the mass media. (Luhmann 2000a, 97; translation modified)

By the mass media, society is informed about itself in a general way, a universally valid reality is constructed. In a functionally differentiated society, the mass media system seems to provide a "background reality" that all the other function systems rely on. This general reality is not a fixed entity but a communicative sequence that autopoietically unfolds in time. It is not "the" social reality and *not all of reality*—each system produces its own reality—but it is the common reality or the common memory that enables society "to take certain assumptions about reality as given and known about in every communication, without having to introduce them specially into the communications and justify them" (Luhmann 2000a, 65). Because of the mass media, we all know—no matter which country or culture we come from—about 9/11, about the movie *Terminator*, and about Coca-Cola. In the same way, the mass media let all of the other function systems know what "is going on." The core function of the mass media is thus to provide society with a specific form of reality. We will discuss this in further detail in the following chapter.

Luhmann explicitly stresses—and we will also return to this aspect in the next chapter—that the common or general reality produced by the mass media is *not based on consensus*. Traditional theories of society—up to and including the Habermasian one—imply that the stability of society depends or should depend on some kind of consensus, on some kind of "social contract" or rational understanding among the individual citizens. If so, Luhmann says, "the mass media would be a destabilizing factor"

(2000a, 100) because they present us with (limited) variation. We are confronted with conflicting views and opinions, different values and choices (for instance, in the movies we watch), and various kinds of goods (like cars or soft drinks) that pretend to be better or "cooler" than the others. There will never be a rational consensus between Coca-Cola and Pepsi. The mass media do not present us with a final consensus on which view of 9/11 is the correct one, nor do they tell us once and for all which movie star or film is the best—as in the case of an airplane wing, social stability is produced through flexibility. Luhmann says that it "would be much too risky to rely primarily on contracts or consensuses that can be called for as a normative requirement" (2000a, 100). It is much less risky for society to pair redundancy with variety. The autopoiesis of communication can go on much smoother if there is some "freedom" of choice involved. We can like Coca-Cola more, but we can also drink Pepsi. We may love Arnold Schwarzenegger, but it is also perfectly acceptable to prefer Robin Williams. We can disagree with a view of 9/11 as long as we still agree with another opinion that is also presented as respectable in the mass media.

On the basis of total consensus, the mass media would lose their function. The mass media in the Soviet Union were quite consensual—but they soon lost all credibility and social efficacy. No one accepted their reality as real. In order for a mass reality to be real, it has to go beyond the limits of consensus. A Habermasian theory is not complex enough, at least from Luhmann's point of view, to do justice to this characteristic of the mass media and of society in general.

The final systemic feature of the mass media that I would like to discuss in this chapter is their *medium*. The medium that the mass media deal with and produce through their communicative operations is *public opinion*. In direct relation to what has just been said in regard to the nonconsensual character of mass media reality, it must be stated right away that here "public opinion" does not mean an opinion that is shared or agreed on by the "people." For Luhmann, public opinion rather means something like a set of nonconsensual and nonpersonal data or ratings. One may say that, for instance, public opinion in America regarding the invasion of Iraq consisted at a specific time of 68 percent approval as well as of

32 percent disapproval—and was of course changing itself on a daily basis.

Like all other communication systems, the mass media system is mainly concerned with its own autopoiesis, with the continuation of its operations by providing *connectivity*. The medium of public opinion is very efficient in this respect. It never grows tired; you can always connect it with itself. A poll can be done and redone—it is usually slightly different the next day, and even if it is the same as yesterday, this is still new information! Today's public opinion is the basis of tomorrow's and the continuation of yesterday's: "The respectively current public opinion . . . is as the result of previous communication the condition for future communication" (Luhmann 1997a, 1104). Public opinion regarding news items, regarding both the products that are advertised and the advertisements themselves, and regarding TV shows, new movies, and new books are the material out of which new mass media communication is made. Public opinion is not the sum of individual mental contents—how could this sum ever be calculated in communication?—it is a communicative product of the mass media. Luhmann explains:

> Public opinion is, after all this, neither the mere fashion of opinions as it was believed in the seventeenth century nor is it the medium of rational enlightenment or the "puissance invisible" which were expected in the eighteenth century to leave tradition behind. It is the medium of the self-description and the world-description of modern society. It is the "Holy Spirit" of the system, the communicative availability of the results of communication. (1997a, 1108)

In metaphorically calling public opinion the "Holy Spirit"[37] of society, Luhmann highlights its functional importance. Public opinion has nothing to do with human subjectivity or with the exercise of human reason; it is a communicative medium that becomes possible through the development of the mass media into an autopoietic and global function system. With the production of a general memory there arises a need for a "currency." The memory has to somehow take shape; it needs to assume forms. Like the economy needs the medium of money, so a general reality needs a medium to manifest itself. Public opinion is this communicative medium, and it is produced within the mass media system. Just like money allows for an incessant continuation of financial transaction—the money I earn today is the same that I spend tomorrow—so public opinion is the "stuff" with which society manufactures its general self-descriptions. It is the flesh and bone through which today's news, TV shows, and ads turn into tomorrow's. With public opinion, mass communication can revolve around itself and continue its on-going self-reproduction. Public opinion transforms itself in eternal spirals. It is indeed the "Holy Spirit" of mass media reality, though not the spiritual spirit envisioned by the Church Fathers, Hegel, and other sacred or secular theologians.

6

Beyond Manipulation

Another systemic characteristic of the mass media is their structural coupling—both with other social function systems and with systems in the environment of society (with the psychic systems as the most important among the latter). Here I will concentrate on the intrasocial structural couplings of the mass media, and its coupling with minds will be the topic of chapter 8. I will thus first deal with an issue that runs like a red thread through Luhmann's book on the mass media: the question of mass media "manipulation." Do the mass media "manipulate," and if not, then why is such an impression so widespread?

In the first paragraph of *The Reality of the Mass Media* Luhmann mentions a quite puzzling phenomenon:

> we know so much about the mass media that we are not able to trust these sources. Our way of dealing with this is to suspect that there is manipulation at work, and yet no consequences of any import ensue because knowledge acquired from the mass media merges together as if of its own accord into a self-reinforcing structure. One will qualify all knowledge as potentially dubitable and still one will have to build on it, to connect to it. (2000a, 1; translation modified)

On the one hand, we certainly accept the mass media reality as our common reality. When Baudrillard provocatively titles his book *The Gulf War Did Not Take Place* (1995; he was talking about the Gulf War of Bush, the elder) or when others claim that the moon landing never happened, this may provide some intellectual stimulation, but it is certainly not accepted as a general truth. We know better: we've seen it on TV and read about it in the papers. A billion readers and viewers cannot err. Even Baudrillard does not literally intend to say that there was never such a thing as the Gulf War. On the other hand, claims like Baudrillard's do not totally contradict "common sense." We all know it happened, because we saw it on TV, but we also know that it did not happen just as we saw it, because we only saw it on TV. We all doubt that what we see on TV and what we read in the papers is a hundred percent accurate—we all have, in greatly varying degrees, a "suspicion of manipulation" (*Manipulationsverdacht*) when it comes to mass media communication, especially regarding the news. However, this manipulation is unable to uproot our trust in the reality presented by the mass media as such. We do not react with a Cartesian methodological skepticism and say: because the media do not always tell the truth, everything they show can be doubted. Someone who acts like this and steadfastly denies the Gulf War or the moon landing will not be able to communicate successfully with most other people. In fact he/she may well be sent to a psychiatrist. The mass media present us with the only general reality there is. So if we do not somehow accept this reality, we will not be accepted as competent communicators. One has to share this general reality in order to be able to communicate in society.

The mass media continue their construction of reality on the basis of their autopoiesis. Their reality is a reality in sequences. Tomorrow's reality follows and connects to today's that in turn follows and connects to yesterday's. If we deny today's reality, we cannot smoothly continue with tomorrow's. Even though we might doubt certain aspects of mass media reporting on the Gulf War, we have to generally accept it as reality in order to function tomorrow as we do today. If we do not accept today's reality, it will be even harder to accept tomorrow's. This is somewhat similar to the confusion one might experience when coming back to a soap opera after missing several weeks of it.

This "suspicion of manipulation" is therefore not as fundamental as is suggested by a literal reading of the title of the book by Baudrillard mentioned above. Still, there is a "limited" suspicion—the suspicion that the mass media present reality, but that they do not present it correctly, that their manipulation presents a slightly skewed picture.

As far as I can tell, regarding the mass media there are two main types of suspicion. The first type assumes that we must trace the manipulation of the mass media further back. According to this view, it is not the mass media themselves that fake reality, but some force *behind* them which actually *controls* them. In this version both the audience and the mass media are victims of manipulation. Manipulated by more or less evil forces, the mass media deceive us about the real reality by presenting us with an edited one. Theories of this kind tend to focus on politicians and capitalists (either in combination or separately) as those who employ the mass media as a means to rule and exploit society. An exemplary study that represents this kind of "suspicion of manipulation" is the book *Manufacturing Consent: The Political Economy of the Mass Media* by Edward S. Herman and Noam Chomsky. The authors show rather convincingly and on the basis of many case studies how the American mass media were and are influenced by political and economic interest groups. In order to maintain and increase their power and wealth, these groups "manipulate" the mass media so that these present the American public with incorrect views of the (political and economic) state of the world. According to this theory pattern, we would be presented with the real view of reality if only we could get rid of these evil manipulators. If we had truly democratic and *liberated* mass media, manipulation would disappear, and only then would we be able to finally see the world as it is. Here I will call these kinds of ideas the "liberation theory of the mass media."

The second type of theory works the other way around. While it agrees with the idea of an ultimately manipulated mass media reality, it sees the mass media not as the victim, but as the villain. Here, the mass media are the origin of manipulation because they do not neutrally serve the legitimate information interests of the people. They influence reality by their own powers—for instance, by manipulating politics and elections through their reporting. The mass media are understood as having partially taken control of the political (and economic) process. From this point of view, political elections, for instance, are ultimately decided by how the mass media present the competitors. In order to win an election, a party or a candidate has to adapt to the mass media and please them—the best adapted, and not the most qualified candidate will win. In this way, an Arnold Schwarzenegger can become governor, and a Ronald Reagan can become president. The mass media may also run the economy. A company that is presented with a bad image in the mass media will hardly make a profit, a country that is portrayed as unsafe will lose its tourism business, and so on. These theories—as, for instance, presented by the German researcher Hans Mathias Kepplinger (1998)—claim that there is an increasing *dominance* of the mass media system over other systems such as politics or the economy. Here, I will call this kind of theory the "domination theory of the mass media."

Social systems theory, as I see it, can well agree with some of the common findings of both theories—namely, with the observation that the mass media system does not "truly" present an "essential" reality, and that it has many links with the economy and politics. However, it cannot agree with the particular assumptions about "manipulation" that both—each in its own way—make. Social systems theory tries to go further than both theories by attempting to explain the phenomena they describe with concepts that go beyond "simple" one-way manipulation.

From the point of view of systems theory, there are at least three major problems with the "liberation theory of the mass media." First, it is much too humanist. According to this theory, the sins of the mass media are to be blamed on a group of evil people. If only the powerful politicians and rich capitalists would stop manipulating the media, then everything would be okay. Neither the media, nor the economy or politics are conceived of as function systems, but as something that is handled by individuals. The problems of the mass media are then finally reduced to the ethical errors of some certain human beings. Secondly, the "realism" of liberation theory is much too simple. It assumes that if manipulation stopped, then the mass media would present the real reality. It assumes that there is one correct version of the Gulf War, and that this one correct version can potentially be presented by the ethically correct mass media. The constructivist view of reality that systems theory adopts does not share the belief in such an essential reality and it does not believe that the functioning of the mass media can ever be "liberated." Thirdly, liberation theory forgets about itself. There is a very noteworthy book by Noam Chomsky entitled *9/11* in which, among other things, he explains the distortion of political reality by the mass media. Interestingly enough, this book was a bestseller for many months here in Canada and, what is even more baffling, its criticisms rely heavily on information from the mass media. It consists in large part of quotations from news reports. It is itself through and through a mass media product. But there is no reflection on this strange phenomenon in Chomsky's version of the liberation theory of the mass media. How can a theory of the mass media totally neglect the fact that it itself takes part in the mass media communication that it pretends to objectively analyze?

The problems with "liberation theory" mentioned above apply to "domination theory" only to a lesser degree. This theory is, for instance, much more willing to concede the systemic character of the mass media, of politics, and the economy. It also does not suppose that there is a "true" reality that the mass media should present—but it seems to assume, for instance, that if the mass media left politics alone, we would have truly democratic elections instead of media spectacles. It seems to say that the world or society would be more fair or authentic without mass media manipulation.

The suspicion that systems theory has in regard to the mass media goes beyond the suspicions of *manipulation* expressed by theories of liberation and domination. Social systems theory does not assume that the mass media system is either directly manipulated by other systems such as politics or the economy nor that it can directly manipulate them. Instead, it tries to explain with its own conceptual apparatus the mutual influences between these systems. It thus also offers a solution to the contradictory conclusions of those theories. It is neither the economy nor politics that manipulates reality through the mass media, nor the mass media that manipulate reality through politics and the economy. It is rather the *structural coupling* between these systems that produces effects which can be perceived as "manipulation" or which cause the "suspicion of manipulation."

The mass media are structurally coupled to many other social function systems—most importantly by *topics* (*Themen*) which is their way of performing "other-reference" (*Fremdreferenz*, see Luhmann 2000, 12–13). News reports about politics or the economy, for instance, and the topics of advertising are, of course, the products or brands of the economy. As discussed above, through a variety of "mutual borrowings" entertainment, too, can well address current political topics. Of course, the mass media can also refer to other systems such as law, religion, or medicine, to name only a few. But since all of these systems are autopoietic and operationally closed, their mutual dependency by structural coupling is not a total or one-way dependency. Structural coupling does not dissolve the operational "integrity" of the systems involved, but only increases their mutual irritability and construction of complexity.

Of course, political news immensely irritates political communication. How the media report on a candidate influences the election. But, on the basis of operational closure, this is a two-way process. If Arnold Schwarzenegger were to say in a *Terminator* movie, "Vote for me," this statement would independently function in the two systems of politics and the mass media. It would be both a political and a mass media statement, and it would elicit a set of entirely different responses in the sphere of the movies and in the election. The box office and the election numbers would still function differently. The systems would still operate on the basis of their own code, albeit under very tight structural coupling. The tighter the structural coupling, the more obvious it becomes that the systems cannot dominate one another. Does the fact that Schwarzenegger is a governor prove that entertainment dominates politics, or does it prove that politics heavily influences Hollywood?

Of course, the economy heavily influences the mass media through payments for advertising. But the economy is also dependent on the mass media for producing effective spots. If a TV network were to boycott a company this would be as devastating as a boycott of the TV station by the same company. Luhmann explains:

> Within the strand of advertising, then, the economy is just as dependent upon the system of the mass media as the latter is upon it, and, as is typical in cases of structural coupling, no logical asymmetry, no hierarchy can be detected. One can only establish, as with a thermostat, a cybernetic cycle, where it then depends on the observer whether he or she thinks that the heating is regulating the temperature of the room by means of the thermostat, or the temperature of the room is regulating the heating system by means of the thermostat. (2000a, 66)

The example of the "cybernetic cycle" including the mutual but nonhierarchic regulation, dependency, and influence of the room temperature and the heating system is a perfect example for illustrating what goes on with social systems under the condition of structural coupling. They cannot do without one another—they constantly irritate each other, they cannot evade this irritation, but are still bound to perpetuate their own autopoiesis by their own means. The room temperature does not manipulate the heating system any more than the heating system manipulates the room temperature. The concept of "manipulation" is much too simple to explain the intensity of a "cybernetic cycle."

Yes, Chomsky is absolutely right: the mass media are highly dependent on politics and the economy—but because of this dependency (and not despite it!) the same is true vice versa! Politics "controls" the media—but by controlling them it cannot but be itself controlled by them. Yes, a president exerts pressure on the media, but, in turn, he has to act like a media puppet if he wants to win the next election. Yes, the broadcasting of the Gulf War is censored and edited ("saving Private Jessica Lynch!") by politics—but, in turn, politics and the military have to follow media scripts to create their public reality. They cannot simply say what they "really" do and what the reality of the war "really" is (what is it?)—they have to follow the conditions of reality set by mass media communication. They have to construct a war that can be shown on TV.[38]

It is particularly the "liberation theory" in Chomsky's version that suffers from the Old European illusion that the mass media (and politics) are not a communication system but actually "made" by people and that they could be "democratic." Under the conditions of functional differentiation there cannot be any social structure that provides for "human" agency and for a "rule of the people"—neither in the mass media nor in politics. People cannot communicate, only communication can. And there is hardly any function system where this is more obvious than the mass media.

There is no "freedom" for the mass media from politics or the economy, and there is no "freedom" for politics or the economy from the mass media either when these systems are structurally coupled. Systems theory explains why the mutual influence of these systems goes *beyond manipulation*.

7

The Reality of the Mass Media

The "cybernetic cycle" of the mass media and other social function systems such as politics and the economy has led our analysis beyond the too simplistic notion of "manipulation." We are now faced with a more complex view of the mass media and their construction of reality. The question is no longer: "How do the mass media distort reality through the manner of their representations? For that would presuppose an ontological, available, objectively accessible reality that can be known without resort to construction; it would basically presuppose the old cosmos of essences" (Luhmann 2000a, 7). Instead, a new question has to be asked: "How do mass media construct reality? Or, to put it in a more complicated way (and related to one's own self-reference!): how can we (as sociologists, for example) describe the reality of their construction of reality?" (Luhmann 2000a, 7). The mass media obviously cannot "distort" reality—because there is no such "essential" thing that is simply distorted. All social function systems are observing systems—in the double meaning of the term. All social function systems construct the reality they observe by developing themselves as autopoietic systems of "cognition." The mass media observe reality and thereby cannot but construct reality. There is not one simple reality of the Gulf War. Every perspective on the war—the political, the economic, or the perspective of a soldier, or of a civilian—is valid and not reducible to any of the others. There is not simply one "authentic" war. How can you possibly present the true reality of the Gulf War in its entirety? This would fail in the same way that the attempt of Tristram Shandy in

149

Laurence Sterne's novel (to which Luhmann refers on various occasions) failed to give a complete account of his life. In his "autobiography," Tristram Shandy, after a few hundred pages, has still not arrived at his birth—he began with his conception and then things turned out to be so complicated that his story became endless and "beginningless." A structured and nonchaotic reality is based on the reduction of complexity, on selection, on systemic observation. Memory is based on forgetting. A coherent reality— be it the reality of a life or a war—can only be constructed from a certain perspective and this perspective has to be itself highly structured in order to be able to present a well-structured picture. If you want to see everything "as it is," you will see nothing. How could one possibly give an account of all the events that led to, happened during, and followed from the Gulf War? There is no unconstructed reality of the Gulf War. The Gulf War—like any other reality, can only become a reality by being observed in a selected and "edited" way. So the question for the mass media, like for all observing systems, must be: how do the mass media construct reality? And the question must "autologically" take into account that its answer will itself be a construction/observation. Unlike Chomsky, Luhmann does not want to ignore the fact that his own observations must necessarily have a systemic "location." He does not deny that his second-order observation is itself also a first-order observation and that it unavoidably has its own blind spots. As noted earlier, Luhmann acknowledges that he becomes himself "a rat in the labyrinth and has to reflect on the position from which he/she observes the other rats" (Luhmann 1988b, 24).

The mass media construct a reality—they construct the common reality of society. What we know in general about our society we know through the mass media. But while the mass media construct a reality for the entire society, this reality is of course not the "entire reality." And so its description cannot claim to be a description of the entirety of reality. The mass media construct a "public" reality. But this reality is not more or less real than the reality constructions of other observing systems.

The title of Luhmann's book on the mass media, *The Reality of the Mass Media* is grammatically ambiguous (which is more obvious in German—*Die Realität der Massenmedien*—than in English), and this ambiguity reflects the "operational constructivism" that underlies the systemic concept of reality. The mass media are the grammatical subject and object of this expression. If the mass media are the grammatical object, then reality is the subject, and thus the reality of the mass media is simply the reality that they "objectively" constitute. As a grammatical subject, the mass media "subjectively" produce a reality—they present us with a reality that is their production or "object." What is meant by the expression in the first sense are the operations proper to the media: the broadcasting and printing as it is performed (Luhmann 2000a, 3). What is meant in the second sense is the reality that "*appears to them*, or through them to others, to be reality" (Luhmann 2000a, 4). Luhmann further explains: "For the approach introduced first above, first-order observation is sufficient, as if we were dealing with facts. For the second approach, it is necessary to adopt the attitude of a second-order observer, an observer of observers" (2000a, 4). The question of the construction of reality by the mass media is a complicated issue of second-order observation. We must observe the mass media as an observing system that produces both its own reality and the reality of what it observes by its observations. Here, we arrive at the heart of "operational constructivism." This theory

> does not lead to "loss of world," it does not deny that reality exists. However, it assumes that the world is not an object but is rather a horizon in the phenomenological sense. It is, in other words, inaccessible. And this is why there is no possibility other than to construct reality and perhaps to observe observers as they construct reality. (Luhmann 2000a, 6)

Because of this complex situation, the mass media's "construction of reality" takes on a double meaning: the construction of reality performed by the mass media is at the same time also a "reality of construction." That the mass media construct a reality through their own observations does not take away the reality of the real— exactly the opposite is the case. Construction of reality always implies the reality of construction. Radical constructivism does not diametrically oppose realism. It is a more complex type of realism than traditional forms for it integrates the notions of reality and construction.

The chapter on "the construction of reality" in Luhmann's mass media study explains some characteristics of this construction that the mass media perform within and for society. The mass media system constructs our common reality through its modes of selection. It presents reality, for instance, on the basis of attributing causes. It presents possible causes for the Gulf War, it shows the reasons the Terminator has for his actions, and it provides us with certain clues why we should prefer this car to another. It also infuses, as discussed above, discontinuities and conflict into reality. Events are presented, especially in the news and in the movies, but also in advertisements as some kind of competition; and today's situations are presented as "new" in comparison with yesterday's. This is quite different from earlier general constructions of reality before the advent of the mass media. Some Old European cultures, but also traditional Chinese society, tended more towards presentations of the common reality as one of harmony and repetition. General events in society or in the world—such as the relations between family members, between rulers and subjects, or the unfolding of time through the seasons—were presented as patterns of stability and sameness rather than of conflict and novelty.

Luhmann also points out that the mass media observe/construct reality moralistically. We learn to distinguish between good and bad governments, between good and bad protagonists, and between good and bad products. The construction of reality by the mass media thus also implies that something should be done, and that it should be done rather soon. It infuses activism and speed into our general reality. The news reports present us with "immoral" behavior of politicians—so that there is a need to replace these politicians with better ones. They present us with negative data concerning the economy (again a rise in prices!)— and suggest that we need to take some measures. Films show us how protagonists solve gigantic problems—and mostly in less than two hours. Advertising also reminds us that we have to act soon if we want to get that thing that will quickly and significantly improve our lives.

This kind of construction/observation presents society with a specific reality—as opposed to previous specific realities that were accepted as common. Some religious groups in North American society (one may think of the Amish) still try to preserve older forms of a general reality, rely mainly on the Bible for their construction of reality, and consequently avoid mass media communication. These groups do not want to share the general reality constructed/observed by the mass media, so they choose other forms of construction/observation. They prefer religious realities that are distinctively less "novel," "speedy," or "competitive." This is, of course, not to say that these groups are objectively or essentially less "novel" or "speedy" than we mass media communicators are. But their construction/observation certainly is—or at least this is what a second-order observer can observe. Of course, neither their nor the mass media's general reality can claim to be more real or more general. Luhmann explains that the reality of the mass media

> replaces knowledge prescriptions which have been provided in other social formations by privileged positions of observation: by sages, priests, the nobility, the city, by religion or by politically and ethically distinguished ways of life. The difference is so stark that one can speak neither of decline nor of progress. Here too the only mode of reflection remains that of second-order observation, that is, that a society which leaves its self-observation to the function system of the mass media enters into precisely this way of observing in the mode of the observation of observers. (Luhmann 2000a, 85; translation modified)

In this passage, Luhmann comments on the contingency of reality-constructions. A society can describe itself and thus its general reality in various ways and it can delegate this job to various institutions. Earlier societies (of which North American Amish communities are remnants) left the general observation of reality to priests or the Bible; in a functionally differentiated society, this function is taken over by the mass media system. With different types of construction, different realities emerge.

The last sentence of the above quoted passage mentions one more characteristic of the mass media construction/observation of reality. It is not only we (or Luhmann) who observe the mass media by second-order observation, the mass media themselves (like practically all other modern function systems)[39] make use of this type of observation.[40] They observe how other function systems observe. The news reports observe the observations of the political and economic systems. They show us how politicians view the world and our country, and they display how the stocks of companies are evaluated on the market. The movies show us how protagonists "psychologically" observe/construct their reality. We learn about the "motives" of the person on the screen and how that character observes reality. With the Bible, we were not allowed to observe God as an observer—we were not allowed to form an image of him. With the mass media, this has profoundly changed. Now we are informed about how and why others observe/construct the world as they do.

This leads to a second aspect of the construction of reality by the mass media—to the reality of the construction. A second-order observation, like that of the mass media, "has to attribute reality to the observer whom it is observing. It can select him, but not invent him" (Luhmann 2000a, 90). The mass media cannot but see what they see. What they see depends on their observation. But once they begin with observations, once they draw their distinctions (between what they see and the unmarked space), then the line is drawn and the reality emerges. Luhmann explains:

> If you have guests and you give them wine, you will not suddenly be struck by the notion that the glasses are unrecognizable things in themselves and might only exist as a subjective synthesis. Rather you will think: if there are guests and if there is wine, then there must also be glasses. Or if you receive a phone call and the person on the other end of the satellite turns nasty, you're not going to say to him: what do you want anyway, you're only a construct of this telephone conversation! (2000a, 91)

The philosophical "doubts" entertained by philosophers of the human mind do not apply to the social construction of reality. The reality constructed by communication is a communicational reality that autopoietically continues itself. Even *if* you doubted the existence of the guests at your party or of the person at the other end of the phone—this would not end communication. Communication that has begun, observations that have been made have become reality. If you replace one observation with another then you might modify the previous one, but you cannot erase its reality. It might have been "false"—but it was not unreal and it made the present reality possible through its own reality. The observational construction of reality sequentially constructs reality and it cannot but construct reality, regardless if this reality is called true or false. To observe that what used to be certain is uncertain and that what used to be truth is appearance does not put an end to observation, communication, and society but continues communication, observation, and society. Like all the other communication systems, the mass media cannot construct irreality they can only construct reality.

As discussed earlier, the reality constructed by the mass media is "a reality not subject to consensus" (Luhmann 2000a, 92). This reality is not a "one-dimensional" reality with a simple "meaning" or "truth." The communicative reality of the mass media, this self-description of society, is thoroughly dynamic. It is a world of "diversity," a world where standardization and variation are nicely combined: There is a diversity of news, a diversity of movies, a diversity of advertisements. Needless to say, this diversity cannot be adequately described with the Old European humanist semantics of "freedom."

8

Individuality and Freedom

An important element of the social reality constructed by the mass media is "individuality." The different program strands of the mass media confront us with different models of individuality. They portray society by attributing events and communication to individual agency. The news reports present individual politicians and VIPs as if they were individual protagonists. Presidents and media stars are supplied with individual auras and appear to somehow be in control, as if they were "the cause of their own action" (Luhmann 2000a, 72). It is suggested that, for instance, a war is a result of the decisions of a few individuals. As to advertising, "it starts out from the assumption of an individual as a being who calculates his profit" (Luhmann 2000a, 72). We are addressed as individual customers and presented with individuals who make individual choices that we may want to copy. In entertainment "the medium of narrative fictionality is chosen to individualize motivational positions. Individuals appear here with a biography, with problems, with self-generated life-situations and sham existences, with a need (understandable to an observer) for suppression, for unconsciousness, for latency" (Luhmann 2000a, 72). Similar to advertising, entertainment presents us with individual choices, not regarding purchases but regarding personalities. We can choose which models we like and what we find attractive. Luhmann concludes:

> The human being is therefore implied in all program strands of the mass media, but not of course, as a real reproduction of his or her bio-

chemical, immunological, neurobiological and consciousness-related processes, but only as a social construct. The construct of the "cognitively more or less informed, competent, morally responsible human being" helps the function system of the mass media constantly to irritate itself with regard to its biological and psychic human environment. (2000a, 74)

The mass media present human beings as "individuals," as social agents with certain social characteristics. This presentation cannot do justice to the complexity of human existence—the mass media cannot portray biological or psychic operations. Human beings are in themselves too systemically split to "fully" appear in society (as I already discussed in chapter 3). Still, by portraying society as "human" the mass media system provides for structural couplings beyond the merely social environment. As a system, the mass media are not only in structural coupling with other social systems,[41] they are, like society in general, also in structural coupling with people's minds. By presenting human beings as individual agents, the mass media system gives minds something to think about—and gives them guidelines on how to perform self-socialization and on how social inclusion can take place. The individual human beings that appear in mass media reality play an important role in today's co-evolution of social and psychic systems. They help minds and social systems increase their respective operational complexity.

In order to explain the specific structural coupling between the mind and the mass media, Luhmann makes use of psychological terminology and borrows the notions of cognitive map, prototype, frame—and, in particular, of *schema* and *script*.[42]

Schemata allow for cognitive selection. With their help, cognition can sort out both what it takes note of and what it does not. They provide a framework with which information can be categorized and ordered. These schemata are not fixed, they can be varied and altered, they are not so much readymade images but patterns for the construction of images. The schema "circle," for instance, is not the image of one particular circle but the rule for how to draw a circle (Luhmann 2000a, 109). Schemata are not the storehouse of cognitive impressions, but rather the cognitive tools for the production of information—and thus for the performance of cognitive autopoiesis.

Luhmann assumes that "the structural coupling of mass media communication and psychically reliable simplifications uses, and indeed generates, such schemata. The process is a circular one. The mass media value comprehensibility. But comprehensibility is best guaranteed by the schemata which the media themselves have already generated" (2000a, 110). Meaning and language couple minds and communication in general. The mass media and minds are coupled by certain cognitive schemata as well. The mass media provide the minds with the schemata for the cognition of reality—and vice versa. The mental operations of the minds of the producers of the mass media influence the schemata of mass media communication, and the schemata of mass media communication influence the viewer's perception of reality. But, of course, the producer's mind is also a viewer's mind. The mind of a TV or movie producer has already watched TV and films. There is again a "cybernetic circle" that is constituted by the structurally-coupled systems. Minds no more control the mass media by imposing schemata than the mass media control minds by doing the same thing. Schemata are rather the "thermostats" that link the mind and the mass media together.

One of the examples given by Luhmann for the structural coupling of the mind and the mass media through schemata is the schematization of persons—the individuality schema, so to speak. This schema helps us to distinguish ourselves from others, to assume an identity and to ascribe the same to others. Luhmann remarks that it was possible to distinguish oneself from others even before the age of the mass media—in a stratified society, for instance, by the family one was born into. Moreover, psychological research seems to indicate that "the difference of one's own I from other individuals is given from the start, meaning as early as a few days after birth" (Luhmann 2000a, 112). Obviously, we not only perceive ourselves as somehow distinct in all kinds of societies, we even do so "naturally." Still, Luhmann assumes that under the conditions of functional differentiation, peculiar types of identity construction emerge. In early modernity, the theater and the novel (an early example of mass media) presented complex individuals. The audience or the readership witnessed a person's motives and character traits, how an identity was formed and related to other identities. This led to an increasing focus on personality development—besides a social status and its characteristics, one was also expected to have a unique identity, biography, and self. In the nineteenth and twentieth centuries "the problem of 'self-realization' is invented and is taken up and disseminated by the mass media. Individuals are encouraged to believe that, although they have without doubt been really alive since conception, and certainly since birth, they must become even more real (or unreal?) than they already are" (Luhmann 2000a, 114). The mass media present us with the schemata for "self-realization." In order to be a modern personality we have to have a personality that goes beyond our functional identities. It is not enough to simply be a mother, a lawyer, and on the city council—one has to be something "unique" as well. One has to have an identity, a history. One has to be as special and unique as everyone else is. The mass media display all these uniformly unique characters—and the minds resonate with these schemata. And in turn, of course, the mass media resonate with mental individuality schemata. The individuals are both inside and outside the mass media; when you watch a film, the news, or a commercial, then the report, the story, or the spot is not literally, not immediately about you—you are outside. But it is about your world—you are still part of this reality that you observe in the mass media. It is not you—but the schemata and scripts are yours, and since there are no others, you are also inside them. Luhmann explains: "When individuals look at media as text or as image, they are outside; when they experience their results within themselves they are inside. They have to oscillate between outside and inside. . . . For the one position is only possible thanks to the other—and vice versa" (2000a, 115). When structurally coupled with society through the mass media—we are both inside and outside of society. The schemata have these two extremes— our psychic existence outside society and our social existence within it. The "self," the "individuality," and the "identity" that we deal with today are the effects of the social reality of our time and of its specific coupling with psychic reality. There is no essence attached to human existence, and there is also no "existential" human project that we can unfold. Concepts of the human being emerge from complex relations and "cybernetic circles" between complex systems—and they change with these relations. The same is true for reality.

The specific conceptions of individuality and reality are always "unlikely" constructions—in comparison with all the other constructions that would have been possible and that preceded them and will follow them. Our psychic and social self-descriptions emerge in a context of a multiplicity of constructions that lack a central perspective and an essential core or "meaning." Yes—the individual, society, and reality all make sense, but they have no ultimate "meaning." There is nothing fundamental to which they refer; there is nothing essential that they indicate. When we communicate and when we think, we are condemned to make sense of the world and of ourselves, but there is no one meaning that integrates this sense. There are only meanings, in the plural—contingent constructs within horizons of sense.

PART III

Philosophical Contexts

It is not so much the disciplinary tradition of social theory from Comte to Parsons that Luhmann tries to connect up with, as the history of problems associated with the philosophy of consciousness from Kant to Husserl.

—JÜRGEN HABERMAS[43]

The purpose of this section is to locate Niklas Luhmann's systems theory within a larger context, both historically and in contemporary theory.

In line with Habermas's insightful observation quoted above, I believe that although Luhmann understood himself mainly as a theoretician of society and thus as a sociologist, he nevertheless "connects up with" major developments in German philosophy between the late eighteenth and the early twentieth century. This connection is twofold. While he explicitly relates himself to this tradition by taking up some of its main questions, he also attempts to thoroughly reformulate these questions and to answer them with a more or less completely revised set of concepts and new terminology. In the following brief sketches, I hope to show how these two somewhat antagonistic attitudes—a continued interest in a set of issues ranging from epistemology to ethics along with the intention to provide radically new approaches—play out in the cases of a few selected thinkers: Kant, Hegel, Marx, and Husserl. I chose these four theoreticians not only because their ambitious projects may be viewed as models for Luhmann's own endeavor, but also because of statistics. If one simply counts the number of references to individual philosophers of the past in Luhmann's major outlines of his general theory (*Social Systems, Die Gesellschaft der Gesellschaft, Einführung in die Systemtheorie*), then those four are (along with Plato and Aristotle) at the top of the list.[44]

It was through his engagement in a dispute with Habermas that Luhmann became widely known in the 1970s. From this perspective, Habermas could be identified as the most immediate contemporary counterpart of Luhmann. If, however, one were to trace the larger theoretical context out of which Luhmann's theory arose, one would also have to mention sociologists like Parsons and Gehlen, biologists like Maturana and Varela, the cybernetics of von Foerster and von Glasersfeld, the logic of George Spencer Brown and Gotthard Günther, and the "ecology" of Bateson. To trace all these influences and relations would go beyond the scope of this book which is specifically concerned with the philosophical dimension of Luhmann's theory. Within contemporary philosophy, it was, besides critical theory, mostly the heterogeneous postmodernist scene that attracted Luhmann's explicit interest and that, vice versa, found him interesting. I will therefore restrict myself to these two trends in philosophy when outlining Luhmann's contemporary relevance.

I will also restrict myself to an outline of how Luhmann interpreted these thinkers and of the relation of his theory to their projects. This is to say, I will refrain from analyzing how far Luhmann's understanding of them was "correct" or not. I have my doubts in this regard, particularly with respect to Hegel. I think Luhmann is in fact often closer to Hegel—or has borrowed more extensively—than he is willing to admit. It is, however, not my intention in the following pages to comment on the adequacy of Luhmann's interpretation of certain philosophical authors, but on how, in his own works, he attempted to continue or discontinue their discourses.

9

Kant

"Kant's question about the conditions for the possibility of cognition remains. But the answer is now: operational closure; and thus the focus of research shifts from the conditions of possibility to the possibilities of conditioning in increasingly complex relations" (Luhmann 1997a, 127). This sentence nicely summarizes Luhmann's complex indebtedness to Kant and his ambivalent attempt to both carry on and overcome the Kantian project.

Luhmann's most concise treatment of the "Kantian question" is his essay "Cognition as Construction" (included in the present book in English translation). In this short but programmatic text, Luhmann explains very pointedly:

> The tradition of epistemological idealism was about the question of the unity within the difference of cognition and the real object. The question was: how can cognition take notice of an object outside of itself? Or: how can it realize that something exists independently of it while anything which it realizes already presupposes cognition and cannot be realized by cognition independently of cognition (this would be a self-contradiction)? No matter if one preferred solutions of transcendental theory or dialectics, the problem was: how is cognition possible in spite of having no independent access to reality outside of it. Radical constructivism, however, begins with the empirical assertion: Cognition is only possible because it has no access to the reality external to it. A brain, for instance, can only produce information because it is coded indifferently in regard to its environment, i.e. it operates enclosed within the recursive network of its own operations. Similarly one would have to say: Communication systems (social systems) are only able to produce information because the

environment does not interrupt them. And following all this, the same should be self-evident with respect to the classical "seat" (subject) of epistemology: to consciousness. (1988b, 8–9)

Luhmann's systems theory is deeply rooted in Kantian epistemology. Like Kant, Luhmann is concerned with the fundamentals of cognition: What is cognition and how does it operate? For a Kantian "epistemological idealism," however, the concept of cognition was primarily "ideal," that is, cognition was assumed to be ultimately an issue of consciousness. On the basis of this assumption a core problem arose: how can cognition relate to what it cognizes? Kant developed a rather revolutionary answer to this problem when he introduced his "Copernican turn," when he switched from a theory of transcendence to a theory of transcendentality. For Kant, idealism was no longer concerned with describing the universal set-up that allowed the human mind to actually participate to some degree in the divine logos; it rather limited itself to questioning which inherent structures within cognition could be inferred from cognition. Kant was no longer focused on the general structure of the world, but on the structure of cognition that allowed it to operate and conceive of a world. Kant accepted the skeptical argument that nothing could "be realized by cognition independently of cognition" and drew the conclusion that in order to understand reality we must first understand the cognition that provides us with it. This shift introduced a good deal of constructivism into epistemology. While it was still assumed that there was a reality independent of cognition, it was granted that the realization of this reality was contingent upon cognitive structures. Thus the realization of reality was a process of cognitive reality construction.

Luhmann's systems theory takes up both the initial cognitive lay-out of transcendental idealism and its constructivist edge, but it considerably radicalizes these two theorems. From a Luhmannian point of view, the Kantian theory is a sort of "constructivism light." While it concedes that the realization of reality is an effect of cognitive construction, it also alleges that it still makes sense to assume the existence of a world that somehow is as it is—as well as the cognitive structure that is transcendentally given. Luhmann's constructivism goes a step further and assumes that the realization of reality is not only a possible way of relating to reality, but that reality basically consists of its own realization.

Cognition is no longer simply a way of relating understandingly to a reality. Here reality emerges as cognition.

It has to be added immediately, though, that this radical constructivism by no means follows the older idealist pattern of declaring cognition to be essentially ideal or the self-realization of a larger consciousness (as with Hegel). Cognition has no specific "essence" at all. It can operate, for instance, "materially" in the form of biological life, mentally in the form of thoughts, or socially in the form of communication. Cognition arises in the form of cognitive systems that constitute themselves, and there is no singular, general, preestablished rule for how this can be done. Cognitive systems establish themselves *by operational closure.* By differentiating themselves operationally, they construct themselves by establishing a difference between themselves and an environment. Cognition is based on the establishment of this difference— it does not happen *in spite of* this difference, but *because of* it. There is no "ontological" necessity of cognition, but if it is there, and it obviously is, it depends on the differentiation of a cognizing system.

While Luhmann thus relates to the cognitive and constructivist elements in Kant, he refrains from any essential or transcendental understanding of cognition: cognition is not "ideal," it can only be defined functionally or "operationally" because it consists in an "observation that is defined on the basis of the concepts of distinction and indication" (Luhmann 1988b, 14). This allows for a very general understanding of cognition that includes, but is not limited to, biological, mental, and social processes. Cells, minds, and social systems are all observing systems and are thus systems that construct themselves and their realization of reality by their own cognition. They are able to establish themselves as self-referential, operational sequences of their own kind. This "radicalization" of cognitive constructivism leads, in summary, to several major differences from the Kantian theory:

- Cognition is not *per se* an act of consciousness. It can take on any operational mode.

- There is no a priori, transcendental structure of cognition; cognition constructs itself on the basis of "operational closure" and this is an "empirical"[45] process, which varies from system to system.

- No complete description of cognitive structures is possible because these structures are continuously evolving.

- Reality is not singular—there is not one specific reality, but a complex multiplicity of system/environment constellations.

- A description of reality is itself a contingent construction within a system/environment relation.

All these differences combine to form the main way transcendental idealism diverges conceptually from systems theory: the distinction subject/object is replaced by the distinction system/environment. In "Cognition as Construction" Luhmann describes his discomfort with the concept of the subject: "The theory of the subject . . . had to presuppose a common—or at least a commonly observable—world and thus was obstructed from conceiving of the *uncoupling* of each singular cognitive system as the *condition* of cognition" (1988b, 10).[46] The subject "constructs" reality by transcendental unification through self-reference. The system does this by differentiation. The conceptual framework of system/environment is not only radically constructivist, but it is also radically "differentialist." The consciously cognizing subject is replaced by self-generating and self-referential systems of observation that introduce splits into the world which thereby constitute a complex multiplicity of system/environment relations.[47]

Luhmann's abolishment of the subject as an anchor of "pure reason" also has severe consequences for "practical reason." Subjectivity was not only an epistemological concept, but also employed as a cornerstone of ethics and social theory. Luhmann criticizes this "sociologization" of the concept of the subject in *The Society of Society*:

> The term "subject" does not designate a substance that, by its pure being, shoulders everything else, the subject is rather self-referentiality itself as the foundation of cognition and action. The experiences with this figure of thought, however, are not so encouraging that one should give in to the temptation of transferring it to society—by conceiving of society as the true subject and perhaps naming it spirit or intersubjectivity and then ascribing everything to it that was previously ascribed to individual consciousness. One does not have to ignore the results of the philosophy of subjectivity, but

one can view them as shallows that the ship of social theory should avoid. (1997a, 868)

After transposing the core structure of self-reference of "epistemo-logical idealism" from the conscious subject to observing systems, Luhmann strictly denies any application of the traditional concept of subjectivity in regard to social theory. Here, he completely leaves Kantian terrain and thus remains in sharp opposition to later post-Kantian theoreticians of spirit (Hegel), intersubjectivity (Husserl), or rational consensus (Habermas) as will be shown in the following sections.[48]

10

Hegel

Hegel's philosophy may well be understood as a further development of Kantian epistemological idealism, and, consequently, the similarities and differences between Luhmann and Hegel often mirror Luhmann's relation to Kant. However, I would argue that there is a somewhat closer kinship and deeper sympathy for Hegel than there is for Kant.

As in the case of Kant, Luhmann shares very general cognitive interests with Hegel. Still, like Kant, Luhmann departs from Hegel by radicalizing the constructivist view of reality, and, particularly, by broadening the concept of cognition far beyond the realms of consciousness. Luhmann is, after all, not an idealist but mainly a theoretician of society. He does not share Hegel's priorities. While Hegel imports concepts of consciousness (such as "spirit" or *Geist*) into social theory, Luhmann denies any general type of cognition for systemic autopoiesis—it may be consciousness, but it can also be communication, life, or, perhaps, something else. There is no essential unity of systems: "The basic question remains how a unity can be constituted. . . . There are different answers to this depending on whether one is dealing with psychic or social systems. Everything further depends on this difference—and this separates us from a conception like that developed in Hegel's *Phenomenology of Spirit*" (Luhmann 1995a, 363). As mentioned in regard to Kant, Luhmann's shift from subject to system also implies, particularly in comparison to Hegel, a shift from unity to multiplicity, from identity to difference. Luhmann declares in his introductory remarks to *Social Systems*: "In order to work out a theory of self-referential systems that

incorporates system/environment theory, a new guiding difference, and thus a new paradigm, is necessary. The difference
between identity and difference serves for this" (1995a, 10). And
in a note to this passage Luhmann makes it quite explicit that this
means a departure from Hegel (Luhmann 1995a, 498): "An atten-
tive reader will notice that we are discussing the difference between
identity and difference, and not their identity. This is where the
following reflections diverge from the dialectical tradition—despite
similarities that may be noted from time to time." This lays out
quite programmatically a main difference between Hegel and
Luhmann—the shift from "world spirit" to a theory of differentiation—but in regard to the final sentence in this quotation, one
may, however, also ask: What exactly are these "similarities that
may be noted from time to time"? I suggest that the similarities
have something to do with style and theoretical ambition.
Arguably, Luhmann's explicit attempt at a "supertheory"
(Luhmann 1995a, 4–5), a general theory of the construction of
reality, is in its scale comparable only to Hegel. So, as one author
(Winthrop-Young 2000) has phrased it, Luhmann may well have
aspired to succeed "on Hegel's throne." Luhmann admits rather
openly to such a claim of succession in *Social Systems* (1995a, xlix)
when he demands of his own theory: "Every step must be fitted in.
And even the arbitrariness of the beginning loses its arbitrariness
(like in Hegel's system) as the construction of the theory proceeds.
Thus a self-supporting construction arises." Luhmann repeatedly
claimed that his theory is one among very few (if any) that is able
to include itself in itself, that it reaches a higher "self-reflecting
degree of conceptual complexity" (1995a, xlix). It is unclear if
Luhmann believed that this self-inclusion of theory actually followed in Hegel's systematic footsteps—as the just quoted passage
seems to suggest—or even surpassed his great predecessor. In *The
Society of Society*, Luhmann accuses Hegel—alluding once more to
the *Phenomenology of Spirit*—of finally failing to construct a completely self-inclusive theory of observation:

> The novel, the romance, but also Hegel's novel of the love between
> world-history and philosophy localizes the observer who can also see
> what he himself previously could not see at the end of the story. This
> makes it necessary to exclude the narrator who has known everything
> already from the beginning, and thus also Hegel himself, from the
> story.[49] (1997a, 1081)

There is some degree of self-inclusion in Hegel—the subject that Hegel talks about becomes finally fully self-reflective. But Hegel, at least in Luhmann's view, forgot to include himself, the perspective of the theory of subjectivity, into the story. He failed to take into account that the epistemologist is himself within the labyrinth of cognition. Hegel ended with a closure of his theory that, for the sake of completing, unifying, and universalizing itself under a general heading—spirit or *Geist*—excluded its own perspective, and, at least in the *Phenomenology of Sprit*,[50] did not really achieve an "autological" theory of observation.

Luhmann's relation to Hegel remains, therefore, highly ambiguous. He claims: "The ambition of a common foundation, a basic symbol, a final thought has to be given up—or left to the philosophers. Sociology, however, does not discover in this direction what Hegel had called "spirit" (*Geist*). It is not a science of the spirit (*Geisteswissenschaft*) [51] (1997a, 1122). Luhmann's theory is a "supertheory" because it fully includes itself in itself. But this self-inclusion leads to the breakdown of any declarations of finality, completion, or foundationalism. This is how Luhmann claims to surpass Hegel in universality, and, at the same time, gives up his attempt to come up with an all-embracing concept such as *Geist*. The time is over for the discipline of philosophy that is concerned with "final thoughts," and also for the humanities in their literal German sense: "the sciences (*Wissenschaften*) of the spirit (*Geist*)." Luhmann says: "What can now be offered as a universal formula of reality constructions is: that such a universal formula no longer exists. Hegel had, as it is known, no heirs" (1997a, 592). Here, Luhmann paradoxically claims to be Hegel's legitimate heir by pointing out why following him means to depart from him. For Luhmann, philosophy came, strictly speaking, to its end with Hegel and was waiting for its sublation (*Aufhebung*) in another theory that was no longer restricted to spirit. It was, perhaps, in recognition of this that Luhmann was awarded the prestigious Hegel prize in 1989.

11

Marx

As it is generally known, Marx believed that Hegel had to be turned upside down—from his head to his feet. He wanted to transform an idealist dialectics into a materialist one, a philosophy of consciousness or spirit into an analysis of historical, political, and economic development. As with Hegel and Kant, Luhmann's relation to Marx is highly ambiguous. On the one hand he attempts to utilize central theoretical elements of this "supertheory" for his own project, while, on the other hand, he strongly rejects some of the core Marxist dogmas and beliefs.

Luhmann is certainly sympathetic to what Marx tried to do with Hegel—to deconstruct Hegel's primary focus on consciousness and to theoretically emancipate social structures from being mere effects of spirituality. He thus sides with Marx in granting society its own mechanisms that cannot be deduced from nonsocial forces or patterns. Luhmann does not believe, however, that Marx has distanced himself far enough from the Hegelian project and accuses him of a formally similar one-sidedness that differs only in content. While Hegel's system was essentially focused on consciousness, Marx ascribed an essential role to the economical-political structure, or, more precisely, to the modes of production. Such an identification of one basic system that shapes all others makes Marx, in a certain sense, as much of a theoretical fundamentalist or ontologist as Hegel. Like Hegel, he was not able to adequately incorporate difference into his theory. This also prevented him from acknowledging the radical contingency of reality construction that necessarily includes one's own theorizing. In the final analysis "Marx himself, however, seems to have been unable, just as Hegel, to account for his own theory within his own theory" (Luhmann 1997a, 1080, n. 350). Marx's and Hegel's supertheories were, in this regard, not yet complete supertheories. They both suffered from being unable or unwilling to "relativize" themselves and thus to combine their universalism with a renunciation of any attempt to identify a "universal formula."

One of Luhmann's clearest descriptions of both his indebtedness to and difference from Marx that is currently available in English is his essay "Modernity in Contemporary Society" (Luhmann 1998, 1–21). Here, Luhmann states:

> What remains remarkable about the Marxist critique of the political economies of its day is the shift of a knowledge previously justified through nature to a social context. The economic order of capitalism does not, according to Marx, follow the nature of economic action with an innate trend toward individual and collective rationality. It is, rather, a social construct. The reference to nature is presented as "reification;" that is, it is analyzed as a moment of social construction. Economic theory's claim to represent an extrasocial objectivity is contested. It only reflects the logic of a social construct. Even if we give up everything else, we should keep this and further develop it beyond Marx. (1998, 8; translation modified)

According to Luhmann, Marx's understanding of the economy and its functioning as a *social construct* rather than a process based on some sort of natural law was groundbreaking. Marx was thus able to translate—and this is probably one of the most important theoretical preconditions for social systems theory—the constructivist elements already contained in the epistemological idealism of Kant and Hegel into a theory of *social* construction. With Marx it became possible to conceive of society as an autopoietic, self-constructing mechanism that operated on its own accord rather than under the unchangeable laws of some trans-social realm. This theoretical step is wholeheartedly embraced by social systems theory. Only a couple of further steps were needed, and one of these was to deny the primacy of the economic structure for the self-construction of society. Marx was, so to speak, only an economic constructivist. The theory of society had to be broadened beyond this prime focus.

This criticism is further detailed in the following paragraph:

One of the most important criticisms of Marxist social theory is that it overestimates the economy and in doing so, as we can see today, underestimates it. The watered-down versions of Antonio Gramsci and Louis Althusser have not changed this. In the definition of society as a whole in economic terms, what is lacking is a sufficient appreciation for the inherent dynamics of the economy and its effects on other functional areas and the ecological conditions of social evolution. What is lacking above all is a sufficient appreciation for parallel phenomena in different functional areas. Missing is a basis for comparing systems and for distilling abstract characteristics of modernity, which can be found in more or less all function systems. (Luhmann 1998, 9; translation modified)

In Luhmann's view, the Marxist attentiveness to production and thus to the economy overestimates this social system in regard to its constituting power for all of society. It ascribes a central position to one singular system and thus becomes unable to account for the plurality of social function systems—it ignores the radically pluralist character of functional differentiation. According to Luhmann, the differentiation of the economy as a self-constructing social system does not prevent other systems from unfolding their own autopoietic operations, but, on the contrary, goes along with the simultaneous differentiation of other function systems. To reduce the function of other social systems to the systemic mechanisms of the economy means to ascribe to it powers that it does not have while also simplifying social complexity. At the same time, however, the primary focus on the economy also underestimates this system's capacity to continuously change itself and enter into extremely complex structural couplings with other social systems such as law, politics, and the mass media. There is no definite structure to the economy. It is, like all other function systems, dynamic. The dynamics of the economic system allow it to establish and continuously re-establish itself within the incessantly evolving network of functional differentiation that characterizes modern society.[52]

Luhmann does not only disagree with the Marxist focus on the economy as, so to speak, the heart of society, he also disagrees with the tendency to decry the nonhuman character of the economy, as it becomes obvious, for instance, in the concept of alienation. Such a "humanist upholstering"[53] of Marxist terminology is, in Luhmann's view, a theoretical obstacle that falls back into

Old European semantics. This does little to aid the analysis of economic structures—they are, after all, social and not human. Such use of language may lead to hasty adoptions of moralist attitudes and programs rather than an adequate understanding of social mechanisms. The most obvious instances of this were the pogroms against the "enemies of the people" that were justified on humanist and moral grounds. In line with his general suspicion of moralist and activist theories, Luhmann is entirely opposed to such elements within Marxism. In regard to this aspect of "practical philosophy," Luhmann is as much appalled by the presumptuousness of the Marxist call to change the world (rather than to interpret it) as he is with the Kantian claim of having found the principles of goodness, or the Habermasian prescription of specific rules for how to communicate in an acceptable way. Luhmann is not enthusiastic about the self-declared "critical sociology" from "Marx to Habermas" that "replaces methodology with measuring the opinions of its (from its perspective) opponents by their critical ambitions. In this case, the judgment precedes the investigation" (Luhmann 1997a, 36). There is a thorough discomfort about normativity and morality in Luhmann that are, for him, not only simple-minded, but may quickly lead to intellectual and, more dangerously, social totalitarianism:

> Hegel's concept of the state is no better. Nor is Marx's hope for a revolution. In societal reality, one just does not see any prospect for achieving such central fusions of an ultimate unity of difference, from which no distance would be possible any longer, so that everyone would be in perfect agreement as a result of a sense of community. (Luhmann 1995a, 442; translation modified)

12

Husserl

Among all the philosophies discussed in this section, Husserl's phenomenology probably had the most immediate influence on Luhmann's systems theory. Just as in the cases of Kant and Hegel, Luhmann makes use of central elements of Husserl's theory of consciousness and transforms these into constitutive elements for general systems theory. But in contrast to Kant and Hegel, in this case Luhmann not only takes over the structural and methodological aspects of a cognitive and constructivist theory, but also much of the conceptual framework itself. He explicitly borrows Husserl's terminology and integrates it into his own conceptual apparatus. I will trace these borrowings here by primarily relying on a rather short text that represents Luhmann's most comprehensive treatment of his relation to Husserl, a treatise entitled *Modern Sciences and Phenomenology* (*Die neuzeitlichen Wissenschaften und die Phänomenologie*, Luhmann 1996b), which is based on a 1995 public lecture in Vienna.

Luhmann explicitly states in this treatise that it is his aim to "introduce Husserl's theoretical intention into a completely different 'life-world'" (1996b, 52). In addition, he claims to be the first to transpose Husserl's "so highly promising type of theory from 'subject' to the 'social system society'" (1996b, 53). He suggests nothing less than that Husserl had already employed a theory of second-order cybernetics, operationally-closed autopoietic systems and radical constructivism, but that "by using such concepts as 'subject,' 'spirit,' or 'transcendental phenomenology,' (he) attached it to a tradition that even at his times had only meager future prospects" (1996b, 47). By attempting to continue the old project of epistemological idealism, Husserl missed the opportunity to understand the broader functionalist relevance of his own theory. He was too much of an epistemologist, in the traditional sense, to realize that he had already detected some of the more general mechanisms of autopoiesis. Luhmann therefore wants to apply Husserl's terminology not in explaining only the "characteristics of consciousness," but also for "the emergence of order in general" (1996b, 50). Luhmann is no longer mainly interested in how consciousness produces intentions, a world, a horizon, and sense (*Sinn*),[54] but also in how such a cognitive construction functions in a variety of other nonconsciousness systems. Here he is particularly interested in the communication system of society. Instead of being fixated on the realm of consciousness, Luhmann is interested in the general functioning of the making of sense and rejects the concept of a "transcendental subject." He no longer accepts the premise that consciousness is "the" medium of cognition, but insists on "keeping the structure discovered by Husserl, namely the insight into the mutual conditioning of operational ability, the separation and simultaneous processing of other- and self-reference as well as the temporality connected to the standpoint of the respective operation" (1996b, 50).

Luhmann translates a whole set of Husserlian terms into the language of systems theory. He begins with "intention": "The form in which consciousness executes its operations is called by Husserl (in connection to Brentano) *Intention*." Luhmann subtracts the causal attribution implied in this concept, the attribution of a certain purpose, and redefines the term in a purely functional way: "Intention is nothing but the positing of a difference" (1996b, 31). Intention is thus no longer a certain mental interest. It is now the primal operation with which any observing system ignites itself, the first step with which a system differs itself out of an environment and thus begins to establish itself. In line with this functional redefinition of the concept of intention, Luhmann reformulates the Husserlian distinction between noesis and noema, between phenomena and consciousness activity, with the distinction between other-reference and self-reference. Along with its "intentionality," and the corresponding drawing of a distinction, a cognizing system is able to differentiate between its cognition—its own operating—and that which it cognizes outside of itself. Intentionality paves the way for a distinction between a system and its environment. Only through this difference can a system identify itself by distinguishing itself from what it observes. The difference between noesis and noema, or, in systems theory language, other- and self-reference, establishes the "membrane" of a system and allows it to operate: "Intentional operating is a continuous oscillating between other-reference and self-reference and thus prevents consciousness from ever losing itself in the world or coming to a halt" (1996b, 34–35). Of course, this is, according to Luhmann, not only the case with consciousness but with all other self-referential systems. This includes social systems. Such oscillating necessarily needs time and so Luhmann agrees with Husserl that systemic cognition also produces temporality. Once more, however, all these concepts are purely functional and not substantially tied to something such as a consciousness or a subject:

> Husserl obviously believed to be able to guarantee the unity of his transcendental phenomenology by the unity of its object "subject." We can already anticipate that one can dispense with this. The disclosed connection between operation, bistability (self-reference/ other-reference), time, and oscillation supports itself—and can therefore possibly be demonstrated with totally different objects. (1996b, 38)

The functionalization and de-ontologization of Husserlian terminology, its separation from consciousness and the subject, also applies to three other tightly connected Husserlian concepts: sense,[55] horizon, and world. Luhmann stated in *Social Systems* (1995a, 98) that "there is no privileged carrier, no ontic substrate" for sense. In other words, sense does not have to be defined "by reference to a subject or any carrier of sense, a sense-constituting agency," but simply by developing "a sufficiently formalized concept of sense" (Luhmann 2002a, 225). Luhmann then formally defines sense, in immediate connection to Husserl, as the unity of the difference between actuality and possibility—and applies it to all sense-processing systems including social systems. Sense emerges only within a context—it needs a horizon. Sense always refers to something else that would also make sense, and the "circular closure of these references appears in its unity as the ultimate horizon of all sense: as *the world*" (Luhmann 1995a, 69; translation modified; see ch. 2, sec. b above for a more detailed explanation of these concepts).

Luhmann's departure from the concept of the transcendental subject leads quite consequentially—and very much in line with Luhmann's rejection of humanist elements in Kant, Hegel, and Marx—to a complete rejection of Husserl's concept of "intersubjectivity." Luhmann does not believe in the formation of the social by anything nonsocial such as minds or humans. Since this is the case, "what is social cannot be traced back to the conscious performances of a monadic subject. This has been the downfall of all attempts to establish a theory of the subjective constitution of 'intersubjectivity'" (Luhmann, 1995a, 81).

Interestingly enough, Luhmann considerably broadens his criticism of Husserl's philosophy in the Vienna lecture and other late publications[56] beyond the concepts of the subject and intersubjectivity. He first critically analyzes Husserl's aversion to technology—Husserl found it to be some sort of perversion of reason—and then took offense to Husserl's attempt, as an alternative to technology, to promote European "culture" and the revival of an Old European tradition of rationality. Luhmann is particularly unhappy with this self-confessed Eurocentrism:

> Most conspicuous is perhaps a Eurocentrism that one rarely finds elsewhere in the twentieth century. European humankind is in crisis, European humankind is in need of salvation—and this by itself. This has certainly nothing to do with imperialism, colonialism, and exploitation, but obviously with a spiritual consciousness of superiority that not only excludes "the gypsies who constantly vagabond around Europe," but also considers a Europeanization of all other humans "whereas we, if we understand ourselves correctly, will, for instance, never Indianize ourselves." No notice of global political and economical circumstances, no thought given to the possibility that European traditions may gradually dissolve into differently structured circumstances of a global society. (Luhmann 1996b, 18, quoting Husserl 1954, 319–20)

Luhmann's disappointment with this side of Husserl's philosophy is not morally or politically motivated. It is about Husserl's inability to overcome the Old European insistence on reason and his claim to not only possess universal and privileged access to it through philosophy, but to the right of imposing it on all others who have not yet been enlightened by it. Luhmann does not identify his theory with this tradition of reason and he seeks to leave it behind. He has no sympathy for a "monoculture of reason,"[57] be it in Kantian, Husserlian, or, as I will show in the following section, Habermasian terms. Such claims have no place in a "supertheory" that, after all, has to be able to include itself in itself and thus to ironically reflect on its own limitations:

> One can now better understand which perspectives Husserl opens and simultaneously blocks up. Reason is self-critical not because of its European pedigree, but only if and only insofar as it can replace its own belief in reality, this is to say if it begins to not believe in itself. . . . Self-critical reason is ironical reason. It is the reason of the "gypsies who constantly vagabond around Europe." (Luhmann 1996b, 45–46)

13

Habermas

That Luhmann distanced himself rather drastically from Husserl's insistence on "European reason" seems to be reflective of the continuous conflict he had had with Habermas on the same issue. It was in this intellectual confrontation that he had earlier on taken the role of a "gypsy of reason" to oppose the Habermasian mission of the completion of enlightenment.

It was mainly through the controversy with Habermas that Luhmann became generally known in the academic world—at least in Germany. In 1971 they jointly published a volume which presented their divergent views under the title *Theory of Society or Social Technology: What is Achieved by Systems Research?* (Luhmann and Habermas 1971). Luhmann comments on this publication in the preface of *The Society of Society*:

> The irony of this title lied in that none of the authors wanted to defend social technology, but that there were differences of opinion in respect to what a theory of society should look like; and it is of symptomatic significance that, in the public perception, the place of a theory of society was initially taken on not by a theory, but by a controversy. (1997a, 11)

Luhmann's early "fame" was then due not so much to the theory he had to offer, but to the fact that he was part of a debate. In the 1970s this debate was, "in the public perception," probably won by Habermas. The intellectual climate in Germany was heavily influenced by the leftist "revolt" of the late 1960s, and Luhmann, who was not discernibly leftist or "progressive," was branded with a depreciative title: "conservative." This was not very fashionable at the time. Habermas had a Marxist background and argued for social change, for emancipation, and for a better society, while Luhmann took, from the beginning, a rather disengaged stance. In this way the debate was publicly judged less on the basis of theoretical strength and more on where one stood (or was supposed to stand) in a political controversy. Public perception, however, did change in time, and especially after the publication of *Social Systems* in 1984. Here, Luhmann presented the first overall outline of systems theory that was immediately taken note of in a wide range of disciplines. In a somewhat dialectic turn of the tide, Habermasian social theory had become the established creed of aging leftist intellectuals, while Luhmann's work was now perceived as having an innovative and avant-gardist approach. Habermas was more and more identified with the social-political "mainstream." A generation of former leftist activists and/or politicians, the so-called *Altachtundsechziger* (roughly: "the grown-old veterans of the protest movement of 1968"), had completed their "march through the institutions" and occupied leading positions in the universities, the schools, the mass media, and, most importantly, in the federal government constituted by the Green Party and the Social Democrats. At the same time Luhmann became the sexier theoretician. Many younger academics who intended to do something new or provocative took an interest in him. Luhmann was read and applied not only in sociology, but (and perhaps more enthusiastically) in such fields as art, literature, media science, psychotherapy, philosophy, education, economics, and theology.[58] There was even a popular German writer and techno music fan who had himself photographed reading a book by Luhmann[59]— that would have hardly happened to Habermas in the 1990s when he seemed to be gaining the unofficial status of state philosopher.

Given the context of the German academic scene, the controversy between Luhmann and Habermas had been from beginning to end—albeit under changing conditions—not only about content, but also about style and political identification. In fact, their approaches were so dissimilar that their debate could hardly be called a dialogue. It was rather a clash of radically different and incompatible views on society and its theory. In short, Luhmann aspired to create a new theory of society that would explain social structures on the basis of systemic functioning. It would refrain from making any normative claims, particularly because he denied that society consisted of human beings. Habermas, on the other hand, aspired to help modern society improve itself, to infuse more rationality into society by outlining how communication could be made to be less dominated by power interests and thus reach a better consensus. In their illuminating outline of the most common criticisms of Luhmann, King and Thornhill list eight. The following five would also be voiced by Habermas and his followers:[60]

- His reluctance to engage in debates over current political and legal issues

- His refusal to see law and politics as instruments for progress in society

- His failure to account for human agency in directing change through law and politics, or in using law and politics to resist change

- The failure of his theoretical ideas to offer anything more than a new brand of conservatism

- His rejection of rationality as a universal arbiter of validity, value, and legitimacy (King and Thornhill 2003, 204)

From a Habermasian perspective, Luhmann has to be rejected because of his antimoralism (or maybe better: his "antinormativism"), antihumanism, and antirationalism. Habermas himself has outlined his criticism of Luhmann in detail in the "Excursus on Luhmann's Appropriation of the Philosophy of the Subject through Systems Theory" included in *The Philosophical Discourse of Modernity* (1987, 368–85). This text is basically a review of *Social Systems*, and, in my view, one of the best philosophical analyses of Luhmann's theory. As the quote at the beginning of this section states, Habermas locates Luhmann within the context of the German philosophy of consciousness or subjectivity from Kant to Husserl. He says, "It (social systems theory) seeks to inherit the basic terms and problematics of the philosophy of the subject, while at the same time surpassing it in its capacity for solving problems" (1987, 368). I hope to have proven on the preceding pages the adequacy of this statement. Habermas then goes on to analyze how Luhmann switches conceptually from subject to system and how this alters the program of epistemological idealism. Habermas summarizes this shift by ascribing to Luhmann a turn from metaphysics to "metabiology:"

> However the expression "metaphysics" may have chanced to arise, one could attribute to it the meaning of a thinking that proceeds from the "for us" of physical appearances and asks what lies behind them. Then we can use the term "metabiological" for a thinking that starts from the "for itself" of organic life and goes behind it—the cybernetically described, basic phenomenon of the self-maintenance of self-relating systems in the face of hypercomplex environments. (1987, 372)

This switch leads, as Habermas remarks—and I think, perfectly adequately—to a switch from a universal reason that is attached to a rational subject to an entirely contingent "functionalist reason" that can be ascribed in any shape or form to any function system:

> Reason as specified in relation to being, thought, or proposition is replaced by the self-enhancing self-maintenance of the system. By taking this approach, Luhmann also goes beyond a critique of reason that aims at revealing the power of self-maintenance to be the latent essence of subject-centered reason. Under the title of systems rationality, reason, now liquidated as irrational, professes exactly this function: It is the ensemble of the conditions that make system-maintenance possible. (1987, 372–73)

This leads to wide-ranging consequences that are entirely irreconcilable with the Habermasian program: purely functional reason is no longer rational reason, it is totally arbitrary, and the same is true for "sense" (*Sinn*). Therefore, as Habermas once more correctly concludes, the internal connection between sense "and validity dissolves. The same thing happens as with Foucault: the interest in truth (and validity in general) is restricted to the effects of holding-something-as-true" (1987, 373). Without a generally valid reason and sense, there is no solid basis for validating social criticism, for constituting true identity, for improving modernity, for establishing intersubjectivity and norms for rational discourse, or for bringing about rational consensus and understanding.

As pointed out earlier, Luhmann and Habermas are so diametrically opposed in their concepts of reason and society that they do not so much debate as exchange incompatible statements. In order to add to the preceding Habermasian rejections of Luhmann a Luhmannian counter-rejection, I translate a passage from *The Society of Society*:

> Linguistic communication has, we say in summary, its unity in the yes/no coding. This excludes, if taken seriously, the possibility of deducing from language itself an ideal norm of understanding. Only the autopoiesis of communication is necessary, and this autopoiesis is not guaranteed by a telos of understanding, but by a binary code— because for a coded communication there is no end, but only the option that is reproduced in all understanding, namely to continue either by accepting or refusing. Put differently: the coding excludes any meta-rule, since one could once more comment approvingly or disapprovingly on the communication of such a rule. (Luhmann 1997a, 229–30)

Thus, with Luhmann it is not only "as with Foucault." When it comes to the denial of any "meta-rule" of understanding, he also takes sides with Lyotard against Habermas, as he explicitly states in a footnote to the above quoted passage. This leads immediately to the next section.

14

Postmodernity, Deconstruction, and Techno-Theory

Luhmann was convinced that Habermasian and Husserlian beliefs in European reason were out of touch with contemporary society. He asked, "How long, then, will Husserl and Habermas be able to maintain their old or modern idea of critical reasons without becoming conservatives who stick to a tradition that cannot maintain its identity but fades away?" (Luhmann 2000b, 40). Clearly, for Luhmann the "project of modernity" was a no go. How about, then, the "postmodern project?" Luhmann's position here is, once more, ambiguous. On the one hand, he does not subscribe to the label "postmodernity" in the first place—there is for him, as in the title of the last chapter of *The Society of Society*, only "The So-Called Postmodernity." But, on the other hand, as we will see, he is highly sympathetic to many "so-called" postmodern theoretical developments, and, particularly, to one of its most prominent methods, namely "deconstruction." When it came to comparing modern and postmodern positions, Luhmann would usually be more sympathetic to the postmodernists, not only in his later works, as in the paragraph from *The Society of Society* (1997a) quoted in the preceding section, but at least as early as *Social Systems* (first German edition, 1984).[61]

Luhmann makes it very clear that to him the problem of "postmodernity" is mainly one of semantics (see Luhmann 1997a, 1143; 2000b) and not of actual structural changes. In other words, he does not see a recent epochal shift. According to him, the last decisive structural shift in society took place in Europe between the sixteenth and eighteenth century with the change from stratified to functional differentiation. To Luhmann, it does not really matter if one would like to designate a society dominated by functional differentiation as "modern" or "postmodern." None of the two terms has any specific structural meaning. Thus the emergence of the term "postmodern" does not actually go along with a change in social structures, but with a change in semantics. It indicates a loss of trust in the traditional or "modern" self-descriptions of society, and here Luhmann's sympathy for post-modernity—if not for the term itself then at least for the "movement" attached to it—arises. Postmodern theory signals not a structural, but a semantic turn: the concepts of modernity that philosophers like Husserl and Habermas stand for are being over-come. In this sense, Luhmann himself is also a postmodernist. However, as opposed to a rather common attitude among post-modern writers, for him the breakdown of the theoretical assumptions and conceptual frameworks of modernity does not mean the end of "supertheory"—it marks exactly the contrary, namely, its true beginning. The postmodern diagnosis of the end of tradi-tional philosophy is correct, but this end does not mean that all we are left with is "the loose talk of French writers" (2000b, 45). It rather points to a fresh start for an inherently coherent and intelli-gible self-description of society, for a new theory for a new society: "Is this, after all, a postmodern theory? Maybe, but then the adherents of postmodern conceptions will finally know what they are talking about" (2000b, 46).

Possibly the most concise definition of the two aspects of post-modern theory that Luhmann attempts to connect with is found in *The Society of Society*: "renunciation of claims to unity and tran-sition towards radically differentialist concepts" (1997a, 555). These two aspects are, of course, tightly interconnected. With "renunciation of claims of unity" Luhmann refers to Lyotard's declaration of the end of metanarratives, a declaration that he often, and mostly approvingly, quoted.[62] In *The Society of Society* (1997a, 1144), he elaborates on the paradox contained in this dec-laration: It is itself a narrative, so if it is true, it is false. Luhmann therefore suggests a slight variation. The end of metanarratives indicates that the unity of society, or, for that matter, of the world, can no longer be stated as a principle, but only as a paradox. Implicitly agreeing with Lyotard, he concludes: "The final found-ing (*Letztfundierung*) on a paradox ranks as one of the central characteristics of postmodern thought. The paradox is the orthodoxy of our times" (1997a, 1144). With postmodern thought, metanarratives and their "claims of unity" come to an end. It is Luhmann's intention to replace them with "supertheory." This transition is conceptually equivalent to what was identified by Luhmann as the second characteristic of postmodern thought, it is "a transition towards radically differentialist concepts." At this juncture, Luhmann quite explicitly embraces two developments in contemporary theory: Derrida's (and de Man's [63]) deconstruction and various "trends in science" (1997a, 1146) that I will, for the sake of terminological convenience, summarize here as "techno-theory."

Luhmann's article "Deconstruction as Second-Order Observing" (1993a) is a fine example of how he connects his own theory with Derrida's. As the title of this article suggests, Luhmann basically attempts to demonstrate that deconstruction is a more or less immediate predecessor of the theory of second-order observation. Luhmann finds that deconstruction recommends "the reading of forms as differences, to look at distinctions without the hope of regaining unity at a higher (or later) level," and it "is deconstruction of the 'is' and the 'is not,'" because it "deconstructs the assumption of presence, of any stable relation between presence and absence, or even the very distinction between presence and absence" (1993a, 766). To Luhmann, deconstruction thus reflects on the radical contingency of any "ontological" claim, particularly in language. Deconstruction reveals that all statements of an "is" are based on distinctions. Presence is then, both ontologically and temporally, a construct of differentiation. It never gains total self-identity. As the deconstructionist of presence, Derrida implicitly recognizes the functional status of second-order observation. Every presence or "is" is the result of an observation that is different from it. What deconstruction can do is to again observe the observation that observes presence. It observes, from the position of second-order observation, the construction of the "is," and thereby deconstructs this construction. However, deconstruction—and this is most decisive—also applies to itself. Any deconstruction is itself subject to further deconstruction, there can be no final unity that eventually does away with difference. Deconstruction, as well as second-order observation, does not claim to be a privileged method of observation. What Luhmann says about second-order observation is also the case with deconstruction, "At the level of second-order observing, everything becomes contingent, including the second-order observing itself" (1993a, 769).

As stated above, both deconstruction and social systems theory represent "a transition towards radically differentialist concepts." They are therefore not only a part of so-called postmodernity, but of an even broader development. Luhmann diagnoses:

> The deconstruction of our metaphysical tradition pursued by Nietzsche, Heidegger, and Derrida can be seen as a part of a much larger movement that loosens the binding force of tradition and replaces unity with difference. The deconstruction of the ontological presuppositions of metaphysics uproots our historical semantics in a most radical way. This seems to correspond to what I have called the catastrophe of modernity, the transition of one form of stability to another. (1993a, 778)

And he concludes, "Seen in this way deconstruction will survive its deconstruction as the most pertinent description of the self-description of modern society (1993a, 780). Luhmann obviously accepted Derrida's deconstruction, so to speak, as a partner in crime. It is a parallel theory that contributes to the radical uprooting of an old semantics and the establishment of a more adequate self-description of contemporary society.

Deconstruction was not the only postmodern theory that Luhmann felt deeply related to. In connection with his envisioned transition to a new semantics, a new "form of stability," based on "radically differentialist concepts," he also links up with developments in the theory of science and technology. On the final pages of *The Society of Society* he says, "If one conceives of postmodern descriptions as operating within realms of self-produced indeterminacy, then one immediately sees parallels to other trends in science that deal with mathematics, cybernetics, systems theory, or with the characteristics of self-referentially and recursively operating machines" (1997a, 1146). Luhmann refers here to contemporary systems theory developments in fields that do not deal with social—or psychic or biological—autopoiesis, but with technological or machinic autopoiesis.[64] Luhmann's explicit departure from *Geisteswissenschaften* (the "sciences of the spirit") makes it perfectly appropriate to associate his theory of differentiation with similar ones outside the traditional boundaries of the humanities and social sciences.[65] If one were to trace this theoretical line back to philosophy, one would soon find authors such as Deleuze[66] and, via him, Hardt and Negri—with whom this study began. These are more than coincidental parallels, and it is quite interesting to see that in his later work Luhmann referred more and more frequently to Deleuze's concept of *sens* as an antecedent for his own usage of the term *Sinn*. This is done at the expense of the "humanist" Husserl to whom he usually attributed this term in his earlier works.[57] Obviously, it is not only the "radically differentialist concepts" and their nonhumanist approaches that Luhmann and contemporary "techno-theoreticians" have in common, they also share a departure from models of centrality and from the "trivial" cybernetics of steering by input/output. It would have certainly been interesting to see if Luhmann had further moved in this direction had he lived a few years longer.

Luhmann reflected more systematically on *science* than on technology—since, unlike technology, is a social system and consists of communication. Luhmann dedicated one of his lengthy monographic case studies to the analysis of this system (Luhmann 1990c). The outcome is at times very reminiscent of Thomas Kuhn's analysis of *The Structure of Scientific Revolutions*, although Luhmann refers only sporadically to this book (see, for instance, Luhmann 1990, 342). Both Kuhn and Luhmann look at science sociologically and historically. The evolution of science is not so much an evolution of the knowledge of objects, but the evolution of a certain type of communication about objects. An analysis of the history of science therefore becomes for both authors an analysis of the communicative production of truth.

15

Conclusion: From Metanarrative to Supertheory

Some philosophers are now only interested in the textual history of the discipline, others in fashionable topics such as postmodernism or ethics; still others present the predicament of any general view in a literary or feuilleton-like way; and, what is perhaps worst: the strive for precision that borders on pedantry. (Luhmann 1996b, 17)

Niklas Luhmann's relation to philosophy can, in my view, be compared to Hegel's relation to religion (as expressed in the *Phenomenology of Spirit*). For Hegel, religion was, with respect to its highest purpose, a thing of the past. It had reached its end as a satisfactory manifestation of the "spirit." Neither its semantics nor its general structure could be fully accepted any longer. Religion was in waiting, so to speak, for its *Aufhebung* ("sublation")—in the famous threefold sense of continuation, negation, and elevation—in philosophy. According to Hegel, it was time to replace religion as the most general type of world view with an altogether different type, namely, science, and the most profound and fundamental science was philosophy. Religion was not a system of knowledge, it did not work primarily with concepts, but with images and narratives (God, angels, salvation, sin). Its "essence" had to be expressed in a more self-reflective way, in a language and in a form that represented a higher understanding that was capable not only of describing the spirit "out there," but which would go a step further and be a self-description of general consciousness. With Hegel, it was time for religion to understand itself, and thus it would cease being religion and become philosophy, or in postmodernist terms: narrative would become metanarrative.

For Luhmann *philosophy* had become with respect to its highest purpose, a thing of the past. On many occasions, including his acceptance speech for the Hegel Prize, Luhmann pointed out that he did not see himself as a philosopher. He was, nominally, a sociologist and often called himself such. Still, his interest was not sociological "normal science" (and, accordingly, he often met stiff resistance in his own discipline), for he rather aimed at developing a general theory of society. His theory was to be nothing less than a "supertheory," a theory that would be of universal relevance. Luhmann did not believe that such a supertheory, or for that matter, theory itself, still had its home in philosophy. The attempts at metanarrative, having reached their peak, arguably, with Hegel, were no longer convincing. If "so-called postmodernity" had shown one thing, it was that there was no position from which one could claim to come up with a fundamental self-description of all descriptions. There was no privileged point from which a metanarrative could claim to be truly "meta-," to be truly beyond. Academically speaking, philosophers seemed to have become aware of this predicament and, for the most part, decided on one of the four options outlined in the quotation at the beginning of this section. Luhmann did not want to engage in any of these alternatives. Instead of giving up the attempt at a valid, general self-description, he took on the challenge of another *Aufhebung*, now not from religion to philosophy, but *from philosophy to theory*. Luhmann was no longer a philosopher, but I would claim, someone who attempted to continue, negate, and elevate philosophy's essential project.

What does the replacement of "metanarrative" with "supertheory" mean? Like the Hegelian metanarrative, Luhmann's supertheory claims to be thoroughly conceptualized and to return to its beginning—in other words, a coherent whole instead of a linear argument. Like a metanarrative, a supertheory also claims to be able to deal with practically everything. There is nothing that, on principle, it could not cover, be it God or a football game. Unlike a metanarrative, however, a supertheory is built around an ironic or self-ironic core. By including itself "wholly" (and not only its beginning) in itself, it acknowledges not only the general validity of itself, but also the self-dependency of this validity. A supertheory reflects on the fact that it and its validity are its own product—and is therefore absolutely *contingent*. What a supertheory says has to make general sense to it. But this sense itself is not general, it is contingent upon the theory that is constructing this horizon of sense in the first place. A supertheory is a theoretical endeavor, and there is nothing more to it. What it says is relevant only theoretically, only within its own confinements. In this way the claim for a supertheory is both utterly presumptuous and modest: it claims to surpass religious and philosophical attempts in regard to self-inclusiveness and universal validity. But at the same time, it says that this is only possible at the price of the acceptance of total contingency and, in the final analysis, becoming unnecessary. Supertheory does little outside of theory. With supertheory, the world does not become morally better, more rational, or spiritually complete. It only becomes more distinct.

Notes

¹ The philosophy department in which I am teaching recently had to develop a new minor in this field to please higher administrative demands.

² In *Social Systems* (1995a, 2) Luhmann also mentions machines as a fourth type of system. The systemic qualities of machines, however, are problematic. In his later writings, Luhmann sometimes mentions the (future) possibilities of machines, for instance, computers, to become self-referential autopoietic systems (see the last section in this book). At present, this stage does not yet seem to have been reached, and thus Luhmann confines his theory mostly to systems of life, consciousness, and communication. With respect to machines he writes very clearly: "A system is either autopoietic or not autopoietic. It cannot be a bit autopoietic. With regard to 'autos' it is clear that the operations of a system are either produced within the system or that they are, in important ways, predetermined by the environment, for instance through a programme on the basis of which a computer functions" (2002a, 116). Externally programmed machines are not autopoietic systems.

³ An example would be the ancient Chinese philosophy of Daoism. See Moeller (2003).

⁴ In his earlier publications, Luhmann had used Talcott Parsons's concept of systemic "interpenetration" to describe how systems can be closely tied to each other while being operationally closed. In his later works he more and more abandoned the Parsonian concept in favor of Maturana's.

⁵ Psychic and social systems also share the medium "sense," or *Sinn* in German. They are both sense-producing systems, see ch. 2 below.

⁶ According to Luhmann (2002a, 317) the term goes back to Robert Sears and became prominent by being used in Parsons and Shils (1951).

⁷ In some English translations of texts by Luhmann, the words "expression" and "utterance" are used for the German word *Mitteilung*.

I hesitate to use "expression" because it is associated with the expression of "thoughts" or "intentions." Similarly, "utterance" hints at the existence of something beyond communication, which is then uttered in communication. The term "announcement" is a bit more technical and does not necessarily imply a realm outside of communication coming to bear within it.

[8] For a more detailed discussion of this subject see ch. 14 below.

[9] See ch. 1, sec. a above.

[10] *Sinn* is usually translated into English as "meaning." I prefer "sense," first because it is etymologically closer to the German *Sinn* (used by Luhmann in connection to Edmund Husserl) and the French *sens* (as used by Gilles Deleuze to whom Luhmann also frequently referred, see ch. 14 below), and, secondly, because in English one can speak of "making sense," but not of "making meaning." "Making sense" conveys quite well the constructivist meaning that *Sinn* has in Luhmann's theory. *Sinn* is in his terminology an "intentional" *product* ("*making* sense") as opposed to something that a term or life can essentially "have" (*having* meaning).

[11] See ch. 12 below.

[12] Luhmann borrows the concepts of observation, distinction, and indication from George Spencer Brown's *Laws of Form.*

[13] See also ch. 9 below.

[14] Luhmann borrows this paradigmatically ambiguous expression from Heinz von Foerster (1981).

[15] See part 3 below.

[16] On this concept see von Foerster (1981).

[17] Interestingly enough, Buddhist philosophy—from ancient Indian origins to the contemporary Chinese revival of Tiantai-metaphysics by Mou Zongsan—seems to have dealt quite similarly with the same problem, albeit by mostly avoiding notions of subjectivity.

[18] See *Beyond Good and Evil*, 280.

[19] One may detect here a faint resemblance to Freud's famous dissection of the human psychic identity into three noncongruent and rather contradictory forces: the *id*, the *ego*, and the *super-ego*. The *id* has some similarities to the biological systems, the *ego* to the system of consciousness, and the *super-ego* to the social system. For Freud, however, the *id*, the *ego*, and the *super-ego* remain, in the final analysis, psychic phenomena. This is not the case with the different systemic realms of systems theory.

[20] Here, Luhmann seems to give an implicit explanation of brain death experiences. Being an operationally-closed autopoietic system, it is not surprising that consciousness can survive the organism—but it is empirically unsound to assume that it can survive it for more than a very short period.

[21] See Luhmann's article "Beyond Barbarianism" in the translation section of the present book.

[22] For analyses and criticisms of Luhmann's theory of ecological communication in English see: Miller (1994) as well as Peterson and Peterson (2000).

[23] See ch. 1, sec. b above.

[24] See p. 5 of the English translation.

[25] See p. 5 of the English translation.

[26] See p. 36 of the English translation.

[27] See p. 50 of the English translation.

[28] See p. 123 of the English translation.

[29] See p. 116 of the English translation.

[30] See p. 117–18 of the English translation.

[31] For analyses and criticisms of Luhmann's ethics in English see: Dallmann (1998) and Neckel and Wolf (1994). See also Luhmann (1994b).

[32] *Tractatus logico-philosophicus*, 6.42-6.522.

[33] See Moeller (2002) for a discussion of Luhmann's negative ethics—and of another negative ethics, the ethics of ancient Chinese Daoism.

[34] One should add: only in Europe. The historically much earlier invention of mechanical printing in China is a different case. Luhmann discusses the different social effects of the invention of the printing press in East Asia in *The Society of Society*, see Luhmann (1997a, 291).

[35] See also ch. 14 below for a brief discussion of Luhmann's relation to theories of technology.

[36] See Moeller (2002).

[37] Regarding this metaphor, Luhmann refers to V.O. Key Jr. (1961).

[38] This is the topic of the satirical movie *Wag the Dog*. As to the mutual dependency of mass media and politics (and as to the problem of "censorship") in the case of the first American Gulf War and its reporting, Luhmann (2000a, 8–9) explains: "All that censorship had to do was to operate according to the ways of the media; it had to contribute to achieving the desired construction and exclude independent information, that would hardly have been attainable anyway. Since the war was staged as a media event from the start and since the parallel action of filming or interpreting data simultaneously served military and news production purposes, de-coupling would have brought about an almost total loss of information in any case. So in order to exercise censorship, not much more was required than to take the media's chronic need for information into account and provide them with new information for the necessary continuation of programs. Thus, what was mainly shown was the military machinery in operation. The fact that the victims' side of the war was

almost completely erased in the process aroused considerable criticism; but most likely only because this completely contradicted the picture built up by the media themselves of what a war should look like."

39 See ch. 1, sec. b above.

40 Still, the mass media, unlike social systems theory, do not autologically "reflect" on their second-order observation. Or, as Luhmann (2000a, 119) puts it, "In the system itself, there is no final figure of the ambiguous 'observing system', no autological realization that whatever is true for observers is also true for the system that is observing them." Luhmann's theory and the mass media both operate as second-order observations, but of those two only Luhmann's theory practices second-order *cybernetics*.

41 See ch. 6 above.

42 Luhmann refers to a variety of psychological studies by Bartlett, Tolman, Abelson, and many others; see the notes to ch. 15 of *The Reality of the Mass Media* (Luhmann 2000a) for details.

43 1987, 377; translation modified.

44 These books, just as most other works by Luhmann (perhaps because of his antihumanism!?), do not include personal names, but only subjects in their indices. I traced the names myself and came up with these results.

45 In "Deconstruction as Second-Order Observing" Luhmann explains, "Operational closure seems to be the necessary *empirical* condition of observations." He further notes: "I underline *empirical* to insist that it is not a transcendental apriori in Kant's sense, based on the distinction (always distinctions!) between the empirical and the transcendental, the realm of causality and the realm of freedom. But it is a *condition of possibility* in Kant's sense, a condition of the possibility of observations" (1993a, 774; emphases in the original).

46 This relates to an earlier and more complex formulation of the same issue in *Social Systems*: "Kant began with the prejudice that plurality (in the form of sense data) is given and that unity must be constituted (synthesized). Only separating these aspects, thus posing complexity as a problem, makes the subject into a subject—indeed, into a subject of the connection between plurality and union, not only into a producer of synthesis. Systems theory breaks with Kant's point of departure and therefore has no need for a concept of the subject. It replaces it with the concept of self-referential systems. Then it can say that every unity used in this system (whether as the unity of an element, the unity of a process, or the unity of a system) must be constituted by the system itself and cannot be obtained from its environment" (1995a, 28; translation modified).

47 A very comprehensive analysis of Luhmann's conceptual shift from subject to system is presented in Habermas (1987, 368–85).

⁴⁸ Luhmann was extremely critical of the Kantian attempt to establish a practical philosophy grounded on rational principles—he called this flatly a "disaster" (1997a, 555). See ch. 4, sec. b, "Negative Ethics," above for a more detailed analysis of Luhmann's criticism of Kantian ethics.

⁴⁹ Interestingly enough, Luhmann expands this criticism quite broadly when he continues: "But this is not sufficient for answering the question of the observer. Even more of a failure are the presently fashionable replies: the language game pluralism of a Wittgenstein, the thesis of cultural relativism, or the plurality of discourses of so-called 'postmodernism'."

⁵⁰ Luhmann leaves it open whether Hegel corrected this failure in his *Logic*, which "would have to be further examined" (Luhmann 1988b, 27).

⁵¹ The German word "Geisteswissenschaften" ("humanities") literally means "sciences of spirit." Luhmann here clearly implies that theory has lost its home in the traditional humanities or philosophy. His explicit refusal to continue the conceptual tradition of terms of consciousness and subjectivity such as "Geist" is, of course, also a refusal of the conceptual tradition of the "human." Luhmann seems to deny a theoretical future for both *Geisteswissenschaften* and the humanities. This is in line with one of his main theoretical counterparts in Germany, the media theoretician Friedrich Kittler. One of Kittler's works (1980) is programmatically entitled "Exorcising the *Geist* out of the *Geisteswissenschaften*"(*Austreibung des Geistes aus den Geisteswissenschaften*).

⁵² One of the most common criticisms of Luhmann is, quite expectedly, the claim by Neo-Marxists or leftist intellectuals, that in fact Marx was right in ascribing a central role to the economy and that Luhmann makes a decisive error in not recognizing its dominance in capitalist society. See, for instance, Wolfe (1998, 146) who describes Luhmann's unwillingness "to place the economic system at the center of social organization" and his conception of society as "one of horizontal functionally differentiated systems in which no system . . . exerts a centrifugal force" as a "fundamental weakness."

⁵³ The term in German is *humanistische Unterfütterung*. In Luhmann (1998, 6) it is erroneously translated as "humanist malnourishment."

⁵⁴ As explained above, I prefer to translate the German word *Sinn* as used by Husserl and Luhmann as "sense" instead of "meaning." Recent English translations of Husserl also tend to do this.

⁵⁵ See ch. 14 below for Luhmann's later tendency to trace his usage of this term back to Deleuze rather than to Husserl.

⁵⁶ See the text on "barbarism" included in this book.

⁵⁷ See the use of this expression in Luhmann's text on "barbarism" included in this book.

58 See de Berg and Schmidt (2000) for extensive documentation of the reception of Luhmann's theory in Germany.

59 Rainald Goetz, *celebration. 90s. nacht. pop* (Frankfurt/Main: Suhrkamp, 1999), 126–27.

60 The other three concern Luhmann's eclecticism, his lack of empirical research, and an alleged lack of regard for local or historical variations.

61 See section 4, III in *Social Systems* (Luhmann 1995a) for a discussion of Husserl and Derrida.

62 See *Social Systems* (Luhmann 1995a, 431) as a relatively early example.

63 When it comes to deconstruction, Luhmann usually refers to Jacques Derrida, sometimes, however, he also refers to Paul de Man (see, for instance, *The Society of Society*, Luhmann 1997a, vol. I, notes 31, 153, 235 and vol. II, notes 243, 407).

64 In a note to this passage, Luhmann refers to Küppers and Paslack, 1991.

65 See above. Luhmann's relation to "techno-theoreticians," such as the German thinker Friedrich Kittler, is well presented in Winthrop-Young (2000). See also Maresch and Werber (1999) for more materials on this aspect.

66 On Deleuze and Luhmann see Wolfe 1998, 116–27.

67 In *The Society of Society* (1997a, 44, note 44), for instance, Luhmann first introduces the concept of *Sinn* by referring to Deleuze's *Logique du sens* and not to Husserl. Throughout the book he repeatedly refers to Deleuze and his notion of *sens* (1997a, 49, note 54; 140, note 184; 682, note 161; 1040, note 286; 1100, note 372).

References

Baraldi, C., G. Corsi, and E. Esposito. 1997. *GLU. Glossar zu Niklas Luhmanns Theorie sozialer Systeme.* Frankfurt/Main: Suhrkamp.

Baudrillard, J. 1995. *The Gulf War Did Not Take Place.* Sydney: Power.

Bechmann, G., and N. Stehr. 2002. "The Legacy of Niklas Luhmann." *Society* 39, no. 2: 67–75.

Bloom, A. 1991. *The Republic of Plato.* New York, London: Basic Books.

Champion, T. C., ed. 1989. *Centre and Periphery: Comparative Studies in Archaeology.* London, Boston: Unwin Hyman.

Chase-Dunn, C., and T. D. Hall, eds. 1991. *Core/Periphery Relations in Precapitalists Worlds.* Boulder: Westview Press.

Chomsky, N. 2001. *9-11.* New York: Seven Stories Press.

Clam, J. 2002. *Was heißt, sich an Differenz statt an Identität orientieren? Zur De-ontologisierung in Philosophie und Sozial-wissenschaft.* Konstanz: UVK.

Dallmann, H.-U. 1998. "Niklas Luhmann's Systems Theory as a Challenge for Ethics." *Ethical Theory and Moral Practice* 1: 85–102.

de Berg, H., and J. Schmidt, eds. 2000. *Rezeption und Reflexion. Zur Resonanz der Systemtheorie Niklas Luhmanns außerhalb der Soziologie.* Frankfurt/Main: Suhrkamp.

Deleuze, G. 1969. *Logique du sens.* Paris: Éditions de Minuit.

Foucault, M. 1966. *Le mots et les choses.* Paris: Edition Gallimard.

Kittler, F. 1980. *Austreibung des Geistes aus den Geistes-wissenschaften. Programme des Postsstrukturalismus.* Stuttgart: Uni TB.

Habermas, J. 1987. *The Philosophical Discourse of Modernity. Twelve Lectures.* Translated by Frederick Lawrence. Cambridge, MA: MIT Press.

Hardt, M., and A. Negri. 2001. *Empire.* Cambridge, MA: Harvard University Press.

Herman, E. S., and N. Chomsky. 1988. *Manufacturing Consent: The Political Economy of the Mass Media.* New York: Pantheon Books.

Husserl, E. 1954. "Die Krisis des europäischen Menschentums und die Philosophie. " *Husserliana*, vol. 6 (The Hague): 314–48.

Kepplinger, H. M. 1998. *Die Demontage der Politik in der Informationsgesellschaft.* Freiburg: Alber.

Key Jr., V. O. 1961. *Public Opinion and American Democracy.* New York: Knopf.

King, M., and C. Thornhill. 2003. *Niklas Luhmann's Theory of Politics and Law.* New York: Palgrave Macmillan.

Krause, D. 1999. *Luhmann-Lexikon.* Stuttgart: Enke.

Küppers, G., and R. Paslack, 1991. "Chaos—Von der Einheit zur Vielheit: Zum Verhältnis von Chaosforschung und Postmoderne." *Selbstorganisation* 2: 151–67.

Luhmann, N. 1975. *Macht.* Stuttgart: Enke. (English translation: 1979. *Trust and Power.* Translated by Howard Davis, John Raffan, and Kathryn Rooney. Chichester, Toronto: Wiley, 1979.)

———. 1977. *Funktion der Religion.* Frankfurt/Main: Suhrkamp. (English translation: 1984. *Religious Dogmatics and the Evolution of Society.* Translated by Peter Beyer. New York: Edwin Mellen Press.)

———. 1980. *Gesellschaftsstruktur und Semantik. Studien zur Wissenssoziologie der modernen Gesellschaft*, vol. 1. Frankfurt/ Main: Suhrkamp.

———. 1981. *Gesellschaftsstruktur und Semantik. Studien zur Wissenssoziologie der modernen Gesellschaft*, vol. 2. Frankfurt/ Main: Suhrkamp.

———. 1982a. *Liebe als Passion. Zur Codierung von Intimität.* Frankfurt/Main: Suhrkamp. (English translation: 1986. *Love as Passion: The Codification of Intimacy.* Translated by Jeremy Gaines and Doris L. Jones. Cambridge, England: Polity Press.)

———. 1982b. *The Differentiation of Society.* New York: Columbia University Press.

———. 1986a. *Ökologische Kommunikation. Kann die moderne Gesellschaft sich auf Gefährdungen einstellen?* Opladen: Westdeutscher Verlag. (English translation: 1989. *Ecological Communication.* Translated by John Bednarz, Jr. Chicago: University of Chicago Press.)

———. 1986b. "The Individuality of the Individual: Historical Meanings and Contemporary Problems." In *Reconstructing Individualism: Autonomy, Individuality, and the Self in Western Thought*, edited by T. C. Heller, M. Sosna, and D. E. Wellbery, 313–54. Stanford: Stanford University Press.

———. 1987. "The Morality of Risk and the Risk of Morality." *International Review of Sociology* 3: 87–101.

————. 1988a. *Die Wirtschaft der Gesellschaft.* Frankfurt/Main: Suhrkamp.

————. 1988b. *Erkenntnis als Konstruktion.* Bern: Benteli.

————. 1989. *Gesellschaftsstruktur und Semantik. Studien zur Wissenssoziologie der modernen Gesellschaft,* vol. 3. Frankfurt/Main: Suhrkamp.

————. 1990a. *Essays on Self-Reference.* New York, Oxford: Columbia University Press.

————. 1990b. *Paradigm lost: Über die ethische Reflexion der Moral: Rede anläßlich der Verleihung des Hegel-Preises 1989.* Frankfurt/Main: Suhrkamp. (English translation: 1988. "Paradigm Lost: On the Ethical Reflection of Morality." Speech on the Occasion of the Award of the Hegel Prize. Translated by David Roberts. *Thesis Eleven* 29: 82–94.)

————. 1990c. *Die Wissenschaft der Gesellschaft.* Frankfurt/Main: Suhrkamp.

————. 1993a. "Deconstruction as Second-Order Observing." *New Literary History* 24, no. 4: 763–82.

————. 1993b. "The Code of the Moral." *Cardozo Law Review* 14: 995–1009.

————. 1993c. *Das Recht der Gesellschaft.* Frankfurt/Main: Suhrkamp. (English translation: 1985. *A Sociological Theory of Law.* Translated by Elizabeth King and Martin Albrow. London, Boston: Routledge.)

————. 1994a. "How Can the Mind Participate in Communication?" In *Materialities of Communication,* edited by H. U. Gumbrecht and K. L. Pfeiffer, 371–87. Translated by William Whobrey. Stanford: Stanford University Press.

————. 1994b. "Politicians, Honesty and the Higher Amorality of Politics." *Theory, Culture and Society* 11: 25–36.

————. 1995a. *Social Systems.* Translated by John Bednarz, Jr. and Dirk Baecker. Stanford: Stanford University Press. (Translation of: 1984. *Sozial Systeme: Grundriß einer allgemeinen Theorie.* Frankfurt/Main: Suhrkamp.)

————. 1995b. *Die Kunst der Gesellschaft.* Frankfurt/Main: Suhrkamp. (English translation: 2000. Translated by Eva M. Knodt. *Art as a Social System.* Stanford: Stanford University Press.)

————. 1996a. *Protest.* Frankfurt/Main: Suhrkamp.

————. 1996b. *Die neuzeitlichen Wissenschaften und die Phänomenologie.* Vienna: Picus.

————. 1996c. "The Sociology of the Moral and Ethics." *International Sociology* 11, no. 1: 27–36.

———. 1997a. *Die Gesellschaft der Gesellschaft.* Frankfurt/Main: Suhrkamp.

———. 1997b. "Globalization or World Society: How to Conceive of Modern Society?" *International Review of Sociology* 7, no. 1: 67–79. (http://www.libfl.ru/LuhmannlLuhmann2.html.)

———. 1997c. "Limits of Steering." *Theory, Culture, and Society* 14, no. 1: 41–57.

———. 1997d. "Politik, Demokratie, Moral." In *Normen, Ethik und Gesellschaft*, edited by Konferenz der Deutschen Akademie der Wissenschaften. Mainz: Philipp von Zabern.

———. 1998. *Observations on Modernity.* Translated by William Whobrey. Stanford: Stanford University Press. (Translation of: 1992. *Beobachtungen der Moderne.* Opladen: Westdeutscher Verlag.)

———. 1999. *Gesellschaftsstruktur und Semantik. Studien zur Wissenssoziologie der modernen Gesellschaft*, vol. 4. Frankfurt/ Main: Suhrkamp.

———. 2000a. *The Reality of the Mass Media.* Translated by Kathleen Cross. Stanford: Stanford University Press. (Translation of: 1996. *Die Realität der Massenmedien.* 2nd ed. Opladen: Westdeutscher Verlag.)

———. 2000b. "Why Does Society Describe Itself as Postmodern?" In *Observing Complexity: Systems Theory and Postmodernity*, edited by W. Rasch and C. Wolfe, 35–49. Minneapolis, London: University of Minnesota Press.

———. 2002a. *Einführung in die Systemtheorie.* Heidelberg: Carl-Auer-Systeme.

———. 2002b. *Theories of Distinction: Redescribing the Descriptions of Modernity.* Edited by William Rasch. Stanford: Stanford University Press.

Luhmann, N., and J. Habermas. 1971. *Theorie der Gesellschaft oder Sozialtechnologie: Was leistet die Systemforschung?* Frankfurt/Main: Suhrkamp.

Luhmann, N., and K. E. Schorr, eds. 1998. *Reflexionsprobleme im Erziehungssystem.* Frankfurt/Main: Suhrkamp. (English translation: 2001. *Problems of Reflection in the System of Education.* Translated by Rebecca A. Neuwirth. Berghahn: Waxmann Verlag.)

Lyotard, J.-F. 1979. *La condition postmoderne: Rapport sur le Savoir.* Paris: Éditions de Minuit.

Maresch, R., and N. Werber, eds. 1999. *Kommunikation Medien Macht.* Frankfurt/Main: Suhrkamp.

Maturana, H. R. 1981. "Autopoiesis." In *Autopoiesis: A Theory of Living Organizations*, edited by M. Zeleny, 21–32. New York: North-Holland.

Miller, M. 1994. "Intersystemic Discourse and Co-ordinates Dissent: A Critique of Luhmann's Concept of Ecological Communication." *Theory, Culture, and Society* 11: 101–21.

Mingers, J. 1995. *Self-Producing Systems: Implications and Applications of Autopoiesis.* New York: Plenum Press.

Moeller, H.-G. 2002a. "The Revolutionary Insignificance of the Internet. Or: Why Neither Chinese Wall Papers nor the Internet Make People Speak." In *Cultural Attitudes towards Technology and Communication*, edited by F. Sudweeks and C. Ess, 95–209. Murdoch: School of Information Technology, Murdoch University.

———. 2002b. "Moral und Pathologie. Niklas Luhmann, die Massenmedien und der Daoismus." In *Komparative Ethik. Das gute Leben zwischen den Kulturen*, edited by R. Elberfeld, 303–18. Cologne: Edition Chora.

———. 2003. *Laozi.* Freiburg: Herder.

Neckel, S., and J. Wolf. 1994. "The Fascination of Amorality: Luhmann's Theory of Morality and Its Resonances among German Intellectuals." *Theory, Culture, and Society* 11: 69–99.

Parsons, T., and E. A. Shils, eds. 1951. *Toward a General Theory of Action.* Cambridge, MA: Harvard University Press.

Peterson, T. R., and M. J. Peterson. 2000. "Ecology According to *Silent Springs's* Vision of Progress." In *And No Birds Sing: Rhetorical Analyses of Rachel Carson's Silent Spring*, edited by C. Waddell, 73–102. Edwardsville: Southern Illinois University Press.

Rasch, W. 2000. *Niklas Luhmann's Modernity: The Paradoxes of Differentiation.* Stanford: Stanford University Press.

Rasch, W., and C. Wolfe, eds. 2000. *Observing Complexity: Systems Theory and Postmodernity.* Minneapolis, London: University of Minnesota Press.

Rowlands, M., M. Larsen, and K. Kristiansen, eds. 1987. *Centre and Periphery in the Ancient World.* Cambridge, New York: Cambridge University Press.

Spencer Brown, G. 1969. *Laws of Form.* London: Allen & Unwin.

Varela, F. 1997. "Autopoiese, strukturelle Kopplung und Therapie. Fragen an Francisco Varela." In *Lebende Systeme*, edited by F. B. Simon, 148–64. Frankfurt/Main: Suhrkamp.

Viskovatoff, A. 1999. "Foundations of Niklas Luhmann's Theory of Social Systems." *Philosophy of the Social Sciences* 29, no. 4: 481–516. (http://www.libfl.ru/LuhmannlLuhmann2.html)

von Foerster, H. 1981. *Observing Systems.* Seaside, CA: Intersystems.

———. 1985. "Entdecken oder Erfinden: Wie läßt sich Verstehen verstehen?" In *Einführung in den Konstruktivismus*, edited by H. Gumin and A. Mohler, 27–68. Munich: Piper.

Winthrop-Young, G. 2000. "Silicon Sociology, or, Two Kings on Hegel's Throne? Kittler, Luhmann, and the Posthuman Merger of German Media Theory." *Yale Journal of Criticism* 13, no. 2: 391–420.

Wolfe, C. *Critical Environments: Postmodern Theory and the Pragmatics of the "Outside."* Minneapolis, London: University of Minnesota Press.

Glossary of Key Terms

autopoiesis (*Autopoiesis*). This concept was coined by the evolutionary biologists Humberto Maturana and Francisco Varela. It literally means "self-production" (derived from Greek, *autos* means "self" and *poiesis* means "production") or, by extension, "self-reproduction." It was originally used to explain the emergence and reproduction of cells and bodily systems such as the immune system. Luhmann uses it to explain the emergence and reproduction of social systems.

The concept of autopoiesis is about origin and proliferation and can be contrasted with concepts of creation or invention. In Luhmann's sociology the concept makes it possible to conceive of society in terms of the reproduction of life rather than in terms of mechanical manufacturing.

The Confucians in ancient China, for instance, believed that social institutions had been invented by certain sage rulers at the beginning of civilization. For Luhmann, however, social systems cannot be traced back to an external act of creation or invention. Politics, for example, was not invented by a person or a group of people, rather it emerged as a type of communication and proved to be capable of continuing itself. Over time, political structures, organizations, and programs took shape within this communication system, recently, for instance, as parties, ideologies, and elections. These, again, are not invented or created outside the system and then inserted into it, like a new kind of computer chip is inserted into an old computer, but are internal developments within the system. An autopoietic system is its own product; a computer is not. A good example of the autopoietic reproduction of communication systems would be committees. Once committees exist within an organization (such as a university, for instance), they typically proliferate into more and more committees. The autopoietic growth of a social system is its self-proliferation.

An autopoietic system produces and reproduces the elements of which it consists through the elements of which it consists.

blind spot (*blinder Fleck*). The term is metaphorical and articulates a simple fact. Whenever we look at something, there is something behind our back. In order to see something we have to establish a point of view. This point of view is that which we cannot have in view whenever we have something in view. Of course, that point of view can be viewed from another point of view, but this point of view again has its own blind spot, and so on *ad infinitum*.

This concept expresses the idea that the very possibility of cognition always presupposes some conditions of cognition, which are themselves not cognized. There can never be a cognition or a knowledge of everything. The world as a whole can never be seen—it cannot be described by any theory, philosophy, or theology. Thus seeing and cognition are based on not-seeing or not-cognizing. Paradoxically, seeing (something) is based on blindness (of something else).

code (*Code*). Luhmann uses this term to designate the basic distinction that a social system applies in order to communicate. Codes are binary, they consist of a positive and a negative value. The legal system, for instance, operates on the basis of the code or distinction legal/illegal. The mass media system operates on the basis of the code information/noninformation.

If a car drives by on Main Street then the legal system can observe this event on the basis of the code legal/illegal: Is the speed of the car legal or illegal? Does the driver have a license? This can be communicated in a courtroom. The mass media will observe the same event on the basis of the code information/noninformation. If the Queen was a passenger in the car, then that will be information and reported in the news; alternatively, if the passenger was you or me, then this will be noninformation.

cognition (*Erkenntnis*). Luhmann uses this term in a very broad sense. Cognition occurs not only in minds but in all kinds of systems: living systems (cells or immune systems can have cognition of enzymes or viruses), psychic systems (minds, of course, have cognition) and social systems (the news mass media, for instance, have cognition of foreign wars).

Observing systems are cognitive systems. If a system observes something, it has cognition. Cognition is always a construction by means of the operational possibilities of the system. The legal system cognizes everything in legal terms. These terms are not constituted by what is cognized, but by the system itself. Smoking in a restaurant is not legal or illegal as such. It only becomes legal or illegal because it is observed by the legal system in terms of the legal code.

Biologically speaking, how we see the world depends on the cognitive capacities of our eyes and brains to produce images. Cognition is always a construction by an observing system.

communication (*Kommunikation*). Communication is the type of operation that society consists of. All social systems are communication systems and vice versa. Communication is not limited to communication by language. One can, for instance, also communicate with money (in the economy) or with grades (in the education system).

For Luhmann, communication does not consist of a substantial "transfer" of information from sender to receiver. The sender does not hand anything over to the receiver. Instead, Luhmann suggests a purely functional model. Communication consists of the three moments or "selections" of: announcement, information, and understanding. Something has to be announced; in other words, something has to be said or written, or a grade has to be assigned. If you stay silent, no communication will arise. An announcement has to have some informative value. The words have to have a meaning, the grade has to be either A, B, C, D, or F. G does not work. The information has to be understood, too. If no one listens or if the student is not familiar with the grading scale, then communication does not function. You can sing in the shower, but that is not communication.

Luhmann's purely functional definition of communication can be illustrated by his peculiar conception of "understanding." It does not matter if what is understood is understood "correctly." It is only important that the "selection" of understanding takes place at all. When teaching a large class, there are usually many students who "get it wrong." But this does not mean that there is less communication in these cases. Luhmann holds that, typically, understanding is misunderstanding without understanding the "mis" (Luhmann 2000a, 97).

connectivity (*Anschlussfähigkeit*). Connectivity of operations is the key for the self-establishment of an autopoietic system. Operations of the same kind have to be capable of connecting to each other so that a network of operations arises. In communication systems, communication has to be able to be continued. If not, the system stops reproducing itself and thus ceases to exist.

Mass media communication, for instance, is obviously going "to be continued." Today's news continues yesterday's and tomorrow's will continue today's. For the mass media system to preserve itself it has to be able to continue itself by its own means. News has to be continued with news, not with legal or economic communication. Similarly, in the economy, payments have to be continued with more payments. If I receive money, I have to be able to spend it again, otherwise there would be no connectivity and the system would collapse.

constructivism (*Konstruktivismus*). Luhmann subscribes to a "radically constructivist" concept of society—and not only of society. All cognition is, for him, construction.

The term "constructivism" can be contrasted with the term "realism." A simple realism would argue that reality is as it is and that it can be cognized and represented as such. A constructivist view of reality posits that "reality" only emerges as a result of a construction by an observer. This does not mean that there is no reality, but that it emerges as a reality only when it is observed. When a tree falls down in a forest and no one is there to witness the fall, the tree still falls. But its sound is real only if it is heard. And how it sounds depends on the ears of those who hear it. The reality of the sound of the falling tree is a construction by its observer. There is not one "realistic" sound that could be heard as such. In order to be able to hear the sound, one must have a cognitive system that is able to construct sound perception.

contingency (*Kontingenz*). Contingency means that things could have been otherwise. For Luhmann, this is an important concept because observations and distinctions, cognitions and selections are typically contingent. That specific distinctions in society emerge, such as the distinction legal/illegal, or government/opposition, is not dictated by human nature but is the result of a social evolution that could have taken another course. One may well imagine a society that does not apply these distinctions and codes. Native American societies, for instance, did not have a legal or political system in the modern sense. That we now use specific legal and political distinctions and that they play such an important role in our society is entirely contingent upon the specific social circumstances of our times.

The concept of contingency complements Luhmann's constructivism. That we observe in specific ways, that we have specific social systems, and draw specific distinctions (such as legal/illegal) is not because these distinctions are "out there," but because specific systems evolved. The distinctions are made by an observing system and are thus contingent upon it. Other distinctions could have been drawn.

The term "double contingency" (*doppelte Kontingenz*) is often used in reference to the fact that the selections in communication are contingent upon two sides. Luhmann (2002a, 318) gives the example of a warship and a trading vessel that reach an island from different sides. The warship wants to attack the trading vessel. They both have two options: they can either turn southwards or northwards to sail around the island. If the trading vessel turns north, the warship will do the same—but if the warship does so, the trading vessel will turn south.

cybernetics (*Kybernetik*). Cybernetics, as a scientific concept, can be traced back to the mathematician Norbert Wiener who published a book entitled *Cybernetics* in 1948. As conceived by Wiener, cybernetics analyzes control or steering systems (like the term "government," "cybernetics" is derived from the Greek word for "steering") and communication systems that operate on the basis of processing information. These systems can be biological or physiological systems such as the nervous system, but also mechanical or electronic systems such as machines or computers. "Cyberspace" is the realm that is established by processing information.

Luhmann aligns himself with the "second-order cybernetics" associated with Heinz von Foerster, which presents a new development in cybernetics that evolved in the 1960s. Second-order cybernetics differs from "first-order cybernetics" by reflecting on the fact that what is the case for the cybernetic systems that are observed is also the case for the observers of those systems since they themselves also operate as observing systems. Von Foerster uses the term "observing systems" in its double sense, which indicates that a system that observes can, at the same time, be observed. Luhmann is referring to the principle of second-order cybernetics when he says: "In this way, the epistemologist becomes him/herself a rat in the labyrinth and has to reflect on the position from which he/she observes the other rats" (Luhmann 1988b, 24).

environment (*Umwelt*). In Luhmann's systems theory, a system can only exist within an environment that is other than itself. The terms "system" and "environment" are complementary. A system never exists as such but only in distinction from something else. In society, the different social systems are within one another's environment. For the economy, for instance, other systems such as politics or the legal system are in the environment. Since the environment is relative to the system, there is not one single environment, but a different environment for every system. There is also a nonsocial environment for social systems. As communication systems they depend, for instance, on the existence of minds and bodies. Psychic and living systems exist in the environment of social systems. The environment as such is not a specific system, it is everything other than the system for which it is the environment.

evolution (*Evolution*). Systems are not static; they are dynamic and evolve. New systems emerge. In society, for instance, the mass media did not always exist. On a larger scale, functional differentiation, that is, social differentiation into different function systems, did not always exist. Earlier societies were differentiated differently. Native American society, for instance, was a tribal society in which different, but similar social "segments" (the tribes) coexisted; there were no function systems in the modern sense. The shift from one dominant type of social differentiation to another is an evolutionary, but not a teleological, shift. In the process of evolution, structures change, so within evolution there is a "structural drift."

Evolutionary processes can be processes of "co-evolution." Different systems, particularly when they are structurally coupled, evolve co-dependently. The evolution of psychic systems and that of social systems influence one another. How society develops has an effect on how humans think. How human thinking develops, in turn, has an effect on how society evolves.

functional differentiation (*funktionale Differenzierung*). Luhmann argues that societies' types of "differentiation" can distinguish them. "Differentiation" means the way in which society is divided. The basic type of differentiation in a tribal society, for instance, is "segmentary"—different tribes are segments that exist next to each other and the basic dividing lines in society are those between the tribes. In a society based on "stratified differentiation," the basic divisions are those between the social strata or classes. Here it matters not so much which tribe you belong to, but rather whether you are an aristocrat or a peasant. Today's "world society" is dominated by functional differentiation, that is, by the dividing lines between the different function systems, namely, the economy, politics, the education system, and so forth. One studies in the education system, shops in the economy system, and watches TV in the mass media system.

information (*Information*). Luhmann uses the term "information" in two different senses. First, it is one of the moments or "selections" that constitute communication (see the entry for "communication" above). Second, the distinction information/noninformation is the basic code of the mass media. Everything that is selected and reported or broadcast by the mass media is information. Once it is broadcast, it turns into noninformation. Today's news is information. Tomorrow, tomorrow's news will be information and today's news noninformation.

irritation (*Irritation*). "Irritation" is the somewhat problematic translation of a German word that is spelled identically. In German, however, to irritate (*irritieren*) does not mean "to bother" or "to annoy," but, more precisely, "to distract" or "to perturb." "Perturbation" might therefore be a less misleading translation.

Luhmann uses this somewhat odd term to avoid the implication of any "simplistic" cause-effect or input-output pattern when it comes to describing how two or more systems affect each other. Operationally-closed systems cannot immediately interfere with one another's operations. They do not function like a pop machine that will invariably give you the same drink every time you insert a dollar and push a certain button. What happens in one system does not, in the strict sense, "cause" a specific reaction in another system, but rather triggers certain developments or "resonance." When, for instance, the mass media system reports a political scandal, it does not cause one and only one specific effect in the political system. It rather "perturbs" the political system so that, most likely, politics cannot go on as if nothing had happened. It cannot be predicted with certainty whether the president will step down or whether he will lose the next election. This is decided in the political system alone.

medium (*Medium*) **and form** (*Form*). Luhmann's specific usage of the term "medium" (and its conceptual brother "form") is borrowed from a rather obscure theorist of the early twentieth century named Fritz Heider. A medium consists of elements in "loose coupling" that can take on forms in "strict coupling." Sand on the beach, for instance, is a medium that exists in loose coupling. If you walk on it, then there will be footprints; in other words, the medium will take on specific forms in strict coupling. Another, more scientific example is the medium of light. In strict coupling, the forms of visible objects can be perceived. A medium provides for an extremely wide but nevertheless limited realm of forms to take on shape.

The most general medium for Luhmann is "sense" (see entry below). It is a medium that is used in communication as well as in thought. It is shared by psychic and social systems. A thought or a gesture is a specific "form" that the medium of sense can take on.

Language, too, is a medium. Every word or sentence is a "form" that language takes on. Language, as well as the more general medium of "sense," can be used in social as well as in psychic systems. We can communicate and think in language. Language is therefore a medium for communication.

In communication, there are media of dissemination (*Verbreitungsmedien*) such as writing, print, TV, or radio.

Luhmann also speaks of "symbolically generalized communication media" (*symbolisch generalisierte Kommunikationsmedien*). Like all media, these specific media serve the function of increasing the likelihood of successful communication. The symbolically generalized medium of money, for instance, makes economic communication more likely to succeed. By spending money—and thus by communicating economically—one allows those who receive the money to continue economic communication by spending it again. Without money, it is difficult to have an economy as a social system. Other such media are power in politics and truth in science.

memory (*Gedächtnis*). Luhmann uses this term primarily in a metaphorical sense. Memory, for him, is not (so much) the individual's mental capacity to literally keep things in mind, but the social capacity to produce general knowledge, to produce that which is known to be known about in society.

For Luhmann, social memory is not a "storehouse," it does not keep alive what was in the past, but provides options for the present. The mass media system illustrates this very well. The mass media do not store all the facts of the past, but they present what is presently known to be known about. They perform a daily production of memory. They inform society of what is fashionable, ethical, funny, and so forth on a daily basis.

observation (*Beobachtung*). An observation is an act of distinguishing (*Unterscheiden*) and indicating (*Bezeichnen*). In order to watch TV, for instance, you have to be able to observe the TV screen; that is to say, you have to be able to distinguish the screen from the flowerpot behind it. An observational distinction indicates that which is observed and does not indicate that which is not observed. When you watch TV, you can indicate what is happening in the movie, but you cannot indicate what is happening in the flowerpot behind it.

Luhmann is particularly interested in "observing systems." Social systems are observing systems. The legal system, for instance, observes what is happening by applying the legal code. It can, for instance, observe a car crash in legal terms. It will observe if the driver was intoxicated, if she had a valid license, and so on. A doctor will look at other aspects such as which inner organs have been injured or how much blood was lost. By observing something, that which is observed and indicated is distinguished from what is not observed and indicated.

Observing systems can in turn be observed. This is second-order observation, namely, the observation of an observation. Many contemporary social systems observe in the mode of second-order observation. When we watch TV coverage of a war, we do not watch the war but the observation of the war by the TV station or network. In the science system, academics typically observe how other academics have observed. This book, for instance, observes Luhmann's observations.

operation (*Operation*). Operations are what systems consist of; operating is what systems do. Different types of systems consist of different types of operations. Psychic systems, for instance, think and feel, whereas living systems consist of biological operations, and social systems communicate. Your mind consists of the thoughts you think and the emotions you feel. Legal communication consists of what is said in the courtroom and what is written in legal documents.

Autopoietic systems are operationally closed. No other system can interfere in their operations. They can only continue their operations by themselves. No one, for instance, can think or feel for you; there is no immediate external interference possible. The same is true, according to Luhmann, for social systems. You can only continue economic communication by further economic communication. You can only buy something by spending money, not by watching a commercial on TV or by making a political speech.

Operational closure goes along with cognitive openness. By being operationally closed and differentiated from its environment, a system can have cognition of its environment. Once a system has reached operational closure, it can observe the environment in its own terms. Once the legal system has closed itself operationally, it can observe everything as being either legal or illegal.

re-entry (*re-entry*). Luhmann borrows this term from the logician George Spencer Brown. Formally speaking, it designates the re-entry of a distinction into what is distinguished.

A system distinguishes itself from its environment and thereby constitutes itself as a system. This is true for a cell or a mind as well as for social systems. Once a system has established itself by distinguishing itself from the environment, it can reintroduce this distinction within itself. It can, so to speak, become aware of this distinction. In the mass media system, for instance, the editors of a newspaper can reflect on the possible effects that exposing a political scandal will have on the political system as well as on their own newspaper. These effects will, of course, be different. When the editors discuss their decision at a meeting, they will do this by re-entering the distinction between the mass media and the political system into the mass media system.

The concept of re-entry is closely related to the concepts of self-reference and other-reference (see below).

self-reference and **other-reference** (*Selbstreferenz, Fremdreferenz*). These concepts are rather simple although they sound very technical. A system that has distinguished between itself and its environment and, by way of re-entry, has copied this distinction into itself, can, quite naturally, distinguish between itself and its environment. It can therefore refer to itself or to its environment when communicating (if it is a communication system). The mass media system can refer to itself by apologizing for an error in a news report or by sending a spot that advertises a new program. These would be instances of self-reference. It can also refer to its environment, for instance, to politics, when reporting on an election, or to sports, when showing a hockey game. These would be instances of other-reference.

semantics (*Semantik*). Semantics is the general term for the specific ways in which society produces meaning or how it makes sense of things. Intimate relationships, for instance, are nowadays usually made sense of in terms of passion, love, trust, partnership, and so on. These notions constitute the semantics of love. This was not always the case. In other societies, intimate relationships were not so much based on love but on economic or other social considerations. In Chinese society, for instance, the phrase "I love you" was not used between partners until recently. The semantics of intimacy was different in China—but now, under the influence of the global mass media system and other social factors, the semantics has changed. In politics, to give another example, the currently dominant semantics is centered on notions such as democracy, liberty, and freedom. This semantics can be viewed as a product of Western modernity.

Semantics usually changes with a change in social structures such as the family and politics. When the family structure changed to the modern Western type of "core family," semantic changes in love were introduced. Structural changes often precede semantic changes. It usually takes time for a new semantics to develop when structural changes have taken place. In politics, for instance, there has been a shift from national structures to global structures. Still, the traditional semantics of democracy and liberty that were developed in connection with the nation-state continue to dominate public discourse.

sense (*Sinn*). When Luhmann uses the German term *Sinn* in his earlier works, he often refers back to Edmund Husserl's phenomenological concept of *Sinn*. In his later works he sometimes refers to the (French) notion of *sens* developed by Gilles Deleuze. Because of these connections, it is more appropriate to translate Sinn as "sense" than as "meaning" (as most other translators do).

Sense is the "universal medium" (*Universalmedium*) shared by psychic and social systems. Both thinking and communicating operate on the basis of sense. Relating back to Luhmann's understanding of the term "medium" (see entry above), we may say that sense is the "sand" into which each concrete thought or communication imprints a specific footprint. A specific sense is therefore always produced or constructed. It is not already "out there," but a production of psychic or social systems. Minds and social systems "make sense" in the literal meaning of this phrase.

Since the making of sense is always a construction by a system, it can also be defined as a selection within a horizon of what is possible. By thinking this specific thought (for instance, "I should leave now, otherwise I will drink too much") we do not think another thought ("I should stay longer because it's getting fun") that is equally within the horizon of the possible.

society (*Gesellschaft*). Society, for Luhmann, is not constituted by human beings, but by communication. It consists, functionally speaking, not of you and me, but of the different communication systems, such as politics, the economy, and education. These are, to use a biological metaphor, the "organisms" that constitute society. Just as a body consists of the biological "operations" that go on within it (blood circulation, metabolism, brain activity) and a psychic system consists of the thoughts and feelings in the mind, society consists of the communications that go on within it—of what is said, printed, and broadcast.

structural coupling (*strukturelle Kopplung*). In his later works, Luhmann increasingly uses the term "structural coupling" (borrowed from the biologist Humberto Maturana) to replace the term "interpenetration" (borrowed from the sociologist Talcott Parsons). In his *Introduction to Systems Theory*, Luhmann states that he is not sure whether it is necessary to distinguish at all between these two concepts (Luhmann 2002a, 268).

The concept of structural coupling serves the purpose of explaining how systems that are autopoietic and operationally closed (see above) can still be connected and, what is more, how they "existentially" depend on each other. Without the existence of bodies and minds, that is, of biological and psychic systems, there cannot be communication. The dead cannot speak. This interdependence of different operationally-closed systems is called "structural coupling." Structural coupling not only means that the existence of two systems is codependent, but also that what happens in one system will have a great effect on the other system—these systems will co-evolve (see the entry for "evolution" above). Our minds are structurally coupled with social systems. Our thinking develops or evolves along with social evolution.

There are also numerous structural couplings between social systems. The mass media system is structurally coupled with, for instance, the political system and the economy. News serves the function of structurally coupling the mass media with politics, and advertising structurally couples the mass media with the economy.

system (*System*). Luhmann is particularly interested in autopoietic and operationally-closed systems (see entry above). Such systems can be biological (cells, the immune system), psychic (the mind), or social (the economy, politics). As a social theorist, Luhmann focuses largely on social systems. Social systems consist of communication, not of people (see entry for "society" above). Within the social system as a whole there are numerous "subsystems" such as the mass media, the economy, and politics. These subsystems are function systems because they all have their specific function within society.

The concept of the system is relative to the concept of an environment (see entry above). A system is always within an environment. The two concepts are interdependent.

unmarked space (*unmarked space*). This term is closely related to the concept of the "blind spot" (see entry above). Luhmann borrowed it from George Spencer Brown.

Like the "blind spot," the concept of the "unmarked space" expresses the idea that whenever something is observed, something else remains unobserved. In order to focus on something, other things have to be excluded from sight.

The mass media system, for instance, tends to observe scandals and thereby tends to ignore what is not scandalous.

APPENDIXES

Translations
of Key
Luhmann Texts

Appendix A

From
The Society of Society
NIKLAS LUHMANN

Translated by Hans-Georg Moeller

In the currently dominant conception of society, . . . epistemological obstacles[1] are found in the form of four connected and mutually supporting assumptions, namely the supposition

1. that a society consists of concrete human beings and relations between human beings;[2]

This excerpt is a translation of pages 24–35 of *Die Gesellschaft der Gesellschaft* (Frankfurt/Main: Suhrkamp, 1997). Used by permission of Suhrkamp.

[1] Luhmann refers to a concept of Gaston Bachelard and to Bachelard's study *La formation de l'esprit scientifique; Contribution à une Psychanalyse de la connaissance objective* (Paris: 1947). He also refers to Anthony Wilden, *Systems and Structure: Essays in Communication and Exchange* (London: 1980), 205ff.— Trans.

[2] Actually, the problem connected with this supposition was clear to sociology from the beginning. In Durkheim's work, for instance, one reads: "la société n'est pas une simple somme d'individus, mais le système formé par leur association représente une réalité spécifique qui a ses caractères propres." ('Society is not a simple sum of individuals, but the system formed by their association which represents a specific reality with its own characteristics.') In *Les règles de la méthode sociologique*, 127, quoted from the eighth edition (Paris, 1927). The unclarity only consisted in determining the specificity of this association. Because: can one conceive of association without the associated? As long as this theoretical gap is not filled, there will always be relapses. Even newer types of systems theory that introduce the concept of self-reference sometimes work with the assumption that social systems consist of human beings. To quote a philosopher, a physicist, a biologist, and a sociologist: cf. Pablo Navarro, *El holograma social: Una ontología de la socialidad humana* (Madrid, 1994); Mario Bunge, "A Systems Concept of

2. that society is consequently constituted or at least integrated by consensus between human beings, correspondence of their opinions, and complementarity of their goal definitions;

3. that societies are regional and territorially limited units, so that Brazil is a different society from Thailand, the US different from Russia, and then, supposedly, also Uruguay a different society from Paraguay;

4. and that therefore societies can be observed from the outside just as groups of people or territories.

The assumptions made in (1) through (3) prevent a more exact conceptual definition of the object of society. Tradition had described "the human being" (as distinct from animals) with the help of distinctions (such as reason, rationality, will, imagination, emotion, morality) that, as transmitted ideas, were revised but not specified, neither empirically nor in their manner of operation. These distinctions seemed to be sufficient for mutual clarifications,

---

Society: Beyond Individualism and Holism," *Theory and Decision* 10 (1979): 13–30; Humberto R. Maturana, "Man and Society," in *Autopoiesis, Communication and Society: The Theory of Autopoietic System in the Social Sciences,* ed. Frank Benseler, Peter M. Hejl, and Wolfram K. Köck (Frankfurt, 1980), 11–13; Peter M. Hejl, *Sozialwissenschaft als Theorie selbstreferentieller Systeme* (Frankfurt, 1982). Such a confusion, however, makes it impossible to precisely indicate the operation that performs the autopoiesis in the respective cases of organic, neurophysiological, psychic, and social systems. Typically, the concession is still made that the whole human being is not part of the social system, but only insofar as the human being interacts with or actualizes sense-identical (parallel) experiences with others. See for instance Peter M. Hejl, "Zum Begriff des Individuums—Bemerkungen zum ungeklärten Verhältnis von Psychologie und Soziologie," in *Systeme erkennen Systeme: Individuelle, soziale und methodische Bedingungen systemischer Diagnostik,* ed. Günter Schiepek (Munich, 1987), 115–54, esp. 128. This does not help the case, but worsens it, because then one can less than ever before indicate which operation processes this "insofar" distinction—obviously neither cellular chemistry nor the brain nor consciousness nor social communication, but if need be, an observer who distinguishes accordingly. The typical escape route is then to not discuss at all the operations that constitute the system, but rather to construct the theory only on the level of "variables" whose selection, however, can no longer be theoretically controlled. As an example see B. Abbott Segraves, "Ecological Generalization and Structural Transformation of Sociocultural Systems," *American Anthroplogist* 76 (1974): 530–52.

but they did not allow for a clarification of their neurophysiological basis.[3] As "anthropological" concepts they offer even fewer possibilities for being connected with the distinction psychic/social. Difficulties only increase when one gives up these distinctions and instead ascribes importance to the possibility of scientific and empirical labeling. Human individuality starts to become an issue in the mid-eighteenth century—and thus significantly earlier than the industrial revolution—with respect to the peculiarities of the associations and emotional activity of the singular being.[4] This leads to the breakdown of the traditional cosmological placement of humans within an order that assigns them a rank and a lifestyle. Instead, the relation between the individual and society now becomes a problem. In whatever way the traditional concepts, especially "reason," are continued, obviously not everything that individualizes humans (if anything) belongs to society. Society does not weigh exactly as much as all human beings together, and its weight also does not change with every birth and every death. It is not reproduced by an exchange of macro-molecules within singular human cells or with the exchange of cells within the organisms of individual people. Society is therefore not a living thing. The neurophysiological processes of the brain that are inaccessible even for consciousness will not be seriously regarded as social processes; and the same is true for all that goes on in the form of perceptions and sequences of thoughts within the actual area of awareness of a single consciousness. In this situation, Georg Simmel, who attributed this problem to modern individualism, preferred to sacrifice the concept of society over the sacrificing of the sociological interest in individuals. Aggregated concepts—and this was what the problem looked like to him—were altogether problematic and should be replaced by relational theories. After all, astronomy too was not a theory of "the firmament."[5]

---

[3] On the basis of contemporary research one presumably has to declare that that which is experienced and designated as reason, will, emotion, etc., is a subsequent interpretation of already present results of neurophysiological operations, and thus seems to serve their further conscious treatment, but is by no means the decisive origin of human behavior. See for instance Brian Massumi, "The Autonomy of Affect," *Cultural Critique* 31 (1995): 83–109.

[4] Cf. James L. Clifford, ed., *Man versus Society in Eighteenth Century Britain* (Cambridge, 1968).

[5] Thus in: *Über soziale Differenzierung*, quoted from Georg Simmel, *Gesamtausgabe*, vol. 2 (Frankfurt, 1989), 109–295, esp. 126.

When it is no longer evident that society naturally consists of concrete human beings to whom solidarity is prescribed as *ordinata concordia* and, especially, as *ordinata caritas*, a theory of consensus can be a conceptual replacement. This leads to a revitalization and radicalization of the teachings of a social contract in the seventeenth and eighteenth century.[6] The concept of nature, at least for Hobbes, is reduced to something external to society, while others (Pufendorf, for example) reduce it to an inclination to make contracts. This theory, however, had to be discarded promptly. It was juridically circular and thus it could not explain the inviolable and irredeemable mandatoriness of the contract, and historically, in the face of quickly increasing historical knowledge, it could only be treated as fiction lacking any explanatory merit. Its heirs in the nineteenth century were theories of consensus and conceptions of solidarity and integration that drew on consensus. Once more thinned out, there finally comes the call for the "legitimacy" of those institutions that can enforce order even when consensus is lacking, i.e., in the face of resistance. Sociology begins in this way with Emile Durkheim and Max Weber. Notwithstanding all concessions to reality, integration based on consensus was and continues to be the principle by which society is identified as a unity or, one could say, as an "individual."

This body of teaching, however, collapses when one asks more persistently how consensus, in a psychologically realizable sense, should be possible at all, and also how a sufficiently harmonized direction of coordinated expectations should be attained in this way. Max Weber had already made a first step when he reduced the problem to type-coercion (*Typenzwang*) as the condition for understanding any sense that is meant socially. Parsons, here more a follower of Durkheim, sees the solution in a consensus of values that reacts to increasing differentiation with increasing generalization. With these built-in renunciations of concretizations one can take into account the individuality of actors as well as the complexity of the social system, but one also addresses that which can still be called society with such thinned-out concepts that the theory can only work in regard to sufficiently dense parts of society. Moreover, it would have to be denied, consequently and against

---

[6] In regard to contemporary discussions cf. A. Carbonaro and C. Catarsi, eds., *Contrattualismo e science sociali* (Milan, 1992).

better knowledge, that social conflicts, dissention, and deviance belong to society, or one would have to be content with assuring that even this would imply some kind of consensus (for instance, in regard to the offense factor of specific insults). Conversely, John Rawls feels himself forced to postulate a "veil of ignorance" for the initial situation of a contract-like establishment of principles of justice, a veil that prevents individuals from knowing their position and interests[7]—and he thus assumes individuals without individuality. But this is obviously only another way of making the paradox of any recourse to origins invisible.

Another consequence of the assumption that individuals materialize society through their actions lies in the hypothesis that structural problems of society (for example, too intense differentiation without sufficient integration, or contradictions in the structures and behavioral demands of society) appear as *individual abnormal behavior* and that this is how they can be empirically observed. With respect to this, the classic work is Durkheim's book on suicide[8]—but instability of families, criminality, drug abuse, and the retreat from social engagement could also be listed. Individuals may choose their own personal reactions to "anomy," but basically these cases represent functionally equivalent attitudes that, to the sociologist, serve as indicators of problems with roots that have to be traced back to society. But even if such connections can be statistically established, the question of why individuals show symptoms of social pathologies, or why they do not, remains. One would have to reflect primarily on the structural problems of society that are prone to be transformed into individual abnormal behavior. The ecological problems at the very least make it imperative to face this question.

All this should make sociology doubt whether it should ascribe any role at all to consensual integration in *constituting* society. It would suffice to assume that communication, in the course of its own continuation, produces identities, references, its own-values (*Eigenwerte*), and objects—no matter what individual human beings experience when they are confronted with these.[9]

---

[7] See in German translation, John Rawls, *Eine Theorie der Gerechtigkeit* (Frankfurt, 1975), 27 ff.

[8] See Emile Durkheim, *Le suicide: Etude de sociologie* (Paris, 1897).

[9] This interpretation is crucially inspired by the "social behaviorism" of George

This line of argument converges with a version of systems theory that (in regard to concept and reality) relies on the distinction between system and environment. If one proceeds from the system/environment distinction, one has to assign the human being, as a living and consciously experiencing being, either to the system or to its environment. (A division into two or three and a corresponding distribution is empirically impossible.) If one would consider human beings a part of the social system, then this would force one to interpret the theory of differentiation as a theory of the distribution of human beings—be it into strata, nations, ethnicities, or groups. In this way one would end up with a blatant contradiction of the concept of human rights, especially the concept of equality. Such a "humanism" would consequently fail as a result of its own concepts. The only remaining possibility is to conceive of the human being altogether—with body and soul—as a part of the environment of society.

The fact that a humanist concept of society is still supported,[10] even in the face of all the evident discrepancies and in spite of the well-known philosophical criticisms of anthropological founda-

---

Herbert Mead who, nevertheless, is continuously reintegrated into the common consensus theory and thus misunderstood in regard to his decisive point. Still, Mead is interested primarily in the production of permanent objects as stabilizers of the behavior that flows from event to event, and only secondarily in the fact that such objects can also function as symbols of conforming views—but as symbols precisely because consensus can never be controlled under the condition of the simultaneous event-likeness of experience and action. His focus is mainly on a theory of time and only secondarily on a social theory based on necessary fictions. The question is how sociality is possible at all under the condition of simultaneousness ("incontrollability"); and the answer is: through the constitution of objects as "own-values" (*Eigenwerte*) of behavior that flows in time. See most importantly the essay "Eine behavioristische Erklärung des signifikanten Symbols," and (referring to Whitehead) "Die Genesis der Identität und die soziale Kontrolle," both quoted from the German translation in George Herbert Mead, *Gesammelte Aufsätze*, vol. 1 (Frankfurt, 1980), 290–98 and 299–328. For a criticism of social contract theories that uses the concept of a *quasi-objet* see also Michael Serres, *Genese* (Paris, 1982), 146 ff. What Serres has in mind, however, is only the exceptional case that symbolic objects are specifically constructed to enable social coordination. The discussion in the text above goes far beyond this.

[10] Thus today in an especially focused (and exactly therefore rather untypical) manner: Günter Dux, *Geschlecht und Gesellschaft: Warum wir lieben: Die romantische Liebe nach dem Verlust der Welt* (Frankfurt, 1994).

tions,[11] is presumably due to the fear that otherwise one would lose any basis for evaluating society and thus any right to demand that society should be "humane." But even if this were the case, one should still, in the first place, be able to determine independently of those criteria what society makes out of human beings and why this happens.

Similarly evident objections speak against the territorial concept of society.[12] More than ever before, worldwide interdependencies interfere in all details of social processes. If one were to ignore this, one would have to retreat to a concept of society defined on the basis of domination or cultural nostalgia. One would have to make the concept of society dependent on arbitrarily drawn borders between states[13] or one would have to relate it—in spite of all the implied vagueness—to a unity of a regional "culture," to language, or to similar things. All important conditions for further development would then be left to other concepts such as the "global system."[14] For Anthony Giddens, the concept of society is synonymous with the nation-state and therefore nearly superfluous; consequently there is only talk of the "world-embracing"

---

[11] See Martin Heidegger, *Sein und Zeit*, 6th ed., §10 (Tübingen, 1949), 45ff. for the best-known case.

[12] The objections are certainly familiar and especially fostered by authors who start with the assumption of individuals/persons. See, for instance: Tim Ingold, *Evolution and Social Life* (Cambridge, England, 1996), 119 ff. These objections are, however, typically presented against a systems theoretical concept of society—as if systems theory was supposed to indicate spatial and temporal borders of systems. We thus have a twofold problem, namely (1) to explain why sociologists do not take notice of evident reservations against the territorial concept, and (2) to formulate systems theory as a foundation of social theory in such a way that it is not dependent on time and space in its definition of the borders of society.

[13] A sharp critic of this concept of a state society points out that according to it in the present century the Federal Republic of Germany, the German Democratic Republic and Austria would have been at various times one society and several societies. See Immanuel Wallerstein, "Societal Development, or Development of the World-System," *International Sociology* 1 (1986): 3–17, reprinted in *Globalization, Knowledge and Society*, edited by Martin Albrow and Elisabeth King (London, 1990), 158–71. On the other hand, Wallerstein especially holds on to a regional understanding of society and otherwise only speaks of a "world-system."

[14] See only Wilbert E. Moore, "Global Sociology: The World as a Singular System," *American Journal of Sociology* 71 (1966): 475–82; Roland Robertson, *Globalization: Social Theory and Global Culture* (London, 1992).

character of modern institutions.[15] However, the concept of the global system would thus be the true successor of that which was traditionally called "society" (*societas civilis*). If one ties the concept of society to premises centered on domination or values, then one is underestimating not only the complexity and variety of communicational compounds, but also, and primarily, the degree to which the "information society" communicates worldwide without a center and in a connectionist fashion through networks—a trend which in the foreseeable future will certainly be amplified by computerization.

Humanist and regionalist (national) concepts of society no longer qualify as serious theoretical competitors; they only survive in linguistic conventions. Thus today's sociological theory leaves an ambiguous, two-faced impression: it makes use of concepts that have not let go of their connection with tradition, but still allows questions that may go beyond the traditional scope.[16] It employs the concept of action as a fundamental notion so that it can deal with event-like final units—and to be able to remind us over and over again that only individual human beings can act. It forms the concept of the global system in order to acknowledge globalizations—and to leave the concept of society to the level of the nation-state. In the case of a humanist concept of society, too much is included; in the case of a territorial one, too little. In both cases clinging to such unusable concepts might be explained by the wish to think of society as something that can be observed from the outside. With these concepts, however, one is forced to rely on an epistemology that has long become obsolete—an epistemology that proceeds from the distinction thought/being, understanding/thing, subject/object and that thus can only conceive of the real process of cognition on the one side of the distinction as reflection. At least since the linguistic turn in philosophy this has

---

[15] Thus in: *The Consequences of Modernity* (Stanford, CA: 1990), 12ff, esp.16; furthermore 63 ff. in detail on "globalization."

[16] See in this regard (as concerns its application in the development of cybernetic systems theory) the concept of a "skeuomorph" taken from archeological anthropology in N. Katherine Hayles, "Boundary Disputes: Homeostasis, Reflexivity, and the Foundations of Cybernetics," *Configurations* 3 (?) (1994): 441–67; "A Skeuomorph is a design feature, no longer functional in itself, that refers back to an avatar that was functional at an earlier time" (446).

been abandoned—notwithstanding all the logical problems that one trades in by the switch to a "naturalized epistemology" (Quine). But why is it so hard for sociology to make this turn too?

Perhaps the reason is that it knows society too well (or at least that it has to pretend this) to find it attractive to conceive of itself as a part of its reality. One wants to oppose society or at least to remain in resolute resignation in the Frankfurt style. But this would also, and especially then, be possible if sociology would recognize its own theory as a part of its object. It could copy the lightness and indirectness of the facial expression with which Perseus beheaded Medusa (and sociology too is only about heads).[17] Remember that theology invented the figure of the devil for the purpose of observing God and His creation, and that the great Sophists of the nineteenth century, like Marx, Nietzsche, and Freud, have been characterized by their "incongruent perspectives."[18] Thus, the problem rather seems to have to do with the logical and theoretical difficulties that one has to face when one works, as linguistics says, with "autological" concepts and forces oneself to discover oneself in one's object—and to discover sociology as a self-description of society. In its final consequences this leads to a situation in which one can hold on to the idea that reality can be recognized by the resistance it offers, but has to admit that such resistance against communication can only be achieved through communication. If one could accept this, the subject/object distinction could thus be "deconstructed,"[19] and the hidden foundation of the dominating epistemological obstacles would be taken away. Then, one could let the humanist and regionalist conceptual traditions collapse under their own uselessness.

Given the present understanding of science, sociology can hardly refrain from the claim to explain phenomena of social reality. This again requires that the phenomena that are to be explained are distinguished, and that the characteristics by

---

[17] This is suggested by Italo Calvino in his *Lezioni Americani: Sei propost per il prossimo millenio* (Milan, 1988), 6f. See also Niklas Luhmann, "Sthenographie," *Delfin* X (1988): 4–12, also in Niklas Luhmann et al., *Beobachter: Konvergenz der Erkenntnistheorien?* (Munich, 1990), 119–37.

[18] Kenneth Burke, *Permanence and Change* (New York, 1935).

[19] See only Paul de Man, *The Resistance to Theory* (Minneapolis, 1986); formulated in the terminology of language and text.

which they are distinguished are pointed out as precisely as possible. *What-is*-questions such as: what is a company?, what is a social movement?, what is a city?, already require, simply as questions, the indication of essential characteristics, i.e., essentialist concepts that today are no longer grounded in nature but in the methodological demands of scientific research. Therefore it has to be asked: *how* is sociology supposed to formulate a theory of society if it cannot indicate *what* it is looking for with such a concept?

Note, however, that with this type of *what*-question sociology is brought to a state of permanent restlessness, *i.e., that it establishes itself as an autopoietic system.* There can be no final answer to such questions, no fixed point beyond the reach of further research, but only the observation of which effects the various conceptual decisions have. In the mode of second-order (self-) observation, i.e., in the mode of constructivist epistemology, all the provided characteristics are thus dissolved again so that one can see both their necessity for the conduction of research and their contingency. They are, so to speak, self-determinations to experiment with; they are research programs that are indispensable but exchangeable, if it is at all about the distinction between truth and falsity.

In the broad field of interdisciplinary studies today there is an ample supply of research that accounts for this situation, for instance, the explanation of all kinds of cognition on the basis of the operational closure of cognitive systems; or the mathematics of nonlinear functions and of the prognosis of the unpredictable called chaos theory; or the evolutionary theory of the accidental initiation of structure formations. We will, when necessary, make use of these. In the case of sociology, especially, these desiderata contribute to a theory of society, since with society sociology is given an object that always has already produced by itself that which research needs as the determination of its object (or as essential characteristics). It can therefore only be the question *how* this fact can be accounted for by determining *what* the concept of society is to designate.

The following investigations venture this transition to a radically antihumanist, a radically antiregionalist, and a radically constructivist concept of society.[20] Of course, they do not deny that

---

[20] One can, of course, deny that the expectations of a theory of society can be

human beings exist, and they also do not deny the stark differences in living conditions in the different regions of the earth. They only abstain from inferring from these facts a criterion for the definition of society and a determination of the limits of the corresponding object. And it is exactly this abstention that makes it possible to recognize normative and evaluative standards for dealing with human beings—for instance, human rights or communication norms oriented towards understanding in the Habermasian sense—and, finally, the attitudes towards the developmental differences between regions as society's own products instead of assuming that they are regulative ideas or components of the concept of communication. The preliminary question still remains: how does society induce itself to make this and other topics critical?

Nietzsche had already (in *On the Use and Disadvantages of History for Life*) rebelled against his contemporaries' dependency on history and diagnosed their ironic if not cynical consciousness by pointing out: it no longer works in this way, but it does not work in any other way either. This diagnosis may still be accurate, but instead of irony one rather finds a theoretically helpless predicament. Therefore it does not help if one opts for life instead of history and ties life to the ability to forget. The suggestion for today is instead to make better use of the theoretical resources that are actually available—not least for the sake of restoring the relation to history and the semantic burdens inherited from it.

---

fulfilled in this way. Thus Thoman Schwinn, "Funktion und Gesellschaft: Konstante Probleme trotz Paradigmawechsel in der Systemtheorie Niklas Luhmanns," *Zeitschrift für Soziologie* 24 (1995): 196–214. But then what is expected as a theory of society should be more precisely indicated and *justified*.

Appendix B

Cognition as Construction
NIKLAS LUHMANN

Translated by Hans-Georg Moeller

I

It is an old rhetorical technique: when assertions cannot be proven or are hard to prove, amplify the assertion. Thus in late Latin rhetoric, one goes from virtue to *true* virtue; in today's politics there is a demand for *real* reforms. One finds in today's stores *naturally pure* fruits. And the latest fashion in epistemology is called "*radical* constructivism." The more such amplifiers are added, the more suspicion is aroused. The more constructivism distinguishes itself from other epistemologies by naming itself "radical," the more one will therefore doubt if this theory has now (for the first time) found a solution to the problem of cognition, and even whether it has done its homework properly. Those who remember what Kant (in regard to Descartes) called "problematic idealism,"[1] will find it hard to discern what is principally new about what radical constructivism says.

One understands how it comes to a self-designation as radical: in fact there are weaker, undecided yes/but versions of constructivism. One takes note of all arguments that seem to lead toward this direction, but then one says that one should not express oneself so harshly, that cognition could not be understood as exclusively constructive, because, after all, one would have to assume some kind of relation to reality.[2]

This is a translation of a work originally published as *Erkenntnis als Konstruktion* (Bern: Benteli, 1988). Used by permission of Veronika Luhmann-Schröder.
[1] *Kritik der reinen Vernunft*, 274f.
[2] See, for instance, Michael A. Arib and Mary B. Hesse, *The Construction of Reality* (Cambridge, England, 1986).

It is well known that Kant had accordingly inserted a recantation in the second edition of the *Critique of Pure Reason* in which, in an unclear manner, he at least weakened, if not abandoned, the position reached in the transcendental aesthetics.[3] Recantations of this kind are, however, not very convincing; they are only symptoms of insufficiently grasped problems. One could consequently close the file. If epistemology cannot offer any solutions, it also has no problems anymore. It can then either declare itself content or it can deal with empirical research. The question is whether the situation warrants this recantation.

If one pays attention to how the problem of epistemology is formulated, one can in fact discover a radicalization. The tradition of epistemological idealism was about the question of the unity within the difference of cognition and the real object. The question was: how can cognition take notice of an object outside of itself? Or: how can it realize that something exists independently of it while anything which it realizes already presupposes cognition and cannot be realized by cognition independently of cognition (this would be a self-contradiction)? No matter if one preferred solutions of transcendental theory or dialectics, the problem was: how is cognition possible *in spite of* having no independent access to reality outside of it. Radical constructivism, however, begins with the empirical assertion: cognition is only possible *because* it has no access to the reality external to it. A brain, for instance, can only produce information because it is coded indifferently in regard to its environment, i.e., it operates enclosed within the recursive network of its own operations. [4] Similarly one would have to say: communication systems (social systems) are only able to produce information because the environment does not interrupt them. And following all this, the same should be self-evident with respect to the classical "seat" (subject) of epistemology: to consciousness.

---

[3] I am referring to the section "Refusal of Idealism" and especially to the proposition: "The mere, but empirically (!) determined consciousness of my own existence proves the existence of the objects (!) (and thus not only of something, N.L.) in the space (!) outside of myself." (274ff.)

[4] Compare Heinz von Foerster, "Entdecken oder Erfinden: Wie läßt sich Verstehen verstehen?" in *Einführung in den Konstruktivismus*, ed. Heinz Gumin and Armin Mohler (Munich, 1985), 27–68.

Obviously, radical constructivists view this step from "in spite of being impossible" to "because impossible" as a liberating radicalization that enables one to leave behind two thousand years of useless reflections.[5] I do not want to doubt the importance of this step from *in spite of* to *because,* and neither will I doubt the necessity for establishing a new epistemological foundation. But one wants to know more precisely what we gain with this step from *in spite of* to *because*; and here we are only at the beginning of a development that is as yet foreseeable only in vague patterns.

Constructivism could achieve a novelty effect if it would pursue the question of how *uncoupling* (in other words: indifference, closure) is *possible.* The *theory of the epistemological subject* never got to this question because it always had to deal with the paradoxical demand to find out by *introspection* how *others* relate to the *world.*[6] It could concede that there is no direct access to the experience of other subjects, but by going back to the factuality of one's own consciousness one should at least be able to find out the principles by which, in the other's consciousness, the objects of the world fall into order. The theory of the subject therefore had to presuppose a common—or at least a commonly observable—world and thus was prevented from conceiving of the *uncoupling* of each singular cognitive system as the *condition* of cognition. But the transition to a *theory of the epistemological object* does not help either (no matter if the cognizing object is described physically, biologically, psychologically, or sociologically). This transition does not succeed because the reduction of the description of cognition to the goings-on of the described object would again jump across the problem of uncoupling.[7] We

---

[5] Thus with admirable boldness Ernst von Glasersfeld, *Wissen, Sprache und Wirklichkeit: Arbeiten zum radikalen Konstruktivismus* (German translation: Braunschweig, 1987).

[6] That "intersubjectivity" is only a word for this problem, but not a solution should be clear. But where there is no solution, there is no problem either; and the newer social phenomenologists thus proceed from intersubjectivity as if it was a fact. See only Rochard Grathoff and Bernhard Waldenfels, *Sozialität und Intersubjektivität* (Munich, 1983).

[7] Compare Arne Ness [Naess], *Erkenntnis und wissenschaftliches Verhalten* (Oslo, 1936), 193 ff., with the demand to deduce all propositions regarding an external situation from descriptions of the processes within the "inner functional circuit" of the observed organism—which at first sounds very constructivist.

therefore suggest replacing the distinction between subject and object by the distinction between system and environment. This distinction remains similar to classical formulations of the problem insofar as it begins with a distinction and then lets one side re-enter the other. It overtakes classical formulations of the problem, because it revises both the subjective and the objective theory. It can ask the question about *uncoupling* by closure as a question about the differentiation (*Ausdifferenzierung*) of systems, and it can replace the premise of a common world by a theory of the observation of observing systems (second-order cybernetics).

II

We assume that all cognizing systems are real systems within a real environment, or in other words: that they exist. This is naive—as it is often objected.[8] But how should one begin if not naively?[9] A reflection on the beginning cannot be performed at the beginning, but only by the help of a theory that has already established sufficient complexity.[10]

The question, how are systems able to produce cognition within an environment? can then be reformulated as the question, how can systems uncouple themselves from their environment? or, with Heinz von Foerster: how is closure by enclosing possible? To merely pose this question means to suppose very sharp limitations of, i.e., highly selective conditions for, such an event. The self-isolation of a cognizing system—a cell, an immune system, a brain, a consciousness, a communication system—does not lead to a free choice of operations which thereby would become possible. The opposite is the case. Any observer of a system that closes itself for cognition can recognize sharp limitations of what is then possible. In any case, there is no arbitrariness in the real world. The supposition of randomness instead always means: observe the system that

---

[8] For example by Danilo Zolo, "Autopoiesis: Critica di un paradigma conservatore," *MicroMega* 1 (1986): 129–73.

[9] It is, just to note this down, equally naive (albeit a more common naivety) to proceed from the subjectivity of consciousness and to avoid asking the question, whose consciousness?

[10] See the relation between distinction/indication as "form" and "re-entry" of the form into the form in George Spencer Brown, *Laws of Form*, 2nd ed. (London, 1971).

you think to be working at random; and then you will see that your assumption was wrong. Arbitrariness is, from this perspective, nothing but a term for the directive, observe the observer.

Because, how is closure possible?—only by a system's production of its own operations and by their reproduction within the network of their recursive anticipations and recourses. The going-on itself creates the difference between system and environment. Maturana has called this "autopoiesis"; but Lyotard too comes, from linguistics, to the same results with concepts such as *phrase, enchainment, differend*.[11] Systems theory, however, makes it possible to formulate the result with particular clarity. No system can operate outside of its own borders, and neither can a cognizing system. These reflections leave it still open whether all operations of autopoietic systems should be called "cognition" or only those of a specific kind which then would have to be defined more precisely. Maturana opts for congruency under the provision that the concept of cognition also takes into account that autopoiesis—even though it is blind—is performed within a realm of interaction. This is distinguished from a concept of observation that is defined by the command of language.[12] I for one would like to understand the concept of cognition in a narrower way and proceed from a concept of observation that is defined on the basis of the concepts of distinction and indication.[13] What is supposed to be achieved in this way will become clear in the following.

Accordingly, cognition is manufactured by operations of observing and by the recording of observations (description). This includes the observation of observations and the description of descriptions. In any case an observation of the distinction takes place and, depending on the distinction, the indication of something. The concept is indifferent in regard to the system's type of autopoiesis, i.e., indifferent to the form of operation that may be life, consciousness, or communication. It is also indifferent with

---

[11] See especially Jean-François Lyotard, *Le differend* (Paris, 1983). Lyotard, however, rejects (orally) the interpretation of *le differend* as system/environment difference.

[12] Compare Humberto R. Maturana, *Erkennen: Die Organisation und Verkörperung von Wirklichkeit. Ausgewählte Arbeiten zur biologischen Epistemologie* (Braunschweig, 1982), 39ff, 34 f. and passim.

[13] Here I rely on the basic operation distinction/indication in George Spencer Brown's works, but without the intention to develop a calculus of formal logic.

respect to the type of recording (memory); it may be biochemical fixations, but it may also be written texts. The observing and describing itself, however, always has to be an operation that is capable of autopoiesis, i.e., of the performing of life or actual consciousness or communication, because otherwise it could not reproduce the closure and difference of the cognizing system; it could not take place "in" the system. This concept, however, does not demand that all operations of the respective system are observing/describing operations; and it also does not demand that the operations which are observations/descriptions can only be observed as observations/descriptions.

With this conceptual framework that conceives of distinguishing and the thereby possible/compelled indicating as the specific characteristics of cognition it is also determined how the uncoupling from an environment and thus the closure of cognizing systems has to be understood. Cognition is different from an environment because the environment contains no distinctions, but simply is as it is. In other words, the environment contains no otherness and no possibilities. It happens as it happens. An observer may find out that there are other observers in the environment. But he/she can only find this out if he/she distinguishes these observers from what they observe—or from events in the environment that he/she does not indicate as observing. In other words: everything that can be observed is the observer's own accomplishment (*Eigenleistung*), including the observing of observers.

Thus there is nothing in the environment that corresponds to cognition, since everything that corresponds to cognition is dependent on distinctions within which cognition indicates something as this and not that. Therefore, there are neither things nor events in the environment if the term "environment" is supposed to indicate that that which is thus indicated is different from something else. There is not even environment in the environment because this concept only indicates something in distinction from a system and thus demands that one identify the system for which the environment is an environment. (We *said* above, *therefore*, that systems exist.) The distinction between system and environment is itself an operation that guides cognition.

This course of reflection does not allow for any conclusions in regard to the irreality of the environment. It also does not allow for the conclusion that nothing exists besides the cognizing system. Such a conclusion, however, would itself be cognition because it is based on the distinction between "nothing" and "something," and thus, speaking traditionally, uses "nothing" as a *nomen*.[14] But as cognition it would also be based on the sacrifice of a correspondence to reality.

Indications such as "reality" (matter, ultimate reality) or "world" are, *for cognition*, themselves based on distinctions. They formulate the unity of that which is distinguished by a distinction—or, if you wish, their spirit.[15] Even they correspond to the closure of the cognizing system because they too can only be attained by the help of a distinction—in our case the distinction between system and environment.

It is only another indication of the same state of affairs when we say that the distinctions with which cognizing systems respectively observe are their "blind spots" or their latent structures—because this distinction can itself not be distinguished; if it could, then another distinction, namely this one, would itself be blindly applied as a guiding distinction. And once more the same is meant when one says that all observing presupposes and produces the drawing of a borderline, a cut through the world, a violation of the "unmarked space."

III

An operative epistemology conceives of cognition as a kind of operation it can distinguish from other operations. As an operation, cognition happens or not depending on whether the

---

[14] Compare—with conclusions regarding the parallel problem of evil—Anselm of Canterbury, *De casu diaboli XI*, quoted from *Opera Omnia* (Seckau, Rome, Edinburgh, 1938+) reprint (Stuttgart, Bad Cannstatt, 1968), vol. 1, 248 ff. As is well known, it was precisely this that forced theology paradoxically to place the distinction *creatum/increatum* above the distinction being/nonbeing even though the former presupposes the latter, because only through creation does the possibility of indicating something negatively arise. Compare for instance John Scotus Eriugena, *Periphyseon* (*De divisione naturae*), I, I and II quoted from the edition by I. P. Sheldon-Williams, vol. 1 (Dublin, 1978), 37ff. We will return to this issue.

[15] This is obviously an allusion to Hegel because Luhmann uses the German word *Geist*.—Trans.

autopoiesis of the system can be continued with such operations or not. The most important consequence of this approach is that it makes no difference whether cognition produces truth or errors. Obviously the physics, the biochemistry, and the neurophysiology of cognition are the same in both cases. We do not have brains (or parts of the brain) for errors and different brains for truths. The same is also true for conscious and communicative operations of cognition.[16] Neither consciousness systems nor communication systems are empirically split along a true/false divide. The same kind of attention and the same kind of language is employed for both truth values. Only thus can it be explained that errors erroneously appear as truths and that the problem lies in the elimination of errors. Initially, the autopoietic system operates indifferently regarding true/false and it is exactly this that makes it possible and necessary to impose on it a corresponding binary code. But who or what imposes?

All distinguishing, including that between true and false, is due to the efficacy of the observer (because we define observation as a distinguishing indication). Observing is also an operation and as such is incapable of distinguishing itself. (When an observer maneuvers the true/false distinction, he/she cannot simultaneously distinguish whether such operating is itself true or false.) The often discussed distinction between the propositions "A is" and "It is true that A is" is thus produced by an observation of the cognitive operation, i.e., by an observation of an observation, while the primal observation only distinguishes "A" from something else.

Here, logicians may feel themselves forced to distinguish between levels. But this only leads back to the paradox of this very distinction. Empirical theories have to ask instead how cognizing systems organize a corresponding self-observation, i.e., how they can distinguish and neutralize continuously produced errors. This question is answered with the concept of *binary coding*.[17]

---

[16] Behaviorist epistemology even asserted that the process of cognition would be psychologically indifferent also with respect to the distinction between cognition and object; an observer of the observer would project it. See Ness, op. cit., especially 131 ff, 163 ff., on the different psychology of true and false judgments as distinguished by the criterion of continuing or interrupting the sequence of behavior (which, however, only allows for conclusions in regard to identified errors).

[17] Compare also Niklas Luhmann, "Distinctions directrices: Über Codierung

There are of course many possibilities for supply systems with the ability for self-observation. The social system science, for instance, does not only observe itself by the code true/untrue, but also—and perhaps predominantly—by the secondary code of reputation. On the level of epistemology, i.e., when observing and describing systems that observe their observing, one has, after all this, to be able to distinguish various distinctions, namely:

1. the distinction between operation and observation, in which case an observation is a specific operation, namely, the operation of distinguishing—which makes the distinction between operation and observation circular (but, anyway, we only regard it as necessary on the level [!] of second-order cybernetics);

2. the distinction between the system-reference (system *and* environment) of the first-order observer and the system-reference (system *and* environment) of the second-order observer which would have to be made by a third-order observer;[18]

3. the distinction between other-observation and self-observation which presupposes the distinction between system and environment,

4. the distinction between an observation of an observation based on what the observed observer observes (what he/she is dealing with) and one based on that which he/she cannot observe (his/her distinction); and finally

5. the distinction between the binary code true/untrue and other forms of self- or other-observation.

Only an epistemology that accounts for all of the above distinctions, relates them to each other, and resolves all occurring paradoxes shall have the right to call itself "constructivist," because only then does it accept the mandate to trace everything that is

---

von Semantiken und Systemen," in Niklas Luhmann, *Soziologische Aufklärung*, vol. 4 (Opladen, 1987), 13–31; and Niklas Luhmann, *Ökologische Kommunikation* (Opladen, 1986), 75ff.

[18] Compare the analyses in regard to the question, which observations are at the basis of a description when it includes sentences on the "limitation" of the reaction capability of an organism? In Ness, op. cit., 56ff.

produced and reproduced as cognition back to the distinction of distinctions (as opposed to a "cause" [*Grund*]). As long as epistemology employs a biological or a psychological concept of cognition, i.e., as long as it relates itself to the autopoiesis of life or to the autopoiesis of consciousness to explain the possibility of cognition, it can claim for itself the status of an external observer. It only has to admit that it itself underlies the same physical/chemical/biological/psychological conditions as the cognition that it observes. This changes with a sociological concept of cognition because there is only one society, only one comprehensive autopoietic system of communication. In this way, the epistemologist him/herself becomes a rat in the labyrinth and has to reflect on the position from which he/she observes the other rats. Then, the reflection no longer leads merely to the common conditions, but beyond these to the unity of the system of cognition, and all "externalization" has to be explained as system-differentiation. Only with the sociology of cognition does a radical, self-inclusive constructivism become possible.

IV

Constructivism, even when pushed so far, is still an empirical theory. Therefore, one can ask why it appears to be "radical." This can only be explained historically.

No traditional epistemology (Hegel's logic would have to be further examined) could dare to go this far—obviously because the position from which it would have had to deal with distinctness was occupied by theology.

In order to see this, it suffices to read Nicolaus Cusanus. God is beyond all distinctions, even beyond the distinction between distinctions, and beyond the distinction between distinctness and indistinctness.[19] He is the *non-aliud*; that which is not different

---

[19] A relatively detailed passage says, for instance: "Est (Deus, N.L.) enim ante differentiam omnem, ante differentiam actus et potentiae, ante differentiam posse fieri et posse facere, ante differentiam lucis et tenebrae, immo ante differentiam esse et non esse, aliquid et nihil atque ante differentiam indifferentiae et differentiae, aequalitatis et inaequalitatis et ita de cunctis." *De venatione sapientiae*, quoted from Nicolaus Cusanus, *Philosophisch-Theologische Schriften*, vol. 1, ed. Leo Gabriel (Vienna, 1964), 58.

from anything different.[20] In him, everything that transcends distinctness coincides insofar as it transcends distinctness—i.e., that which cannot be conceived as greater, as smaller, as quicker, as slower (*coincidentia oppositorum*). However, that which is supposed to be thus designated and impossible to be distinguished has to be compatible with what the Christian dogma teaches about God. God has to be identifiable as a person and as the trinity, and is simultaneously (without distinction) therefore precisely the "mysterious" essence of things. Epistemology thus has to presume that things, although incomprehensible in their essence, have been created as a "contractio" of God and therefore as distinguishable; that God in this way makes himself comprehensible in his incomprehensibility; and that truth, although finally incomprehensible, consists for human beings in the correspondence of their distinctions with those of things.

If one were still to hold on to the prospect of the bliss (*beatitudo*) of the *visio dei*—which could be evidenced by the Scripture—and at the same time insisted on God's indistinctness and consequently on *divinam essentiam per se incomprehensibilem esse*,[21] one had, in God, to save the possibilities of observation and thus on the one hand to be careful not to ascribe to God the impossibility of self-observation, and, on the other hand, to avoid to come close to the devil who was the boldest observer of God. This asked for a highly skillful theology on the level of second-order cybernetics, i.e., in regard to the observation of observers, be it the *electi*, be it the devil, or be it finally God himself. The escape route came fatally close to the assumption that God needed creation and the damnation of the devil in order to be able to observe himself, and it led to writings that Nicolaus believed unprepared minds with their weak eyes had better not read.[22]

The partner for radical constructivism is therefore not traditional epistemology, but traditional theology (a theology which because of its demands of exactness went beyond what theology could bear). One then easily sees that one still has to distinguish

---

[20] See *De non-aliud*, quoted from Nicolaus Cusanus, *Philosophisch-Theologische Schriften*, vol. 2 (Vienna, 1966; reprint 1982), 443–565.

[21] John Scotus Eriugena, op. cit., 54.

[22] *Apologia doctae ignorantiae*, in *Philosophisch-Theologische Schriften*, vol. 1, ed. Leo Gabriel, (Vienna, 1964), 578.

the distinguishing of the distinctions with which observers work and which can be observed in the observations of observers from the indistinct which once was called *God*, and today, if one distinguishes system and environment, is called *world*, or, if one distinguishes object and cognition, *reality*.

V

One would now like to know how distinguishing and indicating is possible as a unitary but two-component operation. This leads one to the already anticipated insight that strongly limiting conditions have to be contributing. What presumably plays a role is that it is just about possible—at least in the realm of the sense operations of consciousness and communication—to view a twoness as a oneness, or, put differently; to see contrasts. Additionally, one will have to take time into account and then one will realize that sufficiently complex systems (and only these) are capable of amplifying small differences (for instance, transitions that become conspicuous along with oscillating self-movements) to large effects with the help of processes that can be called divergence amplifications or, in the terminology of linguistics, hyper-corrections. This also, of course, presupposes the uncoupling of the system, namely, its own time (*Eigenzeit*) for its own operations while there is doubtless a simultaneous environment. This refers again to the necessity of memory, namely, on the one hand, to an ongoing consistency check along with the activation of the respectively appropriate structures, and, on the other hand, to a schema of observation that interprets occurring inconsistencies as distinctions in time or space and thus stretches them apart.

In this way, however, we obviously only arrive at further and further specifications of the evolutionary unlikelihood, but also possibility, of cognizing systems. We could also say that it makes a difference—and perhaps which difference this is—if, in its autopoiesis, the cognitive capability of discrimination is based on biochemical, psychic, or communicational operations. We do not intend, however, to further trace such research programs here, since they would not contribute anything to a clarification of the difference between cognition and object. In this way, we learn something about the reality of the cognizing operations, but nothing about the reality of that which it has to externally presuppose as unknowable and incomprehensible.

In his already quoted "Refutation of Idealism," Kant makes use of an argument from time. Obviously, the environment presents something that appears in contrast to moving operations as persistent and thus allows for a return, a repetition, etc. (even if the thus necessary identifications are again up to the cognizing system). Kant argues vaguely and takes this persisting element to be a condition for its being in time while it should at most be treated as a condition for the identification of its being in time. The reverse time relation should also be taken into account. The cognizing system can deal with the same object while that which has to tolerate to be indicated in this way has already changed itself. And, even more astonishingly, the cognizing system can, insofar as it has language, use constant terms to indicate something that is conceived of as inconstant—for instance, the word "motion" to indicate motions. In other words, it does not have to simulate the changeable through its own change. All these are still rather indefinite clues pointing towards the hypothesis that the differentiating of a cognizing system in any case leads to situations that are ordered simultaneously but no longer rhythmically synchronic with the environment; and this can only be achieved when there are also discontinuities in the environment from which the system can distinguish its own operations.

We can supplement these considerations by recourse to a neglected contribution to academic epistemology by Fritz Heider.[23] At issue are the reality conditions of the possibility of distancing perceptions. Heider assumes that a difference between relatively loose and relatively strict coupling in the external world makes such perceptions possible, i.e., air on the one end, and sounds on the other end of the scale; or light on the one end, and visible objects on the other. The difference is essential; because if air itself would make sounds or if light itself would become visible, distinct perceptions would become impossible. In other words, physical substrates in both loose and strict coupling have to exist for systems to be able to construct themselves. The systems profit from this difference and with its help they can observe one side of the difference, namely, the

---

[23] See "Ding und Medium," *Symposium* 1 (1926): 109–57; English translation (abbreviated) in *Psychological Issues* 1, no. 3 (1959): 1–34.

form. The loosely coupled substrate serves as the medium; the strictly coupled substrate serves as the form. The difference serves as the condition of the possibility of perception while it has to be imperceptible itself. It is the necessarily latent structure of perception, and only a theory of perception on the level of second-order cybernetics, when it observes the perceiving observer, can see that this is so.

It is not difficult to generalize this medium-form difference. One can, for instance, take the acoustically or optically "granular," i.e., loosely coupled, structure of language as a medium which helps form sentences; or money as the medium for constructing prices. Under special conditions, forms (such as words) can thus in turn be a medium for a cognizing system that makes this difference invisible for itself. This demonstrates how far this idea can go, but again it leads away from epistemology. What is decisive is the primary assumption that there is a physically (or in whatever other manner) based difference between loose and strict coupling without which no cognizing system could develop itself or without which it would always be dependent on coincidences in its environment on its own borders which would not allow for any distances in time or space.

A refined conceptual effort could add that the medium is not supposed to be used up by formation, it rather has to regenerate itself; it could add that the form is always stronger (more resistant) than the medium—without a hidden rationality behind this; and it could add that also the respective medium as a loosely coupled substrate is in turn again perceivable as a form if an appropriate medium (for instance, a measuring instrument with high solution capability) can be provided.[24] In this way, one finally gets to quantum physics as a theory which only describes the observations of physicists by physicists, and which is thus established only on the level of second-order cybernetics, and which describes, in correlation with this, reality as indeterminable. This, however, would only mean that the observation of observation, the measuring and prognostication of the results of measurements, produces forms

---

[24] This distinguishes the distinction medium/form from the traditional distinction matter/form that finally arrived at a concept of incorporeal matter, because matter without form was otherwise inconceivable with respect to the quantitative/qualitative determinateness of all bodies.

that make themselves a medium. We know today that this is possible. We experiment with this in other areas too, for example, in modern poetry. But this does not say that the self-observation of the world would be possible without the latent difference between medium and form.

Cognition is therefore not possible in a "random" environment, but only in one that is suitable for cognition. This, however, does not justify assuming any "adaptation" of cognition to reality.[25] Much less can we share the evolutionary optimism of a self-regulatory cybernetics that attempts to explain both increasing efficacy and adaptation with the very same model. In any case, scientific research, viewed in the context of ecology, suggests rather the opposite. Divergence from that which seems to be given is continuously on the rise when cognition in ever more boldly turns corrects itself. This is—as some would still say today—a real possibility; but one could be capable of describing more clearly and with more consciousness of the risks involved that which happens there. Cognition projects distinctions into a reality that does not know of any distinctions. It gives itself a kind of freedom that has not been preconceived. Today, one would no longer suppose that it operates as freedom without cause,[26] because this too would be a judgment with respect to attribution, i.e., it would be cognition. But one can ask oneself, and an epistemology should be capable of this today, which kind of order will be achievable in such a process of continuing divergence amplification.

VI

There are at least some clues indicating that a reality that remained unknown, if it was totally entropic, would not enable cognition to take place. Cognition, however, cannot bring that which, on this side, is the condition for its own possibility into the form of a distinction, because this would again be its own accomplishment and thus in contradiction to the intention of a breakthrough into exteriority. Cognition remains unique as a construction based on distinction. As such it does not know anything external to it which

---

[25] This erroneous conclusion in Ernst von Glasersfeld, op. cit., 80f., 112, 200ff. (which radically deradicalizes his radical constructivism).

[26] Thus the devil in Anselm of Canterbury. See *De casu diaboli*, op. cit.

would correspond to itself. In the realm of this exteriority—that cognition indicates as an "object" through the distinction between self-reference and other-reference—there may be conditions of the possibility of cognition, and we can presume that these will consist in temporal and material discontinuities, in differences of variation speed, or in differences regarding the structural coupling of elements. But if this is the case, then cognition is dependent on *not* using these distinctions because only by such a sacrifice can it achieve an operational closure.

With this we once more return to the question of whether there should be concepts without a difference (which are, therefore, paradoxical). The traditional concept of God had attracted and thus absorbed this question. This may be sufficient to some. We wish, without making a definite decision, to suggest three further concepts, which may very remotely resemble the teaching of the trinity.

We wish to speak of the *world* in order to indicate the unity of the difference between *system and environment*. We wish to speak of *reality* in order to indicate the unity of the difference between *cognition and object*. We wish to speak of *sense* in order to indicate the unity of the difference between *actuality and possibility*. All these concepts are indifferent in the sense of including their own negation. The negation of the world can only be performed within the world. The negation of reality can only be performed as a real operation. Finally, the negation of sense makes no sense if it makes no sense. Undifferentiation therefore means in all these cases that that which is indicated by it cannot be defined on the basis of an antonym, but only on the basis of the very specific distinction on which it is founded.

It has to be stressed once more that these distinctions are necessarily very specific primary distinctions (and by no means random ones).[27] This confirms the thesis that cognition is in spite of, or because of, the necessity of closure, an extremely unlikely type of operation. The aforementioned limiting concepts can only be gained from cognition, and here there are, compared to the immense number of possible distinctions, only a very few possibilities. Additionally, it has to be noted that the aforementioned dis-

---

[27] Insofar as "ultimate reality" is also never the absolute—as for instance in F. H. Bradley, *Essays on Truth and Reality* (Oxford, 1914).

tinctions system/environment, cognition/object, and actuality/ possibility display an obvious asymmetry. There is connectivity only on one of their sides; and they allow re-entry only on one side in the sense of Spencer Brown's logic, i.e., re-entry of the distinction into what is distinguished. In this way the world can only be a concept for orientation within the system, a concept that re-enters the difference between system and environment into the system. In this way the difference between cognition and object is a distinction that is immanent to cognition; and the assumption that reality has to be something that entails both sides is, correspondingly, based on the very practice of cognition. And finally, in this way the difference between actuality and possibility only makes sense if it is practiced *in actu*, i.e., if the momentarily practiced operation refers to a horizon of other possibilities (and here it does not matter if these are real possibilities or possibilities that are only thought of or that can only be fictionally imagined.)

In these analogies one can discern a structure that serves to dissolve the paradox of the unity of the different. Such a paradox is, however, always only visible for an observer. This also means that the form of a theory described on the basis of its ability to resolve paradoxes allows for the question about functional equivalents, or, if it presents the paradox of observation as the observer, the question about God.

In any case the problem is not on the level of the simple practice of the autopoietic operations of those systems that engage in distinguishing and indicating, in observing and describing. Also in this regard one can only say: it happens when it happens; and it does not happen when it does not happen. If one, however, wants to distinguish what happens, one has to observe that which happens as observation. And this is exactly the task of epistemology.

VII

No matter what conditions may have to be fulfilled for cognition to become possible, it can always recognize its conditions through its own possibilities. It can presume this when engaging in its possibilities. It does what it does and thus proves itself to be possible. The problem does not lie here. It lies in the conditions for increase, and today, increasingly, in the conditions for environmental compatibility with an increase in cognitive efficacy. Classic theories assumed such a compatibility with their very concept of cognition, and they articulated it by such formulas as *assimilatio*, representation, or adaptation. Even cybernetic epistemologies sometimes still assume that, in the course of evolution, the adaptation of cognition to an environment is enhanced through an extension and self-referential networking of regulation circuits. We replace this perspective with the question of how a system can build up its own complexity under the condition of cognitive closure and how it can thus increase its cognitive efficacy.

One might think of language here, and indeed there are close connections between linguistic research and epistemological constructivism. As mentioned above, for Maturana, for instance, the concept of observation is dependent on language. Ernst von Glasersfeld too regards linguistic research as the key problem and the empirical foundation of proof for radical constructivism.[28] This is supported by the fact that linguistics, after Saussure, has abandoned a semiotic theory of external reference for language and only continues to use the term "sign" (and its derivates such as "semiology," "semiotics") for operationally-applied systemic elements.

This is exactly, however, how a problem is concealed. The operations of cognition are entirely different depending on the kind of system that is at work. One has to distinguish between psychic and social systems, between actually operating consciousness and communication. Both systems can make use of language to articulate thought as well as communication. For both systems a build-up of complexity to the degree we are familiar with becomes possible only through language. Both systems, however, operate as closed systems under entirely separate operational (autopoietic) and structural conditions. There is not the slightest operational overlap, because the recursive networking with other operations of the respective system imposes entirely different conditions of connectivity on everything that functions as an elementary operation within a system.

Therefore, one cannot, on the one hand, ignore language and should by no means underestimate its effects. But, on the other hand, language is also not the system that enables the construction of cognition as a real operation. It is no system at all. Its efficacy

---

[28] See his collection of essays *Wissen, Sprache und Wirklichkeit: Arbeiten zum radikalen Konstruktivismus* (Braunschweig, 1987).

lies instead in the structural coupling between consciousness and communication. This is to say, language constitutes a particular medium (be it sound, be it optical signs, be it, on this foundation, words), which it couples to its own forms. In this way it provides the partaking systems with a highly specific medium/form difference so that within consciousness as well as within communication language-specific forms can evolve, whether it is thinking linguistically or communication's creating new sentences from moment to moment, i.e., making use of linguistic possibilities through coupling and uncoupling.

These complications—that we cannot avoid if we hold on to the intention to understand systems from the basic operations with which they draw boundaries—let the alliance between linguistic theory and constructivism break down. Language keeps its central function with respect to the ongoing structural coupling of psychic and communicative operations. It fascinates consciousness. It focuses attention on its unique repertoire of conspicuous phonetic or optic forms. It guarantees that when communication goes on the necessary consciousness is activated to a sufficient degree. It limits the degree of freedom of consciousness during ongoing communication, although it is still always possible to simultaneously perceive noncommunicative events, to reflect on uncommunicated sense contents, and, most of all: to consciously deceive through language. During communication, one can also rely on the notation capability of psychic systems, on their memory. And as long as there is no writing, the continuation of communication depends on this precondition, however it may overestimate the efficacy of the factual memory. On the other hand, consciousness would remain extremely dependent on whatever it momentarily perceived if it had no possibility to think its thoughts in the form of phonetic or optic words (if, in this case, one would be willing to speak of consciousness at all).

All these considerations demonstrate the importance of a structural coupling between psychic and social systems that is compatible with gains in complexity. It can only be explained by language. Still, language does not talk to itself. It may supply the construction of cognition with forms, or, more precisely, with a specific difference between medium and form. But for the psychic as well as for the social realization of cognitive operations there are many more limitations that cannot be explained by linguistic analysis but only by psychological or sociological analyses. This is true for the conditions of the self-referential, autopoietic closure of systems as well as its internal consequences.

As long as systems were defined by the vague concept of "connection"[29] the preceding analysis could not be suggested. Consciousness and communication are of course connected, and this to such a degree that even in traditional systems theory it was impossible to conceive of them as different systems. One thus distinguished in an insufficiently explicable terminology between man and nature or between the "humanities" and the "natural sciences." But if one no longer views systems as specific objects with a very dense internal bond, but instead proceeds from the difference between system and environment, then one gets to a completely different theoretical design. The guiding question is then, which (autopoietic) operations close a system? And further, which form of structural coupling takes the connection between system and environment on when such a closure emerges?

Such a switch has far-reaching and currently hardly predictable consequences. For epistemology it leads to the radically constructivist thesis that cognition is only possible when and because systems close themselves operationally on the level of their distinctions and indications and thus become indifferent towards that which is thus excluded as environment. The insight that cognition can only be gained through interrupting all operational relations with an external world does not therefore say that cognition is nothing real or that it would not indicate something real; it only says that there can be no correspondences to the operations in the environment from which a cognizing system differentiates itself, because if this were to be the case the system would steadily dissolve itself into its environment and thus make cognition impossible.

---

[29] Often in such a way that systems are internally more closely or densely connected than with their environment.

Appendix C

Beyond Barbarism

NIKLAS LUHMANN

Translated by Hans-Georg Moeller

I

In view of the changing meaning of important cosmological, social, and political concepts in the second half of the eighteenth century, the question whether old "word-shells" should still be used or instead be discarded frequently arises. We do not have this problem where the words "barbarians," "barbaric," and "barbarism" are concerned. These words are today only used to express disgust and to supply one's disgust with an aura of objectivity. One can do without them; there are countless other ways to do this.

There are, however, also modern concepts of barbarism. One can think of, for instance, the distinction between "savages" and "barbarians" in Schiller's "Letters on the Aesthetic Education of Man": The savages perceive the world sensually, and therefore experience it as a variety of the diverse. The barbarians, on the other hand, have subscribed to reason. They are those who grant absolute primacy to the unity of reason over the variety and individuality of all the phenomena. Barbarians are those who have only one iron left in the fireplace. They cultivate, so to speak, a monoculture of reason. It may be politically convenient to continue this conception of barbarism—but it is not advisable, because nowadays one would no longer associate it with Robespierre—but with Habermas. Robespierre had a guillotine at

The translation follows the German original as found in: Niklas Luhmann, *Gesellschaftsstruktur und Semantik. Studien zur Wissenssoziologie der modernen Gesellschaft*, vol. 4 (Frankfurt/ Main: Suhrkamp, 1999), 138–50. Used by permission of Suhrkamp.

261

hand. The modern adherents of reason distinguish themselves by interpreting provocative and appellative speech as already being politics and are content with this.

Moreover, by continuing that use of language one would lose the possibility of comparing ancient conceptual dispositions with modern ones. If one has such comparative intentions, it is out of the question to conceive of barbarism as a historical universal category. One would no longer have the possibility of doing what is attempted in the following: to investigate the *problem* that came to expression with the distinction between barbarians and Hellenes— a problem which, under the conditions of present-day social structures, is likely to take on a very different shape from Greek antiquity. A supposition arises that this new shape may be the distinction between inclusion and exclusion.

II

In order to reflect on conceptual dispositions in the Old World one can relate to Kosselleck's analysis of asymmetric antonyms[1] or to Louis Dumont's *englobement du contraire*.[2] In this light, the distinction between barbarians and Hellenes is one among many. Such distinctions resulted from the attempt to continue a hierarchical world-architecture in the face of increasing complexity. The world is more perfect if it contains not only angels, but also stones, not only men, but also women, not only Hellenes, but also barbarians. Formally this is about oppositions; or more abstractly, about distinctions by which the higher evaluation of the one side not only underscores the contradistinction of the two elements, but also the fact that they belong to a hierarchical order. The "better" side therefore has a double function in a horizontal and a vertical direction. It represents the hierarchy within the distinction, and this in turn justifies its superiority.

It is important to note that oppositions of this kind are not understood as antagonisms. They are only classifications according to a specific order of species and genus as they were already con-

---

[1] See Reinhart Koselleck, "Zur historisch-politischen Semantik assymmetrischer Gegenbegriffe," in *Positionen der Negativität. Poetik und Hermeneutik*, vol. 6, ed. Harald Weinrich (Munich: 1975), 65–104.

[2] See Louis Dumont, *Essais sur l'individualism* (Paris, 1963).

ceived by Plato and logically elaborated by Aristotle. What matters is to exclude one side of the distinction from the other, one species from the other, one determination from its opposite. Accordingly the barbarians cannot be Hellenes, and the Hellenes cannot be barbarians. This suffices as a logical guarantee for order. If opposition were understood as antagonism, as an invitation to conflict, then a stable order would be impossible and modern conditions would be anticipated—for instance, the Hobbesian constellation of individuals that only allowed for a self-transcending (later it will be called dialectical) solution, or the later attempts at a totalitarian logic that intended to humanize all humans.[3] Only modern society will, beyond barbarism, conceive of such instabilities and try to cope with them.

The stability of the semantic type of asymmetrical oppositions and the variety of its applications allows for the assumption that it had socio-structural correlates that supplied it, despite all its ambiguity, with sufficient plausibility. We can reduce these correlates, by drastic simplification, to three aspects:

(1) These societies are regional societies, but increasing border-crossing contacts force them to develop a consciousness of multiple ethnicities and to provide rules for contacts with different ethnicities, although these rules and designations are not recognized as universal, but as society-specific. No one would have expected the barbarians to describe themselves as barbarians. Corresponding problems finally arise even within the city, as it is evidenced by the formation of a *ius gentium* in Rome.

(2) These societies are *de facto* aristocratic societies, although the importance of birth (ancestry) and bureaucratic positions varies greatly. In Greece, an aristocrat, even when refraining from taking on "political" positions, is still of significant inter-Hellenian importance in the areas of diplomacy and sports, as well as a *theoros* who trustfully reports on foreign affairs. The description of society therefore has to take into account the differences of social status. And this

---

[3] On this issue see Philip G. Herbst's typology of logic: *Alternatives to Hierarchies* (Leiden, 1976), 69ff.

means mainly that human beings cannot be socially excluded simply because they lack social rank, liberty, and *dignitas*. To realize the hierarchy all ranks are necessary. And this has:

(3) consequences for the regulation of inclusion and exclusion. Inclusion is essentially up to the family homes, and thus exclusion also becomes more or less automatically its business, from the killing or exposure of infants to the expulsion of juveniles who then have to somehow make a bare living, for instance, as criminals, beggars, legionaries, or (in England) in the Navy. Since the Middle Ages, corporations were added as absorbing institutions, in the form of guilds, the church, orders, monasteries, and universities, for instance. But, of course, these do not serve the lowest strata, especially not the peasants.

III

This connection between the semantics of asymmetrical oppositions and structural conditions of plausibility loses its meaning with the transition to modernity, and in the beginning practically without any substitution. If in Naples even today people are identified as *saraceni* and accordingly treated without any responsibilities then this can only be characterized as a regional peculiarity.

This change can roughly be conceived of as the transition from a social order of stratification to a society differentiated into function systems. This transition at first de-legitimizes social stratification. Stratification becomes a mere byproduct of the function systems, especially of the economic and education systems. Besides, a regional convergence of the boundaries of function systems can no longer be assumed. The borders between states are not borders of the economic system; the systems of science and mass media are anyways conceived globally. Since the second half of the nineteenth century a world-time exists that allows for everything that happens to happen simultaneously, no matter whether it is, regionally viewed, morning or evening. Communication that transcends regional borders loses its exceptional status. National events are internationally observed. Whether the result should be called "world society" (*Weltgesellschaft*) or "global system" is still disputed, because no sufficient social theory is yet available. Certainly, classifications of identity in the pattern of "we and all the others" lose their meaning. Classifications, for instance, "Serbs and Croats," may still come up, but they represent, at most, a temporal emphasis of specific distinctions in relation to equally possible others.

Along with these structural changes of the primary type of differentiation, the family loses its function to regulate inclusion and exclusion. Families become private, which, among other things, means that they no longer determine the lifestyle of their members and no longer operate under public supervision, but instead are supposed to accept individual life-style choices with sympathy and support. Moreover, the absorption-system of the old-style corporations no longer exists, instead there are modern organizations based on membership decisions, that is to say on the inclusion of a few members and the exclusion of all others.

As opposed to those organizations, the social system and its function systems are laid out to include the entirety of the population. There are no obvious grounds on which one can be excluded from the use of money, from being a legal subject, from having citizenship, from education, or from marriage—or obvious grounds on which all this could be made contingent upon system-internal licenses or special conditions. Given the principal full inclusion of everybody, the function systems themselves decide how far someone gets: if he/she is legally right or wrong, if his/her knowledge is accepted as true or not, if he/she is successful in gaining a reputation in the system of the mass media (that is to say: in attracting public attention), how much money he/she can spend, etc. This sovereignty, regarding the degree of inclusion, guarantees the differentiation of the function systems as such and is symbolically celebrated by being expressed as the freedom and equality of all individuals, which only means that the function systems assume that the population is a homogenous environment and that they can differentiate exclusively on the basis of their own criteria.

Obviously it makes no sense to describe the relations between function systems in the terms of asymmetric oppositions, as if science could classify all nonscientific communication as barbaric. Not even religion designates other function systems as pagan; its worries are more focused on competition within its own function system than on legal, political, or economic events as such.[4] The intersystem relations combine, in the terminology of "pattern variables" (Parsons), universalism and specification, namely encompassing competence—but only for their own function.[5]

IV

Thus, barbarism has disappeared—at least if one understands it to be a form that has another side on which there is *ethos, philia,* beauty of lifestyle, and, especially, a tight connection between these qualities. This, however, does not necessarily imply that modern society can be content with itself. Already the idea (that emerged from Europe, and that Husserl had sketched in his renowned Vienna Lectures in May 1935)[6] that the life-style of the rationally enlightened, socially responsible human being who only worships reason represents the *telos* of humankind ought to be terrifying. This would amount, as stated above, to a totalitarian logic that could no longer recognize any "outside," and that would therefore lack another side which it needs merely on mathematical grounds in order to be a form and to offer possibilities of observation.[7] The consequences begin to take shape in a period of transition that registers changes and their thorough effects, but does not yet possess a social theory that is adequate to the new social conditions. Three aspects are to be especially highlighted: (1) the transformation of earlier exclusions into inclusions, (2) the formulation of philosophical theories that no longer recognize an "outside" (while at the same time concepts such as "environment"

---

[4] "In Toscana ci sono piu maghi che preti"—thus did the bishops in charge express their alarm according to a report in the newspaper *La Republica* from April 23, 1994, while the announcements of the Roman Catholic Church in regard to the simultaneous disturbances sounded rather restrained.

[5] By the way: nothing else conveys, if closely read, Hegel's notorious thesis about the "end of art." Modern art may now take up *everything* as a theme, but only insofar as it can do this *as art.* Cf. Gerhard Plumpe. *Ästhetische Kommunikation der Moderne,* vol. 1 (Opladen, 1993), 302 ff.

[6] See the printed version under the title "Die Krisis des europäischen Menschentums und die Philosophie," *Husserliana,* vol. 6 (The Hague, 1954), 314–48.

[7] This relates to George Spencer Brown, *Laws of Form* (New York, 1979 [reprint]). See also *Kalkül der Form,* ed. Dirk Baecker (Frankfurt, 1993).

enter language as neologisms), and (3) the invention of "culture." All this seems to help draw the barbarians into society.

Deviant behavior is now no longer a reason for exclusion, but rather a reason for special treatment of inclusion. Given the enormous increase of delinquents (that is to say, in the first place, the enormous increase in penal law), there are still penitentiary colonies; but at the same time prisons are built in accordance with new architectonics.[8] Joblessness, begging, etc., is not defined as fate or a plague, but is answered with educational programs, labor houses, industrial pedagogies, etc. Generally speaking, pedagogy switches from households to schools. Hopeless cases are "psychiatrized," i.e., they are conceived of as illnesses or problems that society has to take care of, and that have to be solved with exceptional rights and duties within special institutions. All this was introduced with the new novel, the novel about the individual who showed in *Robinson Crusoe* and *Moll Flanders* how isolation leads to reflection, and how reflection leads to a change in behavior. The individuals lend hope to society, and they do this by being set free from previous restraints, i.e. by being "emancipated" and by being brought to self-discipline. But will they do what is expected? And according to which criteria?

Soon after this, great philosophy catches up by formulating a world without an "outside" for the subject or the spirit. Kant's reduction of the external world to the unknowable thing in itself shows the direction. Schelling's dissolving of all distinctions, including that of inside and outside, into "indifference" (symbolized either by art or religion) is another case. And there is finally Hegel's theory of absolute spirit or Husserl's ontological *epoche*. Can this be interpreted as a new cosmology for a society without exclusion?[9]

In the same context the invention of "culture" takes place. One can speak of "invention" because the modern concept of culture only emerges in the second half of the eighteenth century and has

---

[8] Cf. specifically on this issue: John Bender, *Imagining the Penitentiary: Fiction and the Architecture of Mind in Eighteenth-Century England* (Chicago, 1987).

[9] Without exclusion: this is, by the way, not the case for the philosophy of the late Husserl. Because "the Eskimos or the Indians of the fairs, or the gypsies who constantly vagabond around Europe" (op. cit. 318f.) do not take part in the spiritual entelechy of the European humankind.

no predecessor in Old European semantics. Culture is initially simply a doubling of all artifacts, including texts. Besides their immediate usage, artifacts gain a second meaning as documents of a culture. Pots are on the one side pots, but on the other side they are also signs of a specific culture that distinguishes itself by its kind of pots from another culture. And what is true for pots is also true for religions. Along with the new semantics of culture the old concept of nation that was related to heritage changes too. Comparisons between nations were already common at earlier times (for instance, in the context of different criteria for aristocracy), but now they take on the form of cultural comparisons. Nations have the practical communicative advantage of having proper names, so one can avoid the embarrassment of having to explain what exactly one is talking about.

The interest in culture is therefore rooted in an interest in comparisons—be they national or historical. From the comparison perspective, nothing can be left aside. Or more precisely: what is included and what is excluded is regulated by the point of comparison, i.e., by the comparison itself, and not by innate qualities. Once more we see the replacement of exclusion by mobile, flexible, differentiable inclusion.

Comparisons are, expressed in the terminology that was fashionable in the eighteenth century, "interesting." But that which is interesting can always, as Friedrich Schlegel notes, be more interesting. The interest in comparisons tends to expand itself, and the concept of culture is so conceived that it does not offer any resistance to comparisons. Neither in history nor in ethnology is something found that could not be compared or that would be uninteresting in principle. The regulatory criterion is exclusively the specification and abstraction of the aspects of comparison.

And to whose disposition are these? First: modern Europe, the contemporary Zeitgeist. Now one witnesses a peculiar return of asymmetric oppositions. The point of view of the comparison describes its findings under the aspect of culture while the cultures that are so compared are mostly unaware that they are cultures. One may read Novalis's "Christendom; or: Europe" or Schiller's "On Naïve and Sentimental Poetry." The Middle Ages had not reflected on themselves as a successful spiritual totality; only in that way could they be one. The naive poets did not know that the immediacy of their relation to reality was naive. This was only told to them by the distinctions of modernity, to the effect that modernity with its culture of reflexivity became both presumptuous and melancholic. It began to suffer from itself, and to bet on the future.

The connection between these semantic dispositions of modernity becomes evident when it is observed by the guiding difference of inclusion and exclusion. The existence of hell is denied—but then better and worse places in heaven must be distinguished. One recognizes problematic cases, and has to help out with therapy, social work, or developmental aid. The logic of functional differentiation excludes social exclusion, but then it has to allow distinctions within the function systems according to their criteria. But is this logic sustainable? How can there be inclusion if there is no exclusion?

V

To the surprise of the well-meaning it must be ascertained that exclusion still exists, and it exists on a massive scale and in such forms of misery that they are beyond description. Anybody who dares a visit to the *favelas* of South American cities and escapes alive can talk about this. But even a visit to the settlements that were left behind after the closing of the coal mines in Wales can assure one of it. To this effect, no empirical research is needed. Who trusts one's eyes can see it, and can see it so impressively that all explanations at hand will fail.

We know there is talk about exploitation, or about social suppression, or about *marginalidad*, about an increase in the contradiction between center and periphery. But all these are theories that are still governed by the desire for all-inclusion and therefore are looking for scapegoats: capitalism, the ruling alliance of financial and industry capital with the armed forces or with the powerful families of the country. But if one takes a closer look, one does not find anything that could be exploited or suppressed. One finds existences reduced to the bodily in their self-perception and other-perception, attempting to get to the next day. In order to survive they have to have capabilities of perceiving dangers and of making available what is most needed—or resignation and indifference with regard to all "bourgeois" values: including order, cleanliness, and self-respect. And if one adds up what one sees one can conceive of the idea that this may be the guiding difference of the next century: inclusion and exclusion.

The search for scapegoats and the search for points of attack to bring about changes towards all-inclusion are still based on a primary stratified society. In proportion to the degree to which this assumption becomes inadequate and is passed on as a mere ideal, and the degree to which phenomena can no longer be accurately traced back to the activities of certain ruling circles, the search for a different explanation becomes more worthwhile. At this point, one can make use of the theory of functional differentiation insofar as it is distinguished from the classical theory of labor division (increase in profits with unavoidable costs).

Functional differentiation, as opposed to what the self-descriptions of the systems are claiming, cannot realize the postulated full-inclusion. Function systems, when operating rationally, exclude persons or marginalize them so drastically that this has consequences in regard to getting access to other function systems. No education, no work, no income, no regular marriages, children with no birth certificate, no passport, no participation in politics, no access to legal advice, to the police, or to the courts—the list can be extended and it concerns, depending on the circumstances, all marginalizations up to total exclusion. No one will say that it has to be this way according to some kind of Malthusian population law. It is, however, sufficient to see that it is so and how such an amplifying effect is produced at the margins of function systems. Perhaps religion could offer an exceptional opportunity? But if one inspects more closely the countless new cults of the modern world, based on states of trance as medium, no distinction of black and white magic, healing as a promise without differentiation of medical and other life-problems, then one understands the hesitation of the Catholic Church to espouse religiosity of this type in the churches.

Facts of this kind turn the common theory of integration held by many sociologists upside down. Modern society is indeed highly integrated, but only in its area of exclusion, as negative integration, and above all—without consensus. In the realm of inclusion, however, the normal conditions of stability reign: loose coupling, relatively high capability of coping with errors, careers as the mode of integration of individuals and society, multiple contexts of observational perspectives, and better or worse conditions of life with a high degree of acceptance of individual-ized communication.

Still, the corresponding disintegration of inclusion can also be reflected upon, and this is what present-day theoreticians of modernity are currently focusing on. The integration of the indi-vidual and society no longer finds its principles in common con-sensus; it switched from provenance (and thus, from *ethos*) to career, that is to say, to processed contingency. Moreover, the mutual-increase connection between culture (*Bildung*) and free-dom predicted by neo-humanists did not come true, but has rather been dissolved. In modern supply-society, freedom is not restricted by coercion, but rather structured by supply in such a way that the enacting of freedom can no longer be attributed to the self-real-ization of the individual. One buys for a good price, watches the advertised films, chooses a religion or not as one likes—just like the others. Even God is a supply-God. He offers, and the model is of course Pascal's wager, his love so impressively and so independent of moral judgments that the refusal would be meaningless or, the-ologically speaking, would fulfill the definition of sin. This demon-strates that culture and social conditions have made the enacting of freedom so asymmetrical that the individual is only left with mean-ingless decisions—or with protests that do not change anything.

This was, of course, never different. But in modern society this hits the vital element of the self-description of the system as "humane."

With a certain nostalgia we can now think back to the barbar-ians or to the other ethnicities, the pagans, the savages. They were left with their own social order. We did not have anything to do with it. We were free to convert them or to enslave them, or to cheat them when exchanging goods. And they were our concepts, European concepts, when we spoke of *humanitas*, of *ius gentium*, of humankind or of human rights. All this is no longer adequate in the situation modern society finds itself in—not to speak of con-cepts such as *societas civilis* or *communitas* that we are getting from our basements like *Sauerkraut* to enjoy them reheated.[10]

---

[10] In the oral presentation, I had referred at this juncture to the *Witwe Bolte*. This aroused displeasure. Perhaps I came too close to the matter. [The *Witwe Bolte*— a widow named "Bolte"—is a prominent persona in nineteenth-century German popular literature. She appears in the satirical children's book *Max und Moritz* by

If this diagnosis is only roughly correct, society can neither expect advice nor help from sociology. But it could make sense to search for theories that do more justice to the facts than the optimistic-critical traditional ways of thought within our discipline—justice to those facts with which society constructs itself.

Wilhelm Busch. Max and Moritz, two juvenile "villains," steal Witwe Bolte's chickens from the hearth while she is getting something from the basement. Later in the story, the miller grinds up Max and Moritz because of all the mischief they caused. It should also be noted that Luhmann refers to the oral presentation of the paper at the *Institut für Sozialforschung* in Hamburg, a hotbed of German Critical Theory and leftist thinking. Luhmann, however, was still able to leave the location unharmed.—Trans.

Luhmann
Bibliography

Luhmann Bibliography

1. Works by Luhmann in English

(a) BOOKS

Luhmann, Niklas. *Trust and Power*. Translated by H. Davis, J. Raffan, and K. Rooney. Chichester: Wiley, 1979.

———. *The Differentiation of Society*. Translated by Stephen Holmes and Charles Larmore. New York: Columbia University Press, 1982.

———. *Religious Dogmatics and the Evolution of Societies*. Translated by Peter Beyer. New York: Edwin Mellen Press, 1984.

———. *A Sociological Theory of Law*. Translated by Elizabeth King and Martin Albrow. London: Routledge, 1985.

———. *Love as Passion: The Codification of Intimacy*. Translated by Jeremy Gaines and Doris L. Jones. Cambridge: Polity Press, 1986.

———. *Ecological Communication*. Translated by John Bednarz Jr. Chicago: University of Chicago Press, 1989.

———. *Essays on Self-Reference*. New York: Columbia University Press, 1990.

———. *Political Theory in the Welfare State*. Translated by John Bednarz Jr.. New York: De Gruyter, 1990.

———. *Risk: A Sociological Theory*. Translated by Rhodes Barrett. New York: De Gruyter, 1993.

———. *Social Systems*. Translated by John Bednarz Jr. and Dirk Baecker. Stanford: Stanford University Press, 1995.

———. *The Reality of the Mass Media*. Translated by Kathleen Cross Stanford: Stanford University Press, 1996.

———. *Observations on Modernity*. Translated by William Whobrey. Stanford: Stanford University Press, 1998.

———. *Art as a Social System*. Translated by E. Knodt. Stanford: Stanford University Press, 2000.

———. *Theories of Distinction: Redescribing the Descriptions of Modernity.* Translations by Joseph O'Neil, et al. Stanford: Stanford University Press, 2002.

———. *Law as a Social System.* Translated by Klaus A. Ziegart. Oxford: Oxford University Press, 2004.

Luhmann, Niklas, and Karl-Eberhard Schorr. *Problems of Reflection in the System of Education.* Translated by Rebecca A. Neuwirth. New York: Waxman, 2000.

(b) ARTICLES

Luhmann, Niklas. "Society." In *Marxism, Communism and Western Society. A Comparative Encyclopedia,* vol. VIII, edited by C.D. Kerning, 22–29. New York: Herder and Herder, 1973.

———. "Institutionalized Religion in the Perspective of Functional Sociology." In *The Church as Institution,* edited by Gregory Baum and Andrew Greely, 45–55. New York: Herder and Herder, 1974.

———. "Sociology of Political Systems." *German Political Studies* 1 (1974): 3–29.

———. "The Legal Profession: Comments on the Situation in the Federal Republic of Germany." *The Juridical Review* 20 (1975): 116–32.

———. "Comment (in: Karl Erik Rosengren, Malinowski's Magic)." *Current Anthropology* 17 (1976): 679–80.

———. "The Future Cannot Begin: Temporal Structures in Modern Society." *Social Research* 43 (1976): 130–52.

———. "Generalized Media and the Problem of Contingency." In *Explorations in General Theory in Social Science: Essays in Honor of Talcott Parsons,* edited by Jan J. Loubser et al., 507–32. New York: Free Press, 1976.

———. "A General Theory of Organized Social Systems." In *European Contributions to Organization Theory,* edited by Geert Hofstede and M. Sami Kassem, 96–113. Assen: Van Gorcum, 1976.

———. "Differentiation of Society." *Canadian Journal of Sociology* 2 (1977): 29–53.

———. "Temporalization of Complexity." In *Sociocybernetics,* edited by Felix Geyer and Johannes van der Zouwen, 95–111. Boston: Nijhoff, 1978.

———. "The Actor and the System: The Constraints of Collective Action." *Organization Studies* 1 (1980): 193–95.

———. "Communication about Law in Interaction Systems." In *Advances in Social Theory and Methodology: Toward an Integration of Micro- and Macro-Sociology,* edited by Karin Knorr-Cetina and Aaron V. Cicourel, 234–56. London: Routledge, 1981.

————. "The Improbability of Communication." *International Social Science Journal* 23 (1981): 122–32.

————. "World Society as a Social System." *International Journal of General Systems* 8 (1982): 131–38.

————. "Insistence on Systems Theory: Perspectives from Germany." *Social Forces* 61 (1983): 987–98.

————. "Territorial Borders as Systems Boundaries." In *Cooperation and Conflict in Border Areas,* edited by Raimondo Strassoldo and Giovanni Delli Zotti, 235–44. Milan: F. Angeli, 1983.

————. "The Differentiation of Advances in Knowledge: The Genesis of Science." In *Society and Knowledge: Contemporary Perspectives in the Sociology of Knowledge,* edited by Nico Stehr and Volker Meja, 104–48. London: Transaction, 1984.

————. "The Self-Description of Society: Crisis, Fashion and Sociological Theory." *International Journal of Comparative Sociology* 25 (1984): 59–72.

————. "Complexity and Meaning." In *The Science and Praxis of Complexity,* 99–104. Tokyo: United Nations University, 1985.

————. "Society, Meaning, Religion-Based on Self-Reference." *Sociological Analysis* 46 (1985): 5–20.

————. "The Work of Art and the Self-Reproduction of Art." *Thesis Eleven* 12 (1985): 4–27.

————. "The Autopoiesis of Social Systems." In *Sociocybernetic Paradoxes: Observation, Control and Evolution of Self-Steering Systems,* edited by Felix Geyer and Johannes van der Zouwen, 171–92. London: Sage, 1986.

————. "The Individuality of the Individual: Historical Meanings and Contemporary Problems." In *Restructuring Individualism: Autonomy, Individuality, and the Self in Western Thought,* edited by T. Heller, M. Sosna, and D. E. Wellbury, 313–54. Stanford: Stanford University Press, 1986.

————. "The Self-Reproduction of the Law and its Limits." In *Dilemmas of Law in the Welfare State,* edited by Gunther Teubner, 111–27. New York: de Gruyter, 1986.

————. "The Theory of Social Systems and its Epistemology: Reply to Danilo Zolo's Critical Comments." *Philosophy of the Social Sciences* 16 (1986): 129–34.

————. "The Evolutionary Differentiation between Society and Interaction." In *The Micro-Macro Link,* edited by J. Alexander, B. Giesen, R. Munch, and M. Smelser, 112–31. Berkeley: University of California Press, 1987.

————. "Modern Systems Theory and the Theory of Society." *In Modern German Sociology,* edited by Volker Meja, Dieter Misgeld and Nico Stehr, 173–86. New York: Columbia University Press, 1987.

———. "The Morality of Risk and the Risk of Morality." *International Review of Sociology* 3 (1987): 87–101.

———. "The Representation of Society within Society." *Current Sociology* 35 (1987): 101–8.

———. "The Medium of Art." *Thesis Eleven* 18 (1987): 101–13.

———. "Closure and Openness: On Reality in the World of Law." In *Autopoietic Law: A New Approach to Law and Society*, edited by Gunther Teubner, 335–48. Berlin: de Gruyter, 1988.

———. "Familiarity, Confidence, Trust: Problems and Alternatives." In *Trust: Making and Breaking Cooperative Relations*, edited by Deigo Gambetta, 94–107. New York: Blackwell, 1988.

———. "Observing and Describing Complexity." In *Complexities of the Human Environment: A Cultural and Technological Perspective*, edited by Karl Vak, 251–55. Vienna: Europa Verlag, 1988.

———. "The Sociological Observation of the Theory and Practice of Law." In *European Yearbook in the Sociology of Law* 1 (1988): 23–42.

———. "Tautology and Paradox in the Self-Description of Modern Society." *Sociological Theory* 6 (1988): 26–37.

———. "The Third Question: The Creation of Paradoxes in Law and Legal History." *Journal of Law and Society* 15 (1988): 153–65.

———. "The Unity of the Law System." In *Autopoietic Law: A New Approach to Law and Society*, edited by G. Teubner, 12–35. New York: Walter de Gruyter, 1988.

———. "Law as a Social System." *Northwestern University Law Review* 83 (1988/89): 136–50.

———. "The Cognitive Program of Constructivism and a Reality that Remains Unknown." In *Self-Organization: Portrait of a Scientific Revolution*, edited by Wolfgang Krohn et al., 64–85. Dordrecht: Kluwer, 1990.

———. "The Future of Democracy." *Thesis Eleven* 26 (1990): 46–53.

———. "General Theory and American Sociology." In *Sociology in America*, edited by Herbert J. Gans, 253–64. Newbury Park, CA: Sage, 1990.

———. "The Paradox of System Differentiation and the Evolution of Society." In *Differentiation Theory and Social Change*, edited by Jeffery Alexander and Paul Colomy, 409–40. New York: Columbia University Press, 1990.

———. "Technology, Environment and Social Risk: A Systems Perspective." *Industrial Crisis Quarterly* 4 (1990): 223–31.

———. "Paradigm Lost: On the Ethical Reflection of Morality. Speech on the Occasion of the Award of the Hegel Prize 1989." *Thesis Eleven* 29 (1991): 82–94.

———. "The Coding of the Legal System." In *State, Law, Economy as Autopoietic Systems*, edited by A. Febbrajo and G. Teubner, 145–86. Milan: Giuffre, 1991.

———. "Operational Closure and Structural Coupling: The Differentiation of the Legal System." *Cardozo Law Review* 13 (1991/92): 1419–441.

———. "The Direction of Evolution." In *Social Change and Modernity*, edited by Hans Haferkamp and Neil J. Smelser, 279–93. Berkeley: University of California Press, 1992.

———. "The Concept of Society." *Thesis Eleven* 31 (1992): 67–80.

———. "The Form of Writing." *Stanford Literature Review* 9 (1992): 25–42.

———. "Societal Complexity." In *Concise Encyclopedia of Participation and Co-Management*, edited by Gyorgy Szell, 793–806. Berlin: de Gruyter, 1992.

———. "Operational Closure and Structural Coupling: The Differentiation of the Legal System." *Cardozo Law Review* 13 (1992): 1419–441.

———. "What is Communication." *Communications Theory* 2 (1992): 251–59.

———. "The Code of the Moral." *Cardozo Law Review* 14 (1992/93): 995–1009.

———. "Deconstruction as Second-Order Observing." *New Literary History* 24 (1993): 763–82.

———. "Ecological Thinking: Coping with the Unknown." *System Practice* 6 (1993): 527–39.

———. "European Rationality." In *Rethinking Imagination*, edited by Gillian Robinson and John Rundell, 65–83. London: Routledge, 1993.

———. "Observing Re-entries." *Graduate Faculty Philosophy Journal* 6 (1993): 485–98.

———. "How Can the Mind Participate in Communication?" In *Materialities of Communication*, edited by H.U. Gumbrecht and K.L. Pfeiffer, 371–87. Stanford: Stanford University Press, 1994.

———. "An Interview with Niklas Luhmann." *Theory, Culture and Society* 11 (1994): 37–68.

———. "The Modernity of Science." *New German Critique* 61 (1994): 9–23.

———. "Observing Re-Entries." *Protosoziologie* 6 (1994): 4–13.

———. "Politicians, Honesty and the Higher Amorality of Politics." *Theory, Culture and Society* 11 (1994): 25–36.

———. "Speaking and Silence." *New German Critique* 61 (1994): 25–37.

———. "'What is the Case?' and 'What Lies Behind it?' The Two Sociologies and the Theory of Society." *Sociological Theory* 12 (1994): 126–39.

———. "Legal Argumentation: An Analysis of its Form." *Modern Law Review* 58 (1995): 285–98.

———. "The Paradoxy of Observing Systems." *Cultural Critique* 31 (1995): 37–55.

———. "The Two Sociologies and the Theory of Society." *Thesis Eleven* 43 (1995): 28–47.

———. "Why Does Society Describe Itself as Postmodern?" *Cultural Critique* 30 (1995): 171–86.

———. "Complexity, Structural Contingencies and Value Conflicts." In *Detraditionalization, Critical Reflections on Authority and Identity*, edited by P. Heelas, S. Lash, and P. Morris, 59–71. Cambridge, MA: Blackwell, 1996.

———. "Membership and Motives in Social Systems." *Systems Research* 13 (1996): 341–48.

———. "Modern Society Shocked by Its Risks." *Social Sciences Research Centre Occasional Paper* 17 (1996): 3–19

———. "A Redescription of 'Romantic Art.'" *Modern Language Notes* 111 (1996): 506–22.

———. "On the Scientific Context of the Concept of Communication." *Social Science Information* 35 (1996): 257–67.

———. "The Sociology of the Moral and Ethics." *International Sociology* 11 (1996): 27–36.

———. "The Control of Intransparency." *Systems Research and Behaviour Science* 14 (1997): 359–71.

———. "Globalization or World Society: How to Conceive of Modern Society?" *International Review of Sociology* 7 (1997): 67–79.

———. "Limits of Steering" *Theory, Culture and Society* 14 (1997): 41–57.

———. "Politics and Economy." *Thesis Eleven* 53 (1998): 1–9.

———. "The Paradox of Form." In *Problems of Form*, edited by Dirk Baecker, 15–26. Stanford: Stanford University Press, 1999.

———. "Sign as Form." In *Problems of Form*, edited by Dirk Baecker, 46–63. Stanford: Stanford University Press, 1999.

———. "Morality and the Secrets of Religion." In *Religion and Media*, edited by Hent de Vries and Samuel Weber, 555–68. Stanford: Stanford University Press, 2001.

———. "Notes on the Project 'Poetry and Social Theory.'" *Theory, Culture and Society* 18 (2001): 15–27.

Luhmann, Niklas, and Benjamin Nelson. "A Conversation on Selected Theoretical Questions: Systems Theory and Comparative Civilizational Sociology." *The Graduate Faculty Journal of Sociology* 1 (1976): 1–17.

Luhmann, Niklas, N. Katherine Hayles, William Rasch, Eva Knodt, and Cary Wolfe. "Theory of a Different Order: A Conversation with Katherine Hayles and Niklas Luhmann." In *Observing Complexity: Systems Theory and Postmodernity*, edited by William Rasch and Cary Wolfe, 111–36. Minneapolis: University of Minnesota Press, 2000.

2. Works on Luhmann in English

Albert, Mathias. "Observing World Politics: Luhmann's Systems Theory of Society and International Relations." *Millennium* 28 (1999): 239–65.

Albert, Mathias and Lena Hilkermeier, eds. *Observing International Relations: Niklas Luhmann and World Politics*. New York: Routledge, 2004.

Arato, Andrew. "Civil Society and Political Theory in the Work of Luhmannn and Beyond." *New German Critique* 61 (1994): 129–42.

Arnason, Johann P. "Novalis, Marx and Parsons: Niklas Luhmann's Search for Modernity." *Thesis Eleven* 51 (1997): 75–90.

———. "Binary Codes and Blurred Distinctions: Comment on Luhmann's 'Politics and Economy.'" *Thesis Eleven* 53 (1998): 15–17.

Arnoldi, Jakob. "Niklas Luhmann: An Introduction." *Theory, Culture and Society* 18, no. 1 (2001): 1–13.

Arvidsson, Adam. "From Housewife to Person: Luhmannian Systems Theory and the Semantics of Authenticity in Advertising." *Recherches Sociologiques* 27 (1996): 99–114.

Baecker, D. "Gypsy Reason: Niklas Luhmann's Sociological Enlightenment." *Cybernetics and Human Knowing* 6 (2001): 5–19.

Baecker, Dirk. "Why Systems?" *Theory, Culture and Society* 18 (2002): 59–74.

Bakken, Tore and Tor Hernes, eds. *Autopoietic Organization Theory: Drawing on Niklas Luhmann's Social System Perspective*. Herndon, VA: Copenhagen Business School Press, 2003.

Baldwin, Michael, Mel Ramsden & Charles Harrison. "Roma Reason— Luhmann's Art as a Social System." *Radical Philosophy* 109 (2001): 14–21.

Bailey, K. D. "The Autopoiesis of Social Systems: Assessing Luhmann's Theory of Self-Reference." *Systems Research and Behavioural Science* 14 (1997): 83–100.

Barbesino, P., and S.A. Salvaggio. "How is a Sociology of Sociological Knowledge Possible?" *Social Science Information* 35 (1996): 341–62.

Bechmann, Gotthard, and Nico Stehr. "The Legacy of Niklas Luhmann." *Society* 39 (2002): 69–75.

Bechmann, Gotthard, and Nico Stehr. "Niklas Luhmann." *Convergencia* 10 (2003): 259–76.

Beck, Anthony. "Is Law an Autopoietic System?" *Oxford Journal of Legal Studies* 14 (1994): 401–18.

Bednarz, John, Jr. "Complexity and Intersubjectivity: Towards the Theory of Niklas Luhmann." *Human Studies* 7 (1984): 55–69.

———. "Functional Method and Phenomenology: The View of Niklas Luhmann." *Human Studies* 7 (1984): 343–62.

Beyer, Peter. "The Modern Emergence of Religions and a Global Social System for Religion." *International Sociology* 13 (1998): 151–72.

———. "Relgion as Communication in Niklas Luhmann's *Die Religion der Gesellschaft.*" *Soziale Systeme* 7 (2001): 46–55.

Bleicher, Josef. "System and Meaning: Comments of the Work of Niklas Luhmann." *Theory, Culture and Society* 1 (1982): 49–52.

Bluhdorn, Ingolfur. "Beyond Criticism and Crisis: On the Post-Critical Challenge of Niklas Luhmann." *Review of Contemporary German Affairs* 7 (1999): 185–199.

Bluhdorn, Ingolfur. "An Offer One Might Prefer to Refuse: The Systems Theoretical Legacy of Niklas Luhmann." *European Journal of Social Theory* 3 (2000): 339–54.

Brans, Marleen, and Stefan Rossbach. "The Autopoiesis of Administrative Systems: Niklas Luhmann on Public Administration and Public Policy." *Public Administration* 75 (1997): 417–39.

———. "Luhmannian Perspectives on Public Administration and Policy." In *International Encyclopedia of Public Policy and Administration,* vol. 3, edited by J. Shafritz, 1313–320. Boulder, CO: Westview, 1998.

Calhoon, C. "Social Theory and the Law: Systems Theory, Normative Justification, and Postmodernism." *Northwestern University Law Review* 83 (1988/89): 398–460.

Castellano, Lucio. "Niklas Luhmann's Political Theory." *International Review of Sociology* 23 (1987): 3–31.

Chaves, Mark. "Secularization: A Luhmannian Reflection." *Soziale Systeme* 3 (1997): 439–49.

Chernilo, Daniel. "The Theorization of Social Co-Ordinations in Differentiated Societies: The Theory of Generalized Symbolic Media in Parsons, Luhmann and Habermas." *The British Journal of Sociology* 53 (2002): 431–49.

Christis, Jac. "Luhmann's Theory of Knowledge: Beyond Realism and Constructivism?" *Soziale Systeme* 7 (2001): 328–49.

Christodoulidis, E. A. "A Case for Reflexive Politics: Challenging Luhmann's Account Of the Political System." *Economy and Society* 20 (1991): 380–401.

Clam, Jean. "System's Sole Constituent, the Operation: Clarifying a Central Concept of Luhmannian Theory." *Acta Sociologica* 43 (2000): 63–79.

Clarke, Bruce. "Science, Theory, and Systems." *Interdisciplinary Studies in Literature and Environment* 8 (2001): 149–65.

———. "Mediating the Fly: Posthuman Metamorphosis in the 1950s." *Configurations* 10 (2002): 169–91.

———. "Strong Constructivism: Modernity and Complexity in Science Studies and Systems Theory." In *Democracy, Civil Society, and Environment*, edited by Joseph Bilello, 41–49. Muncie: College of Architecture and Planning Monograph, Ball State University, 2002.

———. "Paradox and the Form of Metamorphosis: Systems Theory in A Midsummer Night's Dream." *Intertext* 8 (2004): 173–87. Cornell, Drucilla. "The Relevance of Time to the Relationship between the Philosophy of the Limit and Systems Theory." In *Deconstruction and the Possibility of Justice*, edited by Drucilla Cornell, Michael Rosenfeld and D. Carlson , 68–91. New York: Routledge, 1992.

Dallmann, Hans-Ulrich. "Niklas Luhmann's Systems Theory as a Challenge for Ethics." *Ethical Theory and Moral Practice* 1 (1998): 85–102.

de Berg, Henk. "A Systems Theoretical Perspective on Communication." *Poetics Today* 16 (1995): 709–36.

———. "Select Annotated Bibliography to Luhmann's Systems Theory and Its Applications in Literary Studies." *Poetics Today* 16 (1995): 737–41.

———. "Luhmann's System Theory and Its Application in Literary Studies." *European Journal of English Studies* 5 (2001): 385–436.

Deflem, M. "The Boundaries of Abortion Law: Systems Theory from Parsons to Luhmann and Habermas." *Social Forces* 76 (1998): 775–818.

Dobbelaere, K. "Secularization Theories and Sociological Paradigms: Convergences and Divergences." *Social Compass* 31 (1984): 199–219.

Dunsire, Andrew. "Tipping the Balance: Autopoiesis and Governance." *Administration and Society* 28 (1996): 299–334.

Elmer, Jonathan. "Blinded Me with Science: Motifs of Observation and Temporality in Lacan and Luhmann." In *Observing Complexity: Systems Theory and Postmodernity*, edited by William Rasch and Cary Wolfe, 215–46. Minneapolis: University of Minnesota Press, 2000.

Esposito, E. "From Self-Reference to Autology: How to Operationalize a Circular Approach." *Social Science Information* 35 (1996): 269–81.

Fuchs, P. "The New Wars of Truth: Conflicts over Science Studies as Differential Modes of Observation." *Social Science Information* 35 (1996): 307–26.

Fuchs, Stephan. "Niklas Luhmann." *Sociological Theory* 17 (1999): 117–19.

———. "Beyond Agency." *Sociological Theory* 19 (2001): 24–40.

Fuchs, Stephan, and D. A. Marshall. "Across the Great (and Small) Divides." *Soziale Systeme* 4 (1998): 5–30.

Fuchs, Stephan, and Jonathan H. Turner. "Legal Sociology as General Social Theory: Luhmann's Sociology of Law." *Virginia Review of Sociology* 1 (1992): 163–70.

Greven, Michael. "Power and Communication in Habermas and Luhmann." *Political Discourse* (1987): 179–93.

Gumbrecht, Hans-Ulrich. "Form without Matter vs. Form as Event." *Modern Language Notes* 111 (1996): 137–80.

———. "How is Our Future Contingent? Luhmann Against Luhmann." *Theory, Culture and Society* 18 (2001): 49–58.

Habermas, Jurgen. "Excursus on Luhmann's Appropriation of the Philosophy of the Subject through Systems Theory." In *The Philosophical Discourse of Modernity: Twelve Lectures*, translated by Frederick G. Lawrence. Cambridge: MIT Press, 1987.

Harrison, Paul. "Niklas Luhmann, Love as Passion." *Thesis Eleven* 27 (1990): 234–39.

Hayim, Gila J. "Postmodern Tendencies in the Sociology of Luhmann: The Self-Thematization of Modernity." *Human Studies* 17 (1994): 307–24.

Hayles, N. Katherine. "Making the Cut: The Interplay of Narrative and System, or What Systems Theory Can't See." *Cultural Critique* 20 (1995): 71–100.

Hess, Andreas. "'What is Actually So Distinctively Societal about Society?' Niklas Luhmann's *Die Gesellschaft der Gesellschaft*." *Schweizerische Zeitschrift fur Soziologie/Revue Suisse de Sociologie* 25 (1999): 123–30.

Hohendahl, Peter Uwe. "No Exit? (Response to Luhmann)." In *Observing Complexity: Systems Theory and Postmodernity*, edited by William Rasch and Cary Wolfe, 51–56. Minneapolis: University of Minnesota Press, 2000.

Holub, Robert. "Luhmann's Progeny: Systems Theory and Literary Studies in the Post-Wall Era." *New German Critique* 61 (1994): 143–59.

Jalava, Janne. "From Norms to Trust: The Luhmannian Connections Between Trust and System." *European Journal of Social Theory* 6 (2003): 173–90.

King, Michael. "The 'Truth' About Autopoiesis." *Journal of Law and Society* 20 (1993): 218–36.

———. "Managerialism versus Virtue. The Phoney War for the Soul of Social Work." *Soziale Systeme* 2 (1996): 53–72.

———. "The Construction and the Demolition of the Luhmann Heresy." *Law and Critique* 12 (2001): 132.

King, Michael, and Chris Thornhill. *Niklas Luhmann's Theory of Politics and Law*. New York: Palgrave MacMillan, 2003.

King, Michael, and Anton Schutz. "The Ambitious Modesty of Niklas Luhmann." *Journal of Law and Society* 21 (1994): 261–87.

King, Michael and Chris Thornhill. "'Will the Real Niklas Luhmann Stand Up, Please.' A Reply to John Mingers." *The Sociological Review* 51 (2003): 276–85.

Knodt, Eva M. "Toward a Non-Foundationalist Epistemology: The Habermas/Luhmann Controversy Revisited." *New German Critique* 61 (1994): 77–100.

Laermans, Rudi and Gert Verschraegen. "The Late Niklas Luhmann on Religion: An Overview." *Social Compass* 48 (2001): 7–20.

Lee, Daniel. "The Society of Society: The Grand Finale of Niklas Luhmann." *Sociological Theory* 18 (2000): 320–30.

Leflaive, X. "Organizations as Structures of Domination." *Organization Studies* 17 (1996): 23–47.

Lewis, J. D., and A. Weigert. "Trust as a Social Reality." *Social Forces* 63 (1985): 283–306.

Leydesdorff, Loet. "Luhmann's Sociological Theory: Its Operationalization and Future Perspectives." *Social Science Information* 35 (1996): 283–306.

———. "Luhmann, Habermas, and the Theory of Communication." *Systems Research and Behavioural Science* 17 (2000): 273–88.

Lieb, Claudia. "Entertainment: An Examination of Functional Theories of Mass Communication." *Poetics* 29 (2001): 225–45.

Machura, Stefan. "The Individual in the Shadow of Powerful Institutions: Niklas Luhmann's 'Legitimation by Procedure' as Seen by Critics." In *Procedural Justice*, edited by Klaus F. Rohl and Stefan Machura, 181–205. Aldershot, U.K.: Ashgate, 1997.

Makarovic, Matej. "Some Problems in Luhmann's Social Systems Theory: Differentiation, Integration, and Planning." *Druzboslovne Razprave* 17 (2001): 59–70.

Miller, Max. "Intersystemic Discourse and Co-Ordinated Dissent: A Critique of Luhmann's Concept of Ecological Communication." *Theory, Culture and Society* 11 (1994): 101–21.

Mingers, John. "Can Social Systems be Autopoietic? Assessing Luhmann's Social Theory." *The Sociological Review* 50 (2002): 278–99.

Misheva, V. "Totalitarian Interaction. A Systems Approach." *Sociologica Internationalis* 31 (1993): 179–96.

Moeller, Hans-Georg. "New Confucianism and the Semantics of Individuality: A Luhmannian Analysis." *Asian Philosophy* 14 (2004): 25–39.

Muller, Harro. "Luhmann's Systems Theory as a Theory of Modernity." *New German Critique* 61 (1994): 39–54.

———. "Indentity, Paradox, Difference Conceptions of Time in the Literature of Modernity." *Modern Language Notes* 111 (1996): 523–32.

Munch, Richard. "The Law in Terms of Systems Theory." *American Journal of Sociology* 92 (1987): 1221–223.

Murphy, John W. "Talcott Parsons and Niklas Luhmann: Two Versions of the Social 'System.'" *International Review of Modern Sociology* 12 (1982): 291–301.

———. "Niklas Luhmann and his View of the Social Function of Law." *Human Studies* 7 (1984): 23–38.

———. "Niklas Luhmann: His Contributions to the Sociology of Religion." *International Sociology* 2 (1987): 205–13.

Murphy, W. T. "Modern Times. Niklas Luhmann on Law, Politics and Social Theory." *The Modern Law Review* 47 (1984): 603–20.

Neckel, Sighard, and Jurgen Wolf. "The Fascination of Amorality: Luhmann's Theory of Morality and its Resonances among German Intellectuals." *Theory, Culture and Society* 11 (1994): 69–99.

Neves, M. "From the Autopoiesis to the Allopoiesis of Law." *Journal of Law and Society* 28 (2001): 242–64.

Nishizaka, Aug. "The Use of 'Power': The Discursive Organization of Powerfulness." *Human Studies* 15 (1992): 129–44.

———. "Religious Faith as a Communicative Practice: Luhmann's Theory of Religion and the Discursive Accomplishment of Indeterminability." *International Journal of Japanese Sociology* 2 (1993): 65–78.

Osterberg, Dag. "Luhmann's General Sociology." *Acta Sociologica* 43 (2000): 15–25.

Paterson, John. "An Introduction to Luhmann." *Theory, Culture and Society* 14 (1997): 37–39.

Paul, Axel T. "Organizing Husserl: On the Phenomenological Foundations of Luhmann's Systems Theory." *Journal of Classical Sociology* 1 (2001): 371–94.

Podak, Klaus. "Without Subject, Without Reason: Reflections on Niklas Luhmann's Social Systems." *Thesis Eleven* 13 (1986): 54–66.

Pottage, Alain. "Power as an Art of Contingency: Luhmann, Deleuze, Foucault." *Economy and Society* 27 (1998): 1–27.

Priban, J. "Beyond Procedural Legitimation: Legality and its 'Inflictions.'" *Journal of Law and Society* 24 (1997): 331–49.

Provost, Wallace H. "Contingency and Complexity in the Social Theory of Niklas Luhmann." *International Journal of General Systems* 11 (1985).

———. "Complex Organization and Niklas Luhmann's Sociology of Law." *International Journal of General Systems* 15 (1989).

Rasch, William. "Theories of Complexity, Complexities of Theory: Habermas, Luhmann, and the Study of Social Systems." *German Studies Review* 14 (1991): 65–84.

———. "Immanent Systems, Transcendental Temptations, and the Limits of Ethics." *Cultural Critique* 30 (1995): 73–99.

———. "The Limit of Late Modernity: Luhmann and Lyotard on Exclusion." *Soziale Systeme* 3 (1997): 257–69.

———. "Locating the Political: Schmitt, Mouffe, Luhmann, and the Possibility of Pluralism. "*Schweizerische Zeitschrift fur Soziologie/ Revue Suisse de Sociologie* 7 (1997): 103–15.

———. "Luhmann's Widerlegung des Idealismus? Constructivism as a Two-Front War." *Soziale Systeme* 4 (1998): 151–59.

———. *Niklas Luhmann's Modernity: The Paradoxes of Differentiation.* Stanford: Stanford University Press, 2000.

Rasch, William, and Eva M. Knodt. "Systems Theory and the System of Theory." *New German Critique* 61 (1994): 3–7.

Rasch, William, and Cary Wolfe, eds. *Observing Complexity: Systems Theory and Postmodernity.* Minneapolis: University of Minnesota Press, 2000.

Rempel, Michael. "Systems Theory and Power/Knowledge: A Foucauldian Reconstruction of Niklas Luhmann's Systems Theory." *The International Journal of Sociology and Social Policy* 16 (1996): 58–90.

Reinfandt, Christoph. "Integrating Literary Theory: Systems-theoretical Perspectives of Literature and Literary Theory." *Literatur in Wissenschaft und Unterricht* 28 (1995): 55–64.

Roberts, David. "Paradox Preserved: From Ontology to Autology. Reflections on Niklas Luhmann's The Art of Society." *Thesis Eleven* 51 (1997): 53–74.

Roberts, David, ed. *Reconstructing Theory: Gadamer, Habermas, Luhmann.* Victoria, Australia: Melbourne University Press, 1995.

Rossbach, S. "Gnosis, Science, and Mysticism: A History of Self-Referential Theory Designs." *Social Science Information* 35 (1996): 233–55.

Rottleuthner, Hubert. "A Purified Sociology of Law: Niklas Luhmann on the Autonomy of the Legal System." *Law and Society Review* 23 (1989): 779–95.

Scambler, Graham. "Theorizing Modernity: Luhmann, Habermas, Elias and New Perspectives on Health and Healing." *Critical Public Health* 8 (1998): 237–44.

Schecter, Stephen. "Culture and Politics in Luhmann's Reading of Contemporary Society." *Schweizerische Zeitschrift fur Soziologie/ Revue Suisse de Sociologie* 7 (1997): 117–26.

Scherr, Albert. "Niklas Luhmann—An Outline of the Theory of Autopoietic Social Systems." *Soziologie* 3 (1994): 149–63.

———. "Transformations in Social Work: From Help Towards Social Inclusion to the Management of Exclusion." *European Journal of Social Work* 2 (1999): 15–25.

Schnebel, Eberhard. "Values in Decision-Making Processes: Systematic Structures of Jurgen Habermas and Niklas Luhmann for the Appreciation of Responsibility in Leadership." *Journal of Business Ethics* 27 (2000): 79–88.

Schofthaler, Traugott. "The Social Foundations of Modernity: Durkheimian Problems and the Vicissitudes of Niklas Luhmann's Systems Theory of Religion, Morality and Personality." *Social Compass* 31 (1984): 185–97.

Schwanitz, Dietrich. "Systems Theory and the Environment of Theory." The *Current in Criticism: Essays on the Present and Future of Literary Theory*, edited by Clayton Koelb and Virgil Lokke, 265–94. West Lafayette, IN: Purdue University Press, 1987.

———. "Systems Theory According to Niklas Luhmann—Its Environment and Conceptual Strategies." *Cultural Critique* 30 (1995): 137–70.

———. "Systems Theory and the Difference between Communication and Consciousness." *Modern Language Notes* 111 (1996): 288–505.

Sevanen, Erkki. "Art as an Autopoietic Sub-System of Modern Society: A Critical Analysis of the Concepts of Art and Autopoietic Systems in Luhmann's Late Production." *Theory, Culture and Society* 18 (2001): 75–103.

Sinclair, M.B.W. "Autopoiesis: Who Needs It?" *Legal Studies Form* 16 (1992): 81–102.

Sixel, Friedrich W. "Beyond Good and Evil? A Study of Luhmann's Sociology of Morals." *Theory, Culture and Society* 2 (1983): 35–47.

Staheli, Urs. "From Victimology Towards Parasitology: A Systems Theoretical Reading of the Function of Exclusion." *Recherches Sociologiques* 27 (1996): 59–80.

———. "Exorcising the 'Popular' Seriously: Luhmann's Concept of Semantics." *International Review of Sociology* 7 (1997): 127–45.

Stehr, Nico. "The Evolution of Meaning Systems: An Interview with Niklas Luhmann." *Theory, Culture and Society* 1 (1982): 33–48.

Stichweh, R. "Science in the System of World Society." *Social Science Information* 35 (1996): 327–40.

———. "Systems Theory as an Alternative to Action Theory? The Rise of 'Communication' as a Theoretical Option." *Acta Sociologica* 43 (2000): 27–39.

Taschwer, Klaus. "Science as System vs. Science as Practice: Luhmann's Sociology of Science and Recent Approaches in Science and Technology Studies (STS)—A Fragmentary Confrontation." *Social Science Information* 35 (1996): 215–32.

Teubner, Gunther. "Economics of Gift-Positivity of Justice: The Mutual Paranoia of Jacques Derrida and Niklas Luhmann." *Theory, Culture and Society* 18 (2001): 29–47.

Teubner, Gunther, ed. *Autopoietic Law: A New Approach to Law and Society.* Berlin: de Gruyter, 1988.

Teubner, Gunther, and A. Febbrajo, eds. *State, Law and Economy as Autopoietic Systems: Regulation and Autonomy in a New Perspective.* Milan: Giuffre, 1992.

Thornhill, Chris. "Systems Theory and Legal Theory: Luhmann, Heidegger and the False Ends of Metaphysics." *Radical Philosophy* 116 (2002): 7–20.

Vanderstraeten, Raf. "Autopoiesis and Socialization: On Luhmann's Reconceptualization of Communication and Socialization." *The British Journal of Sociology* 51 (2000): 581–98.

———. "Luhmann on Socialization and Education." *Educational Theory* 50 (2000): 1–23.

———. "Parsons, Luhmann and the Theorem of Double Contingency." *Journal of Classical Sociology* 2 (2002): 77–92.

———. "An Observation of Luhmann's Observation of Education." *European Journal of Social Theory* 6 (2003): 133–43.

———. "The Social Differentiation of the Educational System." *Sociology* 38 (2004): 255–72.

Verschraegen, Gert. "Human Rights and Modern Society: A Sociological Analysis from the Perspective of Systems Theory." *Journal of Law and Society* 29 (2002): 258–81.

Viskovatoff, Alex. "Foundations of Niklas Luhmann's Theory of Social Systems." *Philosophy of the Social Sciences* 29 (1999): 481–516.

Wagner, Gerhard. "The End of Luhmann's Social Systems Theory." *Philosophy of the Social Sciences* 27 (1997): 387–409.

White, Mary. "Linguistic Norms and Norms in Linguistics." *Journal of Pragmatics* 3 (1979): 81–98.

Winthrop-Young, Geoffery. "Silicon Sociology, or Two Kings on Hegel's Throne?

Kittler, Luhmann, and the Posthuman Merger of German Media Theory." *Yale Journal of Criticism* 13 (2000): 391–420.

Wolfe, Cary. "Making Contingency Safe for Liberalism: The Pragmatics of Epistemology in Rorty and Luhmann." *New German Critique* 61 (1994): 101–27.

———. *Critical Environments: Postmodern Theory and the Pragmatics of the "Outside."* Minneapolis: University of Minnesota Press, 1998.

Zolo, Danilo. "Function, Meaning, Complexity: The Epistemological Premises of Niklas Luhmann's 'Sociological Enlightenment.'" *Philosophy of the Social Sciences* 16 (1986): 115–27.

3. An Annotated List of German Manuals for Luhmann Studies

(a) DICTIONARIES

There are two dictionary-style manuals on Luhmann in German:

1. Krause, Detlef. *Luhmann–Lexikon*. 3rd ed. Stuttgart: Enke, 2001.

   This is a dictionary that lists Luhmann's terminology. Each of the several hundred entries is briefly defined—in strictly Luhmannian terms. The book is therefore of limited use for those who are not already highly familiar with Luhmannian concepts. It is certainly helpful for researchers who need precise clarification in regard to specific terms and want to trace the interrelatedness of various concepts. An introduction presents an overview of Luhmannian systems theory in a language that is often more technical than Luhmann's own writings. An extensive bibliography and index are included.

2. Baraldi, Claudio, Giancarlo Corsi, and Elena Esposito. *GLU: Glossar zu Niklas Luhmanns Theorie sozialer Systeme*. Frankfurt/Main: Suhrkamp, 1997.

   This is a glossary that concisely explicates more than sixty Luhmannian concepts. The explanations are more detailed and accessible than those in the *Luhmann-Lexikon*. They also provide information on texts by Luhmann in which the respective concept is discussed. A bibliography of works by Luhmann is included.

(b) INTRODUCTIONS

There are a number of book-length introductions to Niklas Luhmann in German. Among them are:

1. Margot Berghaus. *Luhmann leicht gemacht. Eine Einführung in die Systemtheorie.* Cologne, Weimar, Vienna: Böhlau, 2003.

This book is exactly what its title promises. It provides easy—and comprehensive—access to Luhmann's work and is a good introduction to systems theory. It is particularly useful for students with a limited knowledge of Luhmann and his writings, but often also helpful for advanced scholars. Like the present study, it includes a specific analysis of Luhmann's theory of the mass media.

2. Fuchs, Peter. *Niklas Luhmann—beobachtet.* 2nd ed. Opladen: Westdeutscher Verlag, 1993.

Peter Fuchs was a student and collaborator of Niklas Luhmann. He not only has a firsthand understanding of Luhmann's theory, but also his book is a very successful attempt to present this theory in a refreshing way while still being academically accurate. The book is written as a fictitious dialogue between a university professor, his students, and a couple of other personae. In a somewhat Socratic way, it explains the core notions of systems theory not only in relation to "real life," but also in an often witty fashion.

3. Reese-Schäfer, Walter. *Luhmann zur Einführung.* Hamburg: Junius, 1992.

This is another well written and adequate introduction to Luhmann. It concentrates on a few core concepts (system, sense, autopoiesis) as well as some major works (*Love as Passion, A Sociology of Risk, Social Systems, Ecological Communication*) and central topics (morality, religion, and the controversy with Habermas).

4. Kneer, Georg, and Armin Nassehi. *Niklas Luhmanns Theorie sozialer Systeme.* Munich: Fink, 1993.

This is a comprehensive analysis of Luhmann's theory of society as presented in *Social Systems.*

5. Gripp-Hagelstange, Helga. *Niklas Luhmann: Eine erkenntnistheoretische Einführung.* Munich: Fink, 1995.

This is an analysis of Luhmann's theory from a philosophical-epistemological perspective.

Other general introductions are:

6. Horster, Detlef. *Niklas Luhmann.* Munich: Beck, 1993.

7. Kiss, Gabor. *Grundzüge und Entwicklung der Luhmannschen Systemtheorie.* 2nd ed. Stuttgart: Enke, 1990.

(c) LUHMANN'S INFLUENCE IN OTHER FIELDS

There is one excellent book that documents the reaction to Luhmann's theory, particularly in Germany and Europe:

de Berg, Henk, and Johannes Schmidt, eds., *Rezeption und Reflexion: Zur Resonanz der Systemtheorie Niklas Luhmanns außerhalb der Soziologie.* Frankfurt/Main: Suhrkamp, 2000.

This book contains detailed articles by leading scholars on the influence of Luhmann's ideas in the theory of law, political science, studies of literature and art, theology, economic theory, pedagogy, philosophy, media science, family therapy, health studies, the sociology of movements, social work, and studies of organizations. Each section contains an often detailed bibliography of works on Luhmann in the respective fields.

(d) BIBLIOGRAPHIES

As mentioned above, Krause's *Luhmann-Lexikon,* the *GLU,* and the volume on Luhmann's influence edited by de Berg and Schmidt contain valuable bibliographies of works by and on Luhmann. There are also two extensive bibliographies of Niklas Luhmann's works:

1. Schiermeyer, Sylke, and Johannes F.K. Schmidt, "Niklas Luhmann—Schriftenverzeichnis." *Soziale Systeme. Zeitschrift für soziologische Theorie* 4, no. 1 (1998), 233–63.

2. "Gesamtverzeichnis der Veröffentlichungen Niklas Luhmanns 1958–1992." In *Die Verwaltung des politischen Systems. Neuere systemtheoretische Zugriffe auf ein altes Thema,* edited by Klaus Dammann, Dieter Grunow and Klaus Japp. Opladen: Westdeutscher Verlag, 1994.

Index

activism
  functionally oriented, 106–7
  in North America, 106
  socially adapted, as conservative,
    107–8
  systems theory critique of,
    102–4
advertising, 128–31
  functions of, 130–31
Althusser, Louis, 179
American Idol (TV show), 134
Amish, 152, 153
Anderson, Pamela, 128
Aristotle, 12, 13, 165, 263
asymmetric antonyms, 262
autonomy model, 14
autopoiesis, 12–13, 14, 245

Baraldi, C., 26, 30, 32
barbarism, concepts of, 261–62
Baudrillard, J., 123, 141–42
  The Gulf War Did Not Take Place,
    141
Bechmann, Gotthard, xi
Bentham, Jeremy, 5, 110
biological systems theory, 12, 15,
    21
Bloom, Allan, 5
Brentano, Franz, 182
Büchner, Georg, 8
Bush, George H., 141

center/periphery differentiation,
    43–44
Chomsky, Noam, 144–45, 147, 150
  Manufacturing Consent, 143
  9/11, 144–45
cognition
  and distinctions, 245–47, 255–57
  and system closure, 260
cognizing systems
  and change, 253
  closure of, 244, 246
communication
  double contingency in, 22–23
  function systems in, 24, 26
  and individuals, 6–9
  as orderly, 22–23
  as sense, 65, 67
  and technology, 124–25
communication media, 26–27
communication systems, structural
    coupling in, 18–20
communicative action, 96–97
Communist Manifesto, 124
Comte, Auguste, 165
concepts, through difference, 256
consensus theories, 232
constructivism
  as empirical, 250
  as radical, 167, 241–43, 250
    cognition in, 169
    and theology, 251
constructivist epistemology, 249–50

Corsi, G., 26, 30, 32
"culture," invention of, 267–68
Cusanus, Nicolaus, 75, 250
cybernetic cycle, 146–47

deconstruction, 193
dehumanization, complaints of, 3
Deleuze, G., 66, 197
de Man, Paul, 195
democracy, as outmoded concept, 117
Derrida, Jacques, 195, 196
differentiation
    center/periphery, 43–44
    segmentary, 42
    stratified, 44–45
Dumont, Louis, 262
Durkheim, Emile, 232, 233

ecological communication, problems of, 105
entertainment, functions of, 132–33
epistemological idealism, 167, 168, 242
epistemology, 257
    problem of, 242
Esposito, E., 26, 30, 32

favelas, 61, 269
Feuerbach, Ludwig, 99
Fichte, Johann Gottlieb, 74
Foucault, Michel, 79, 190, 191
Freud, Sigmund, 75, 237
functional differentiation, 49, 100
    career in, 91–93
    and democracy, 117
    and fundamentalism, 57–58, 95
    in globalization, 56–57
    as historical product, 41
    human rights in, 94–95
    and identity, 159
    imitational person in, 89–90
    inclusion/exclusion in, 93
    individuality in, 87–91

    problems of, 88–90, 92
    intimacy system in, 92
    multiple selves in, 89
    and regional identities, 57
    semantics of freedom in, 90, 94–95
    semantics of subjectivity in, 95
function systems, 24–26, 29, 264–65
    consequences of, for human beings, 46–47
    equality/inequality in, 45–46
    as impossible to direct, 101, 104
    and inclusion/exclusion, 59–62, 265, 270
    as incompatible discourses, 32–33
    inequalities between, 27–28
    influencing each other, 36–37
    neglect of religion and ethnicity in, 58–59
    as nonhierarchical, 45, 48
    and operational closure, 32–33
    and second-order observation, 76–78
    social strata in, 48–49
    structural coupling between, 37–38

Gehlen, Arnold, 165
German Idealism, 87
Giddens, Anthony, 235
Gladiator (movie), 133
globalization, 52–60
    differentiation in, 55–56
    functional differentiation in, 56–57
    and fundamentalism, 58
    regional differences in, 56–57
    and social exclusion, 59–60
global system, concept of, 235–36
global society versus nation-state, 54
God, as beyond all distinctions, 250–51
Gramsci, Antonio, 179
Greek/Barbarian distinction, 93
Green movement, 101, 102
    and nuclear power, 103
Günther, Gotthard, 165

Habermas, Jürgen, 5, 60, 96, 165, 171, 187, 193, 194, 261
and Luhmann, 187–90
The Philosophical Discourse of Modernity, 189
Habermasian theory, limits of, 136–37
Hardt, Michael, 197
Empire, xi
Hauser, Kaspar, 19–20
Hegel, G. W. F., 22, 40, 66, 139, 165, 166, 169, 171, 173–75, 177–78, 181, 250, 267
Phenomenology of Spirit, 174–75, 199
on religion, 199
Heidegger, Martin, 123, 196
Being and Time, 68
Heider, Fritz, 253
Herman, Edward S.
Manufacturing Consent, 143
hermeneutic despair, 8–9
hierarchical distinctions, in Old World, 262–64
Hobbes, Thomas, 5, 232
human being
in social systems theory, 9–11, 79–81, 85
in traditional views, 80, 230–31
humanism, as failed concept, 234
humanist optimism/pessimism, 4–5
Husserl, Edmund, 65, 66, 165, 171, 181–82, 189, 193, 194, 197, 266, 267

identity
and functional differentiation, 159
in social systems theory, 83
in stratified society, 91
individuality
in functional differentiation, 87–92
social semantics of, 84–85
and society, problem of, 231, 233
in stratified society, 86–88
"information society," 236
input-output models, 14

Kant, Immanuel, 99, 110, 165, 167, 173, 181, 189, 241, 267
on cognition, 168
Copernican turn, 168
Critique of Pure Reason, 242
on time, 253
Kepplinger, Hans Mathias, 144
King, Michael, xi, 189
Knodt, Eva M., xi, 8
Kosselleck, R., 262
Kuhn, Thomas
The Structure of Scientific Revolutions, 197

language
as medium, 259
and structural coupling, 38, 259–60
and systems complexity, 19
Luhmann, Niklas
on activism, 106
on advertising, 129–31
antihumanism of, ix–x
on approval and esteem, 111
on autopoiesis, 15–16
on brain, operational closure of, 17
on center/periphery differentiation, 43–44
cognition in, 169
"Cognition as Construction," 70, 167, 170
on communication, 20, 22–23, 191
on communication media, 26
on consciousness, 20, 182
constructivism of, 168
and critical theory, 166
criticisms of, 189
on deconstruction, 193, 195–96
"Deconstruction as Second-Order Observing," 195–96
on difference, 40
on ecological activism, 102, 105
Ecological Communication, 101, 121

on the economic function system,
   179
Einführung in die Systemtheorie,
   165
on entertainment, 132–33
on ethics, 110–11, 113
on exploitation, 61, 269
on function systems, unequal
   growth of, 121
on fundamentalism, 58
and German philosophy, 165
Die Gesellschaft der Gesellschaft,
   165
on the Green movement, 101
on Habermas, 193
and Habermas, controversy with,
   187–88
and Hegel, 175
   difference between, 173–74
as historical thinker, x
on human being, 80
and Husserl, differences between,
   183–84, 193
on Husserl's Eurocentrism, 184
Husserl's influence on, 181–83
on inclusion, in functional
   differentiation, 95–96
on intention, 182–83
Introduction to Systems Theory, xi
and Kant, 167–68
on language, 19
on legal observation, 77
Love as Passion, 51
and Marx, 177–79
and Marxism, 178–80
on mass media, 121, 122, 127–28,
   136–37, 153
   and schemata, 159
   and technology, 122–23
on minds and communication, 81
on modernity, 45, 193
"Modernity in Contemporary
   Society," 178
*Modern Sciences and
   Phenomenology,* 181
on morality, 180
on observation, 72, 75

on operational closure, 15–16
on organizations, 31–32
"Paradigm Lost," 111
on philosophy, 199–200
on political and economic function
   systems, 34–36
and postmodernism, ix, 50, 166,
   193–96
Protest, 108, 121
on public opinion, 137–38
radicalism of, 15–16, 168–69,
   173
on reality, 66
The Reality of Mass Media, xi, 121,
   131, 132, 141, 150
reason in, 190
on science, 197
and self-inclusive theory, 174–75
on semantics, 51
on sense, 65–66, 183, 190
on social differentiation, types of,
   41–42, 85
on social evolution, 41–42
on socialist economy, breakdown
   of, 34
on social movements, 32
on social subsystems, 28–29
Social Systems, xi, 8, 121, 165,
   174, 183, 188, 193
on social systems theory, ix–x
on society, dominant conception
   of, 229–30
The Society of Society, xi, 109, 170,
   174, 187, 191, 193, 194, 196
as sociologist, 200
on sociology, problems of, 236–38
on structural coupling, 19–20
on subject, concept of, 170, 183
supertheory of, 174–75, 195, 200
on symbolically generalized media,
   27–28
system/environment in, 170
*Theory of Society or Social
   Technology,* 187
on Wallerstein, 55
Lynch, Jessica, 134, 147
Lyotard, J.-F., 191, 194, 245

making sense, 65, 67–68
manners, in society, 109
Marx, Karl, 75, 99, 165, 177–78, 237
Marxism, 39, 99–100
  and China, 100
  epistemological optimism of, 100
  impact of, 100
  and Soviet Union, 99–100
mass media
  advertising, 128–30
  as beyond manipulation, 147
  code of, 125–26
  as common reality, 136, 141
  and consensus, lack of, 136–37
  as constructing reality, 144, 150, 152, 154–55
  domination theory of, 144
    problems of, 145
  fields of selection, 128
  as function system, 29
  and individuality, 157–60
  and information/noninformation, 125–28, 135
  and interaction, 123
  liberation theory of, 143
    problems of, 144–45, 147
  and manipulation, 141–44
  memory and forgetting, in, 135–36
  and mind, 158, 159
  as moralistic, 152
  mutual borrowings in, 133–34
  news selectors, 129
  and politics, 76
  program strands, 128–29, 133
  and public opinion, 76, 137–38
  and religious groups, 152–53
  and schemata, 159
  second-order observation in, 153
  social function of, 134–36
  and speed, 135
  structural coupling of, 145–46, 158, 159
  suspicions of, 143
  and technology, 122–25
  and time, 127, 134–35

mass media system, 121
  growth of, 122
Matrix (film), 20
Maturana, Humberto, 12–13, 18, 66, 165, 245, 258
McLuhan, Marshall, 4, 124
Mead, George Herbert, 6, 234n
medieval society, 109
medium/form difference, 254–55
Medusa, 237
metanarrative, 200
Metzger, Thomas, 99
mind
  as filter, 20, 81
  as socialized, 83–84
mind-communication problem, 81
Mingers, J., 12
modernity/modern society, 109
  and exclusion, 269–70
  family in, 265
  functional differentiation in, 49, 50
  function systems in, 45–46, 264–65
  and inclusion, 266–69
  and the individual, 271
  and morality, 110
  as nonhumanist, 122
Moll Flanders, 267
moral discourse, and social conflict, 108–9
morality
  as communication system, 111, 113
  and esteem, 111, 112–13
  in function systems, 111–12
  in modernity, 110
  risks of, 113, 114
  and social conflict, 112–13
moral rules, as manners, 109

nation-state, 54
negative ethics, 109
Negri, Antonio, 197
  Empire, xi

Nietzsche, Friedrich, 74, 79, 196, 237
  On the Use and Disadvantages of History for Life, 239
Novalis, 268

observation
  blind spot in, 73–74
  operation of, 69–70
  second-order, 71–73, 74
  third-order, 73
operational closure, 14, 16–17
  and openness, 16–18
operational constructivism, 151
organizations, in social systems theory, 31

Parsons, Talcott, 26, 96, 111, 165, 232, 266
Pascal, Blaise, 271
perception, and medium/form difference, 253–54
Perseus, 237
philosophy, Old European, 5
Plato, 10, 80, 165, 263
  Republic, 5
  Timaios, 13
poiesis, 12
postmodernism, 49, 79
postmodern theory, 50, 194–95
  as semantic turn, 194
praxis, 12
public opinion, role of, 138–39
Pufendorf, Samuel, 232

Quine, W. V. O., 237

Rasch, William, xi
Rawls, John, xi, 5, 60, 232
Reagan, Ronald, 144
reality, constructivist view of, 68–70, 71, 150, 151, 154
Robespierre, Maximilien, 261

Robinson Crusoe, 267
Rorty, Richard, 6, 111
Rousseau, Jean-Jacques, 5

Sartre, Jean-Paul, 54, 98
Saussure, Ferdinand de, 6, 258
Schelling, F. W. J. von, 267
schemata, in cognition, 158
Schiller, Friedrich von, 261, 268
Schlegel, Friedrich, 268
Schwarzenegger, Arnold, 137, 143, 146
second-order cybernetics, 71–75
segmentary differentiation, 42–43
semantics, 51
  and social structures, 50–52
sense, and self/other reference, 67–68
Shandy, Tristram, 149–50
Simmel, Georg, 231
Social Darwinism, 21
socialization, 83–84
social philosophy, as anthropocentric, 5
social protests, outdated semantics of, 116–17
social structures, and semantics, 50–52
social systems, function-free contexts in, 30
social systems theory, ix–x, 5, 12
  on action, 97
  on activism, 101
  autopoiesis in, 13–14
  on capitalism, 39
  on communication, 6–9, 10–11, 15, 23–24, 97
  difference and distinction in, 40
  disruptive effects of, 116
  epistemological pessimism of, 100
  as event-oriented, 6
  on human being(s), 9, 79–81, 85, 97–98
  as trinity, 10–11
  on individuality, 10, 22
  interactions in, 30–31

on irritation and resonance, in closed systems, 38–39
on Marxism, 39
as nonhumanist, 100
on observation, 75–76
operational closure in, 15
on organizations, 31
on political and economic function systems, 35–36
as radical, 116, 117
skeptical modesty of, 115
on society, 23–24
structural coupling in, 38
task of, 52
on traditional semantics, 117
social theory, early modern, 5
society
  as communications system, 22–24, 29
  as complex multiplicity, 40–41
  dominant conception of, 229–30
  function systems in, 24–25, 29
  as nonhumanist, 116
  subsystems of, 24
  territorial concept of, problems with, 235–36
sociological theory, problems of, 236–38
sociology
  as autopoietic, 238
  beginning of, 232
Spencer, Herbert, 21
Spencer Brown, G., 133, 165
Stehr, Nico, xi
Sterne, Lawrence, 150
stratified differentiation, 41, 44–45
stratified society
  identity in, 91
  individuality in, 86–88
structural coupling, 18–20, 37–39, 147
supertheory, 194, 200–201

and metanarrative, comparing, 200
symbolically generalized media, 26–28
system, as a distinction, 40
system complexity, question of, 258
system/environment distinction, 9, 170, 234, 244, 245
systems, types of, 9, 12
systems theory, 9, 10, 12, 245
  difference and distinction in, 40
  and environment, 16–18
  and ethics, 113–14
  on reality, 70
  self-production in, 16–17
  on sense, 68–69
  larger context of, 165

technology
  and communication, 124
  and society, 124–25
Terminator (movie), 146
theories of action, 96
Thornhill, Chris, xi, 189
true/false distinction, 248

unity of the different, 256–57

Varela, Francisco, 13, 14, 15, 66, 165
von Foerster, Heinz, 165, 244
von Glasersfeld, Ernst, 165, 258

Wallerstein, Immanuel, 43, 55
Weber, Max, 232
Williams, Robin, 137
Wittgenstein, Ludwig, 6, 114
world-society, 52–60
world-system, 55

LaVergne, TN USA
21 November 2010
205790LV00003B/6/P